IMAGES
of America

MEXICAN AMERICANS IN WILMINGTON

I0806299

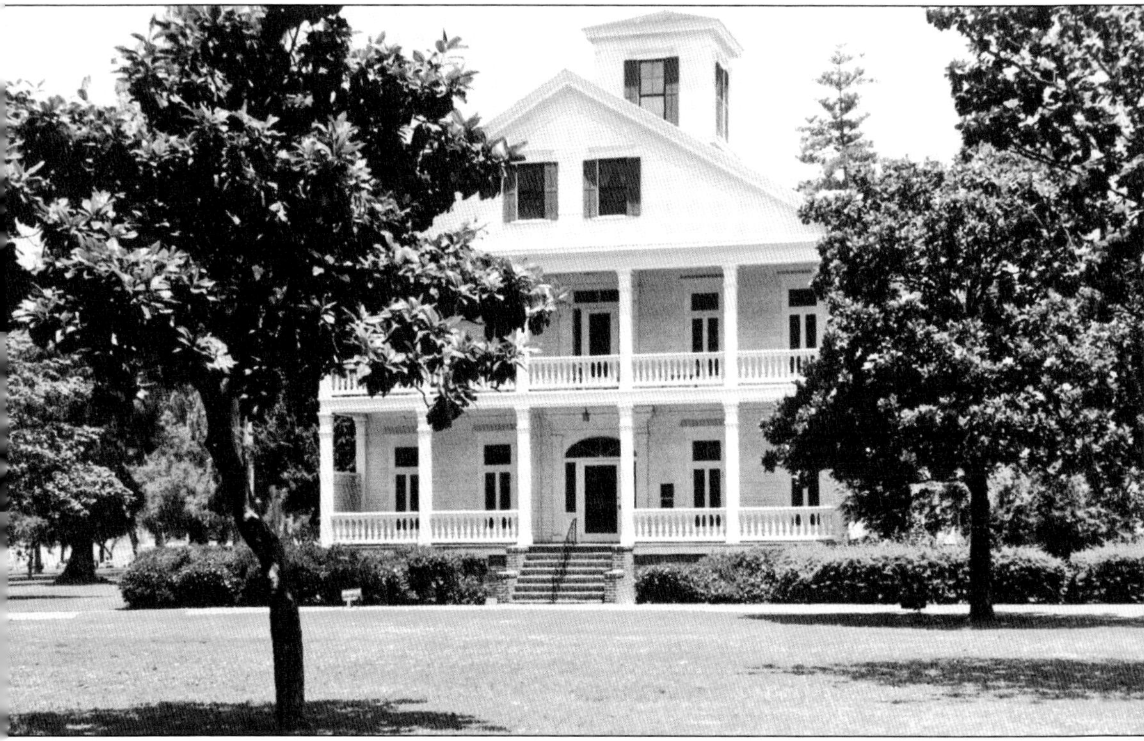

Phineas Banning, the "Father of the Los Angeles Harbor," built his Wilmington home in 1864. Originally situated on 222 acres of land, the residence and 20 acres were sold to the City of Los Angeles in 1929. The grounds of this historical landmark became a center of social life for early residents. The photograph shows the Banning Park home in 1990. (Ramon Quesada.)

On the Cover: Holy Family Church members gathered in 1934 for Thanksgiving Day dinner. It featured roast turkey, *fideo* (vermicelli), and *camotes* (sweet potatoes). Soon afterwards, potatoes and pumpkin pie were adopted into the menu. The day's working group photograph was taken in front of the small wooden framed church on "L" Street, which had begun under a tent across from the Civil War Powder Magazine on Eubank and Opp Streets. The proceeds were designated for a new church building fund. (Ralph Mota.)

IMAGES
of America

MEXICAN AMERICANS IN WILMINGTON

Olivia Cueva-Fernández

ARCADIA
PUBLISHING

Copyright © 2011 by Olivia Cueva-Fernández
ISBN 978-0-7385-8174-3

Published by Arcadia Publishing
Charleston, South Carolina

Printed in the United States of America

Library of Congress Control Number: 2010932244

For all general information, please contact Arcadia Publishing:
Telephone 843-853-2070
Fax 843-853-0044
E-mail sales@arcadiapublishing.com
For customer service and orders:
Toll-Free 1-888-313-2665

Visit us on the Internet at www.arcadiapublishing.com

To my great-grandparents, grandparents, and parents, who came to the United States seeking a better life; to family for everlasting support; to Wilmington friends and families who provided wonderful experiences and memories; and to Marguerite Guidinger, my fifth-grade teacher.

CONTENTS

Acknowledgments		6
Introduction		7
1.	A Community Emerges	9
2.	Family and Friends	19
3.	School and Church	41
4.	Places and Events	63
5.	Work and Play	87
6.	In War and Peace	115

ACKNOWLEDGMENTS

This book was originally inspired by people who voiced a need to document the lives, contributions, and successes of Wilmington's early Mexican Americans. It is a monumental task. Volumes could be written on the subject, and the content of this book only begins to tell the story.

Heartfelt gratitude is extended to the many persons who opened up their hearts, homes, and albums to provide a glimpse of our past. Lost or never-taken photographs of persons, places, and events hampered the telling of a complete pictorial history; however, their stories will be told at another time and space by those inspired by this beginning effort.

This project began with friends and their families, and then friends and relatives of more families aided in providing heirloom photographs, stories, contacts, information, and their time. It has been an honor to have met and worked with so many wonderful people; sadly, it is impossible to acknowledge all those who contributed.

Special thanks to uncle Ralph Violante, who told the first stories, and to Glenn French, who provided the first image. Valuable resources were provided by Hank and Jane Osterhoudt, Wilmington Historical Society; Susan Ogle, Drum Barracks Civil War Museum; Tom Philo, California State University, Dominguez Hills, Special Archives; Anna Machado and Ron Mendez; Simie Seaman; and Alex Areyan.

Special appreciation is extended to Jerry Roberts and Scott Davis of Arcadia Publishing for their technical assistance and to Reynaldo Garay, Ph.D., and Vincent D. Perez for their friendship, encouragement, and help.

Lastly, I give thanks for ongoing support from my daughters, Marisa, Lilia, and Sofia, as well as from Paul and Chris.

INTRODUCTION

Through this visual history about Mexican Americans in Wilmington, the reader will be introduced to the lives of early families of Mexican ancestry. It will provide a glimpse, mainly prior to 1960, into their contributions to the community and the American way of life.

El Pueblo de Nuestra Señora la Reina de Los Angeles (the town of Our Lady Queen of the Angeles) was founded in 1781 by a group of settlers (an ethnic mixture of 44 *pobladores*) who had traveled from Loreto, Baja California, Mexico (New Spain). By 1858, the pueblo needed a port, and south about 20 miles was a mudflat area that could accommodate their needs. Phineas Banning acquired land in San Pedro Bay from Manuel Dominguez and had begun building wharves and warehouses. A port began to emerge.

Years earlier, Juan José Dominguez received a land grant from Spain and built a successful ranch business with horses, cattle, and sheep. His ranch was named Rancho San Pedro, and he set his adobe home on a slope of a hill, now known as Dominguez Hills. Childless, his nephew Cristobal inherited the ranch, and then Cristobal's son Manuel managed the *rancho*. Meanwhile, the Gabrielino natives had lost their holdings throughout the basin and had become laborers along with new inhabitants from Mexico, Portugal, and other parts of the world.

As the port developed, Phineas Banning named the area for his birthplace, Wilmington, Delaware. Wilmington, a strange foreign-sounding place by the water's edge, began to attract more and more people. It was a barren region with favorable climate, resources, and plenty of work. Then, by the turn of the previous century (1900s), Mexico found itself embroiled in conflict. People fled the armies and experienced hunger and religious persecution.

Historically, an important element was the passing of power with the Treaty of Guadalupe Hidalgo, forcing Mexico to cede a vast territory, including Alta California (the state of California) to the United States. The Gold Rush, statehood, and economic interests superseded the personal rights of previous residents. Ethnic tensions rose and violence escalated. As the population changed its face, the Mexicans fell out of the mainstream society, and discrimination gained strength. Spanish-language newspapers were launched to help disseminate information, news, and to keep the cultural identity. Interestingly, an underlying factor remained throughout the state, that is, people were needed for the labor force.

As the situation in Mexico worsened, the demand for labor in the United States increased in the mines, railroads, agriculture, industry, and in factories. Jobs were available in the United States, and the Mexicans came to work. Some people came to Wilmington directly, and some worked in other states and places first, then came to Wilmington. They found a home here, a place so far away from their ancestral roots that most of these pioneers never returned to their homeland. Even though the families faced many difficulties and hardships, they persevered. They had come to provide their families with a better life and pursue the American dream of success.

At school, it was English only or they were punished. Their names were Americanized, and certain curriculum courses were not available to them. Job advancement opportunities were limited and housing was restrictive. Yet, the Mexican Americans found employment wherever they could, in the fields, factories, canneries, and on the docks. They were hardworking, cooperative, and dependable. Families encouraged respect, responsibility, and religion. They played baseball, served in the armed forces, and nurtured family ties and friendships. As in the earlier days of Los Angeles, social, political, and cultural clubs and events were established for their children to know and understand their heritage. Yet, as each generation grew, children knew less and less about their family's past. This is true of any immigrant group as it assimilates into the American way of life.

Before coming under the flag of the United States, and then being annexed to the City of Los Angeles in 1909, Wilmington had gone from the tranquil living of Native Americans, through the transforming influences and periods under the flags of Spain, Mexico, and the Bear Flag Revolt of 26 days. It is now a busy, bustling community, the cornerstone of a large and important metropolis and prominent world port. Its labor force has gone from the days of cattle, ranches, and sheep, from loading tallow and unloading lumber, to its present-day connection with the port's global-related industries.

Descendents of the pioneer families have graduated from colleges and universities to have careers in education, law, medicine, engineering, and other areas. They work as longshoremen, union officials, managers and supervisors, artists, and musicians. They work in technology, and science, and every field imaginable. Ambition, education and skills, earnings, and the automobile have allowed Mexican Americans to expand and develop their potential and talents.

These founding families and their children provide a positive image in society, but who are they? Selecting a title for this book became a challenge. If our grandparents were Mexican, what are we? Americans of Mexican descent, Spanish, Californios, Hispanic, Latinos, Chicanos, Mexicans, or Mexican Americans? Our children may not speak Spanish, we may not live in the *barrio*, and we may not know about our families' contributions, but we carry the heart and soul of our ancestors.

This book will open your eyes to understand and appreciate the sacrifices and contributions of our forbearers. We are proud of them. They will be seen through the stories, photographs, and the lives depicted in this book. It was an honor and pleasure to have met the participants. They opened up their hearts and albums for this portrayal of the early Mexican Americans in Wilmington.

—Olivia Cueva-Fernández

One

A Community Emerges

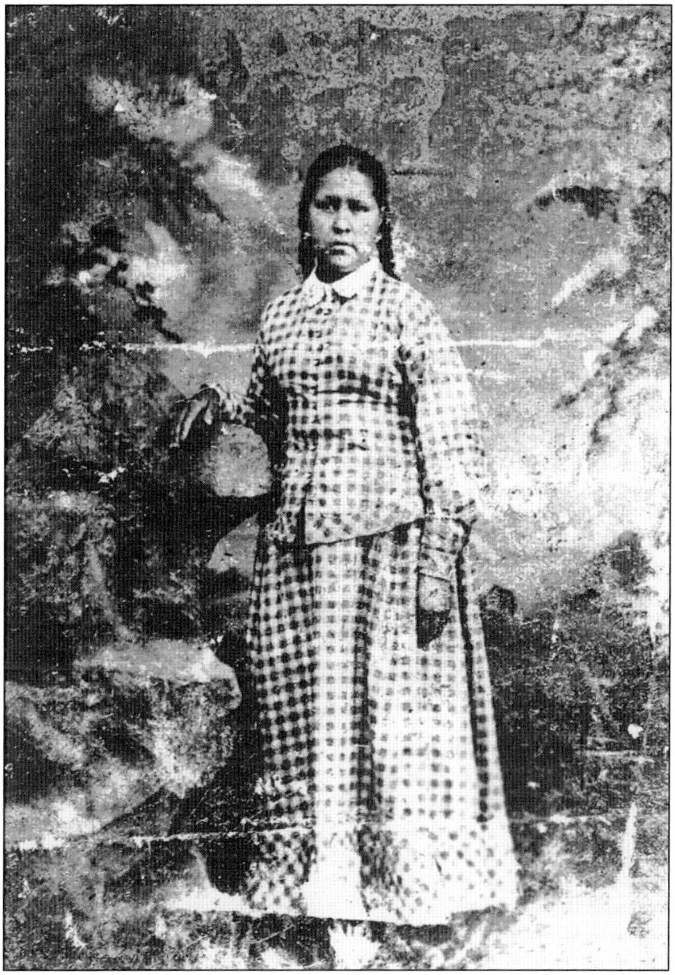

Mexican Americans are a heterogeneous group of people. Some families can identify and are proud of their Native American heritage. Shown here around 1895 is Josefa Apodaca, a full-blooded Apache. She married Juan Rico, of Mexican heritage, whose horses were favorites of Billy the Kid and who once owned a Colt 45 belonging to the outlaw. She lived for a time at 1333 East "M" Street. Several descendants still live in Wilmington. The southwest area of Wilmington was once home to about 500 Suanga natives (Shoshone) who lived along the water's edge. (Carlos Rico.)

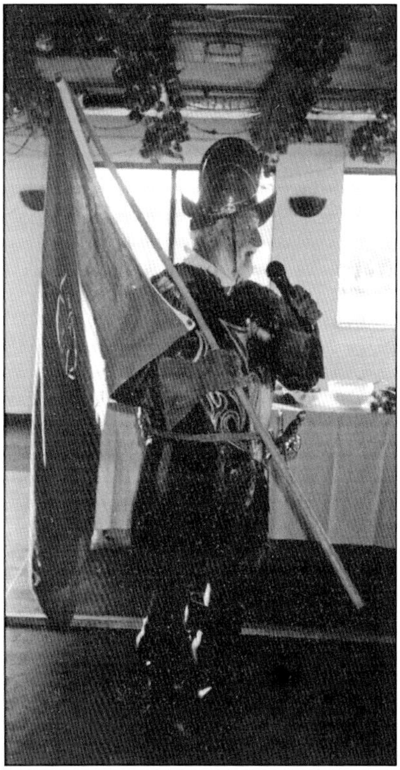

In 1542, Juan Rodriguez Cabrillo arrived at the bay, and seeing smoke from native fires, he called it *Bahia de los Fumos* (Bay of Smokes). John Olguin, founder of the Cabrillo Marine Museum in San Pedro, is seen here as Cabrillo, whom he portrays at historical events. The Olguin family lived for several years in Wilmington near Alameda Street. (Author's collection.)

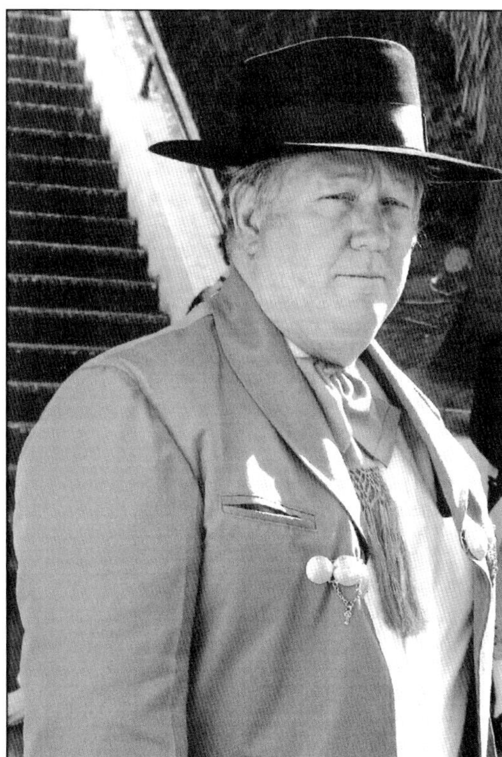

Robert E. Smith resides in Wilmington. He is the past president of *Los Pobladores 200* (The Founders 200), descendants of the founders of Los Angeles. The Pobladores traveled *El Camino Real* (King's Highway) with Captain Gaspar de Portola's expedition to establish pueblos and missions for the Spanish flag. Smith is a direct descendant of Sgt. José Francisco de Ortega, chief scout of the expedition, and from several Spanish families of early California. He is editor of *El Mensaje* (The Message), a publication of *Los Pobladores*. He is shown wearing the dress uniform of a Spanish lieutenant. (Robert E. Smith.)

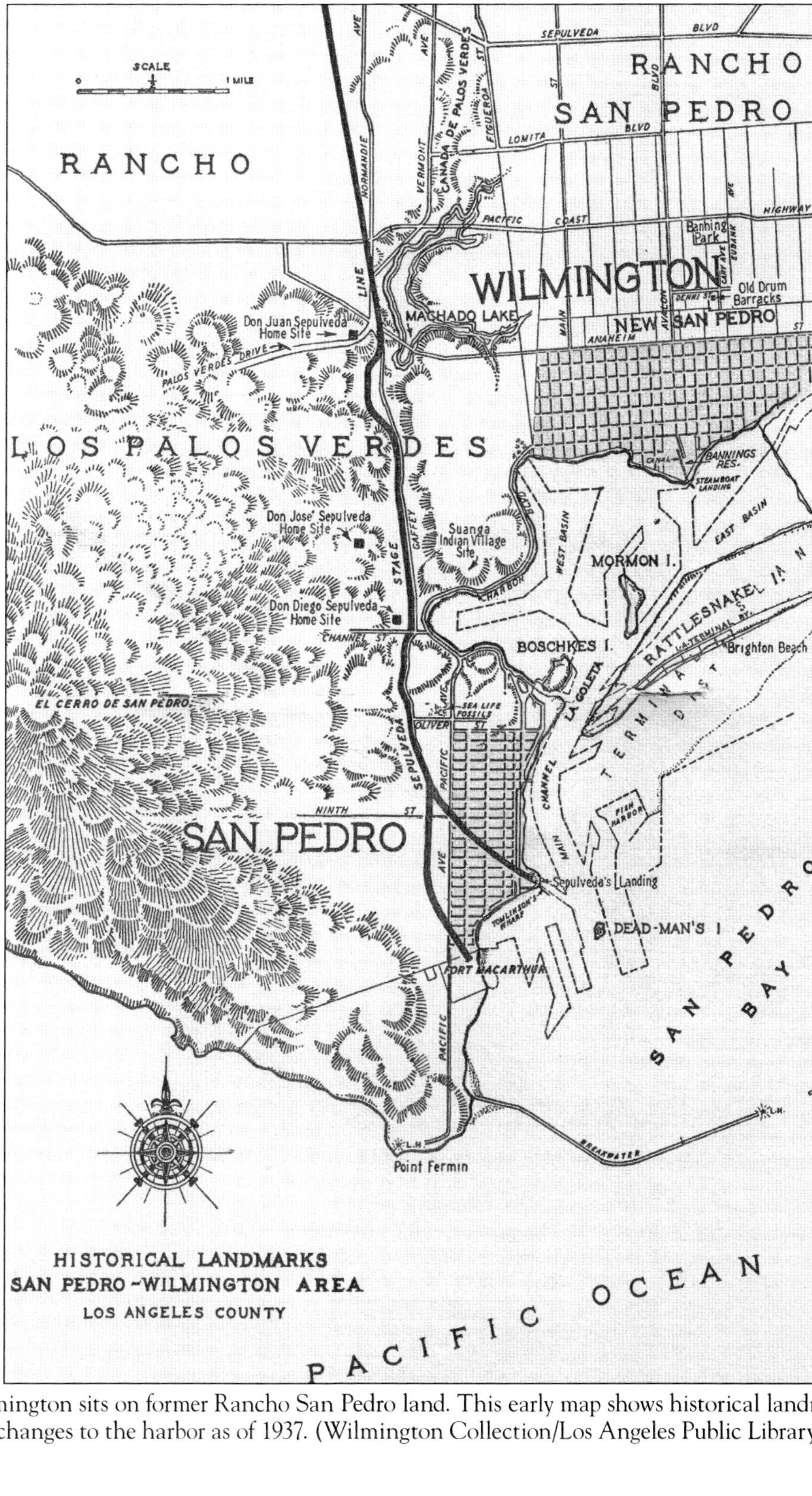

Wilmington sits on former Rancho San Pedro land. This early map shows historical landmarks and changes to the harbor as of 1937. (Wilmington Collection/Los Angeles Public Library.)

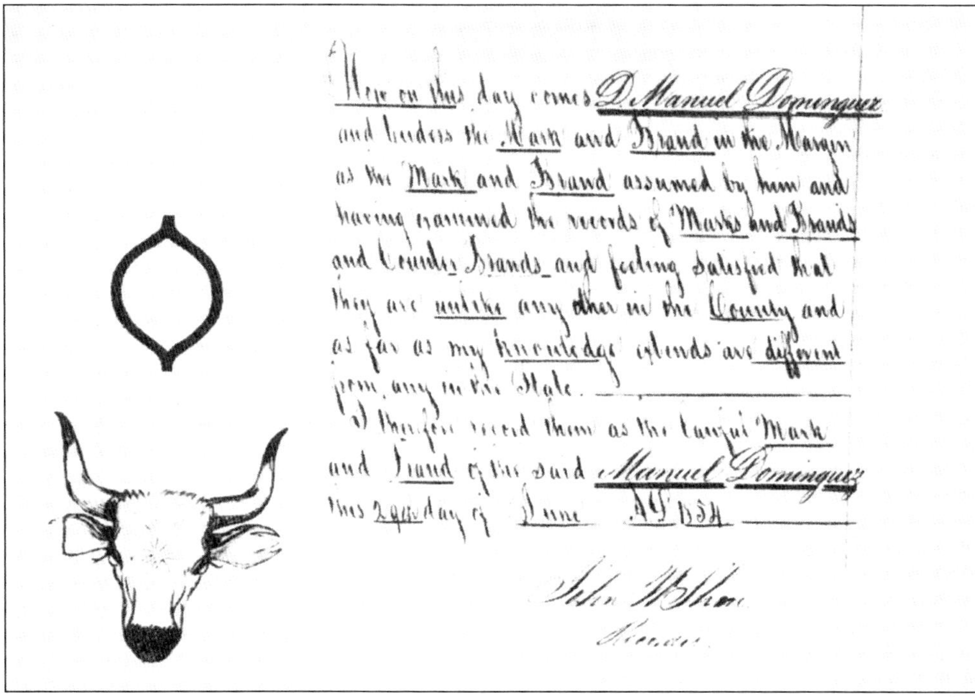

Now on this day comes D. Manuel Dominguez and tenders the Mark and Brand in the Margin as the Mark and Brand assumed by him and having examined the records of Marks and Brands and Counter Brands and feeling satisfied that they are unlike any other in the County and as far as my knowledge extends are different from any in the State.
I therefore record them as the lawful Mark and Brand of the said Manuel Dominguez this 2nd day of June AD 1854.

Recorder

Rancho San Pedro was the land grant of Manuel Dominguez. In June 1854, he registered the cattle brand shown. The primary business of the rancho was cattle raising. The *vaqueros* (cowboys) and most of the farm laborers were Native Americans or of Mexican ancestry. In 1857, Phineas Banning purchased 2,400 acres from Dominguez and began building what was to become Wilmington. (Los Angeles County Recorder.)

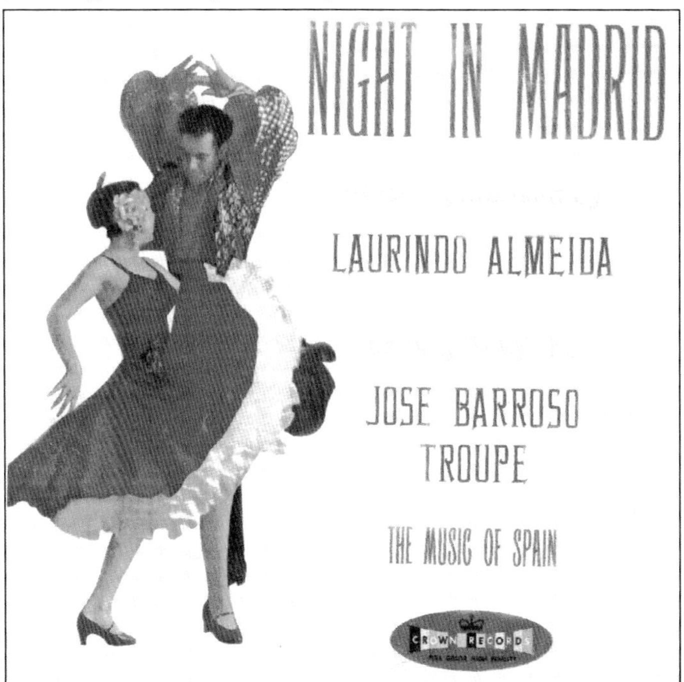

Rancho life inspired Spanish music and dance. This c. 1950 album cover shows Mike Violante as a flamenco dancer, and his castanets are heard accompanying the music. Violante performed professionally, including at the Ramona Pageant in Hemet, California. The play is based on the romanticized and racially sensitive novel *Ramona*, a tale about a rancho owner's daughter who falls in love with Alessandro, a Native American. (Author's collection.)

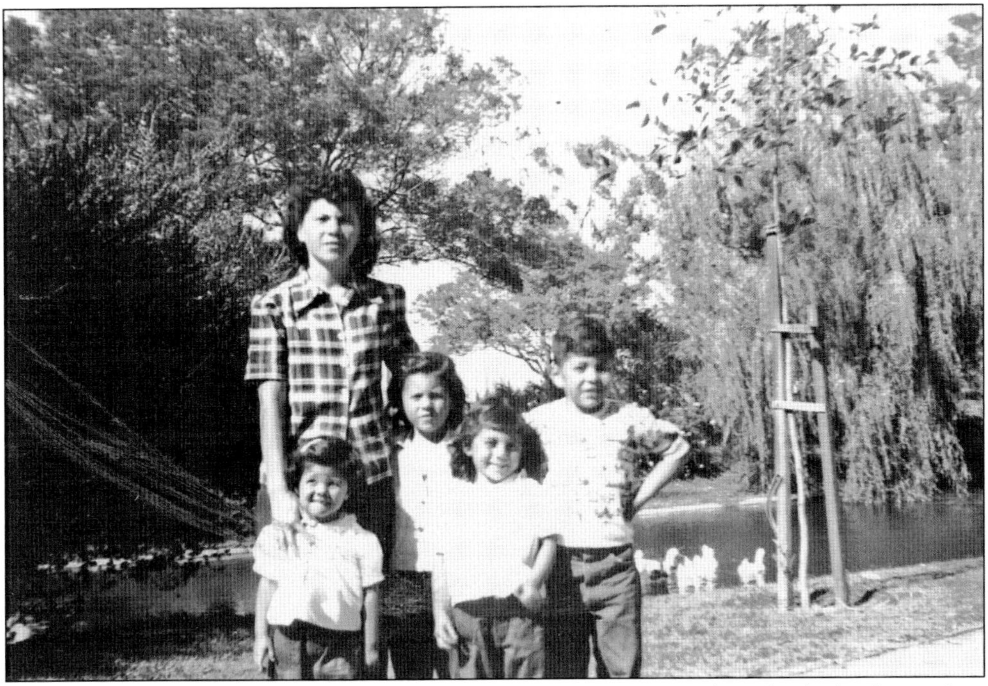

In 1948, Anna Marie Mendez stood with her children at Banning Park as the ducks clustered on the creek's bank. Pictured with their mother, from left to right are (first row) Anna Marie and Rebecca; (second row) Rosalie and George. A descendant of Ignacio Machado, landholder of a Spanish grant, Anna Marie lived with her young children in Wilmington and was raised on the family farm on Wilmington Avenue. (Anna Mendez.)

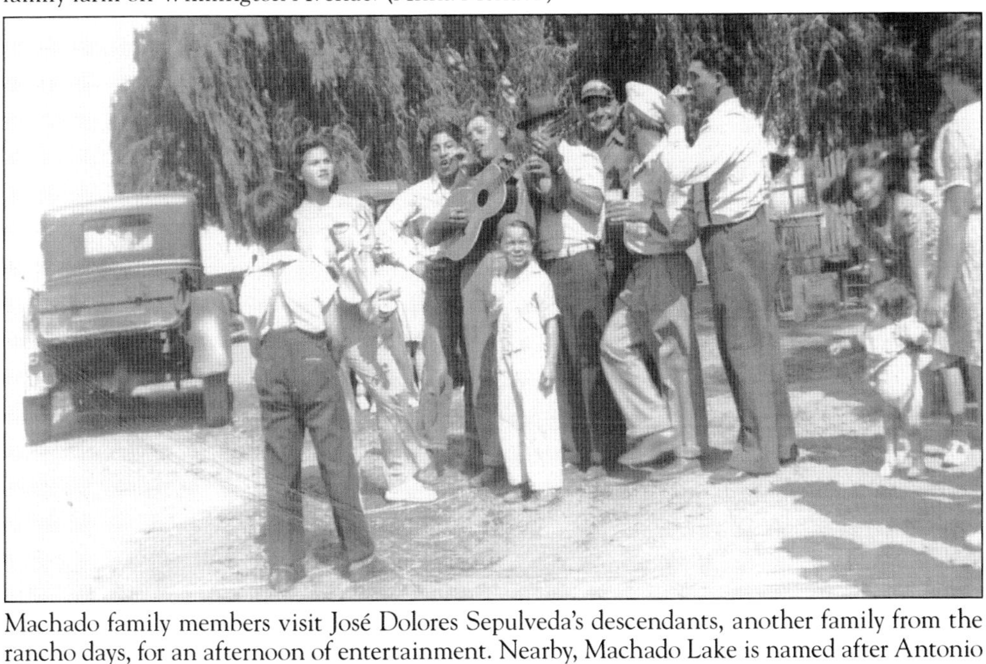

Machado family members visit José Dolores Sepulveda's descendants, another family from the rancho days, for an afternoon of entertainment. Nearby, Machado Lake is named after Antonio Machado, son of José Manuel Machado, who came to help establish missions and settlements. (Anna Mendez.)

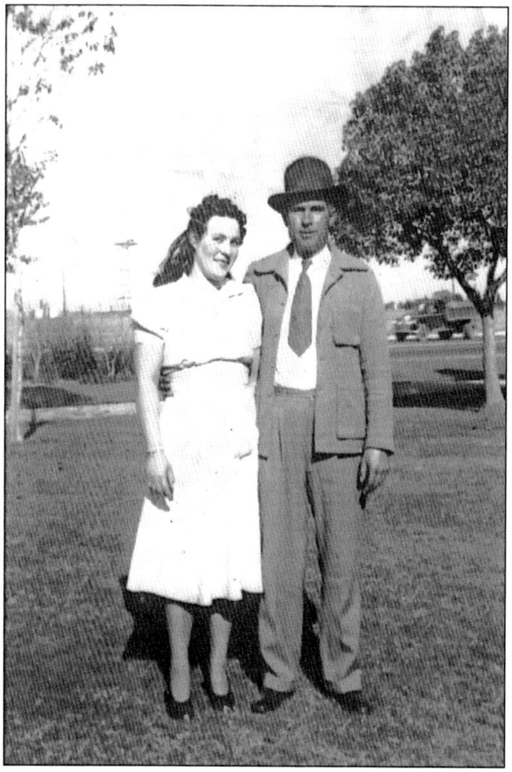

Jose Gallegos and Magdalena Parma married in 1933. They lived most of their lives in Wilmington, where they raised six children. Magdalena was a descendant of Old Town San Diegans and daughter of Petra Crosthwaite, who was of the founding San Diego families—Crosthwaite, Gilbert, and Machado. Jose came from Michoacan and worked at both Blinn and Consolidated lumberyards. (Otila Sorenseene.)

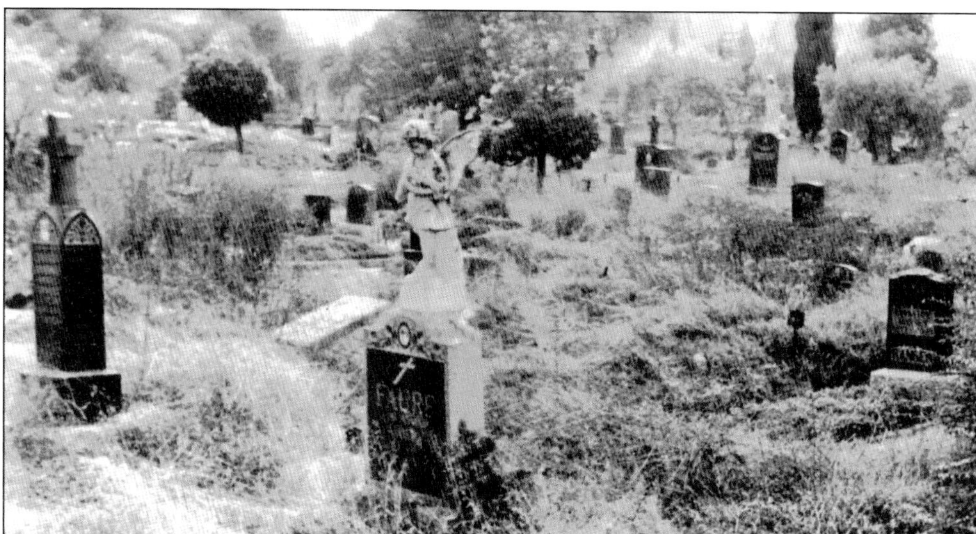

The Wilmington Cemetery began as a private cemetery for the Phineas Banning family. This 10-acre cemetery at 605 East "O" Street is the oldest in the harbor area and the second oldest in the city of Los Angeles. It was established in 1857. It is also the burial site for 26 Civil War soldiers and members of the Banning, Machado, and other early families. The photograph shows the cemetery in a state of neglect, but in 1959, an assessment district was formed for Wilmington property owners to pay for the upkeep through their Los Angeles County property tax bill. (Wilmington Historical Society.)

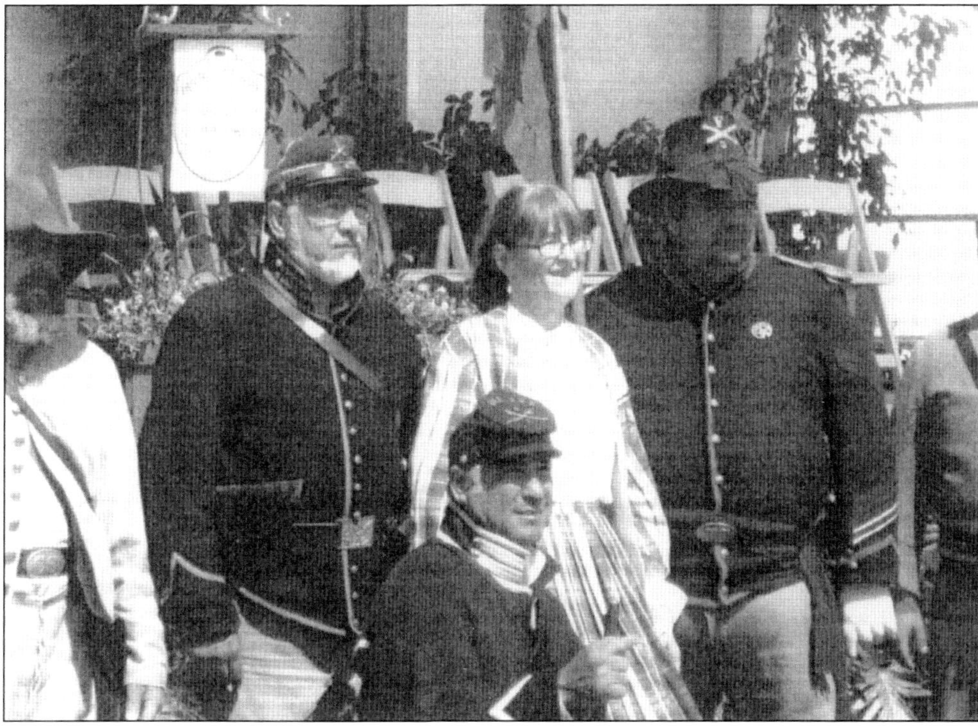

As many as 9,500 men of Hispanic heritage fought in the Civil War. In 1863, four companies of California cavalrymen were authorized, recruited, and sent to Camp Drum (Drum Barracks). These men were noted for their expert horsemanship. In 2007, Rudy Monarraz (front), who grew up near the Drum Barracks and who volunteers in reenactments, is seen with (from left to right) Tom Martinez, Susan Ogle (director), and Joe Justinian. They participated in the museum's program Hispanics in the Civil War. (Drum Barracks Civil War Museum.)

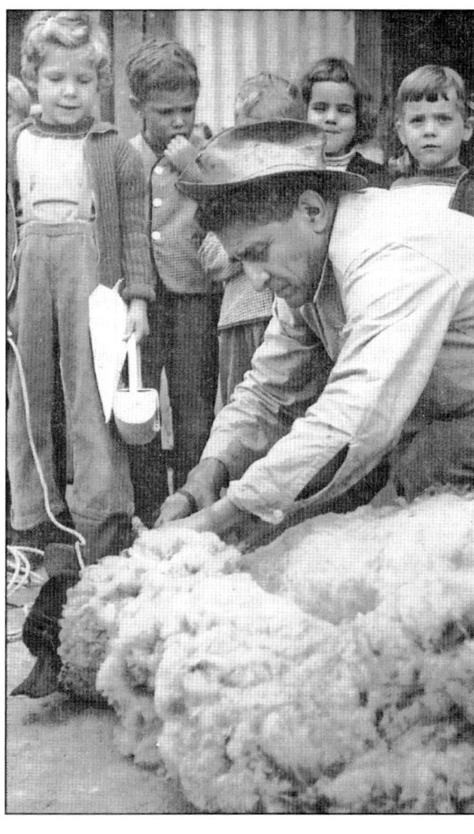

Estanislado Cordero sheers sheep before curious onlookers in the 1920s. Sheepherding and farming were occupations of the Cordero family on Southern California ranchos granted by Spanish and Mexican governments, along with military service under three California flags: Spain, Mexico, and the United States. Estanislado's father, Cpl. Juan de Jesus Antonio Cordero, a Union cavalryman in the 1st Battalion Native California Cavalry, Company C, was based in Wilmington from 1864 to 1866. (James Cordero.)

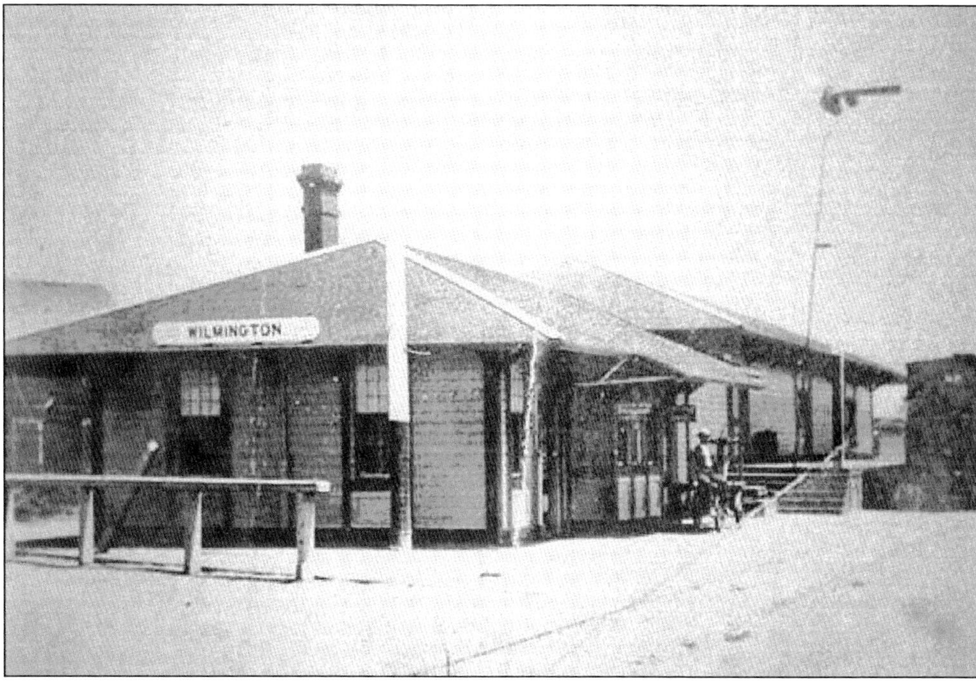

The Wilmington Post Office was established in 1864 at the Drum Barracks. In 1866, it was on Canal Avenue (Avalon Boulevard) at the railroad station. Until 1884, it was one of four post offices in Los Angeles County and served residents from Santa Ana to Compton. The hitching rail shown accommodated horses, stages, and drawn wagons. The signal pole was used for the trains. (Wilmington Historical Society.)

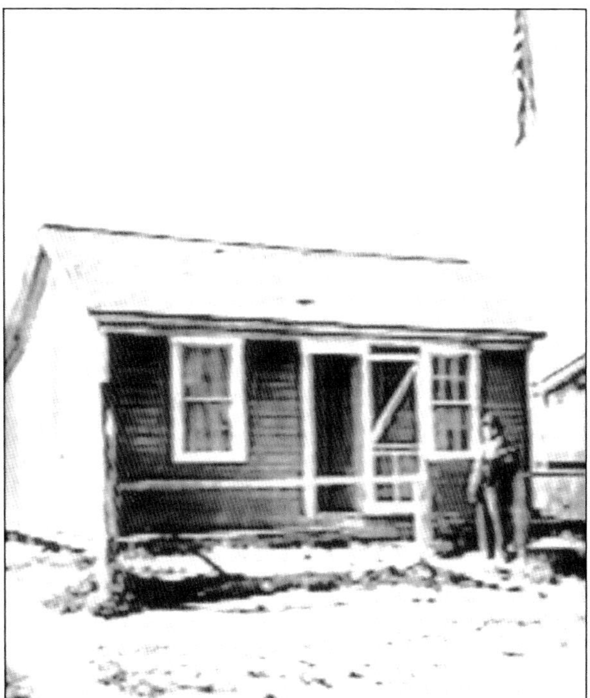

It may be Joe Guerrero standing in front of his home at Third and Canal Streets, now the 100 block of "D" Street, around 1890. An open screen door is visible, and a rail across the front was probably used to secure horses. Houses were raised to avoid water damage, since flooding was a problem in the mudflat areas. Because ducks and other fowl were plentiful, Wilmington was often called "Goosetown." (Wilmington Collection/Los Angeles Public Library.)

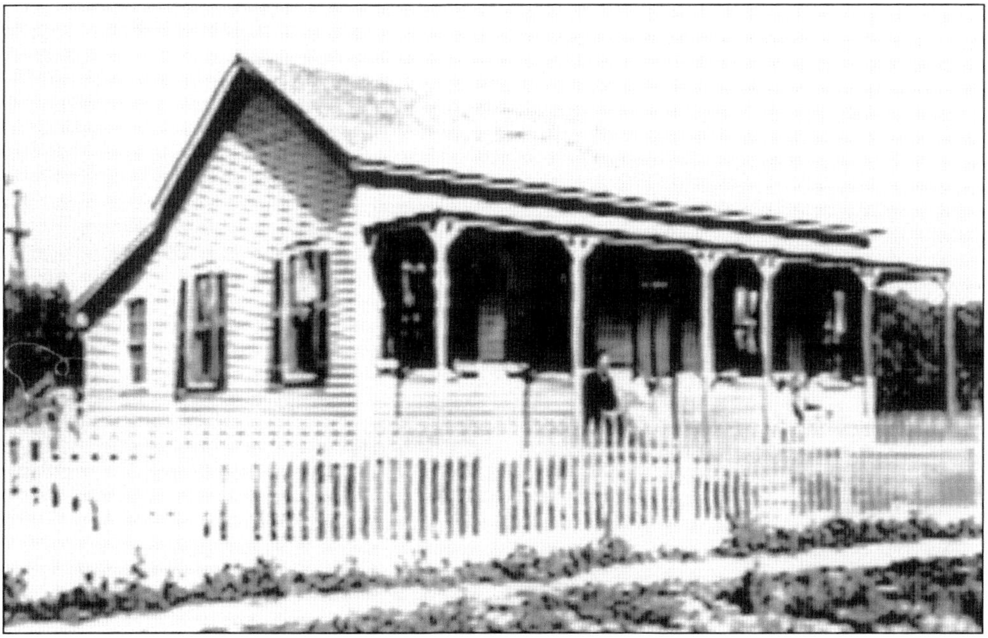

The home of John Diaz was located at 600 Canal Street in 1896. The six front porch pillars and picket fence add to its beauty. Nearby roads were Rocha and Reyes Streets and Machado Avenue, named after early rancho families. In 1926, Canal Street, its name used for 76 years, was changed to Avalon Boulevard. The 19-mile stretch from Los Angeles City Hall to the Catalina Terminal was officially opened in May 1931. (Wilmington Collection/Los Angeles Public Library.)

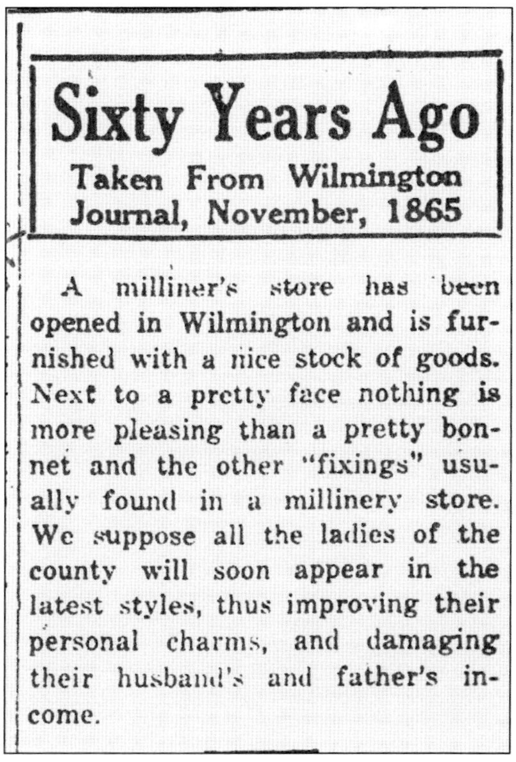

Sixty Years Ago

Taken From Wilmington Journal, November, 1865

A milliner's store has been opened in Wilmington and is furnished with a nice stock of goods. Next to a pretty face nothing is more pleasing than a pretty bonnet and the other "fixings" usually found in a millinery store. We suppose all the ladies of the county will soon appear in the latest styles, thus improving their personal charms, and damaging their husband's and father's income.

This newspaper article was taken from the *Daily Wilmington Journal* in 1925. The 1906 Wilmington Business Directory showed the millinery store was owned by Mrs. M. A. Gonzalves and located at Canal and First Streets. Another 1865 article stated that in a small adobe building 2 miles from town, there were 30 to 40 scholars, mostly Spanish speaking, crowded into one little room. Also, the 35-member volunteer fire department in 1909 included J. Varela, John and Tino Ramirez, L. Garcia, and three Lopez members. (Wilmington Historical Society.)

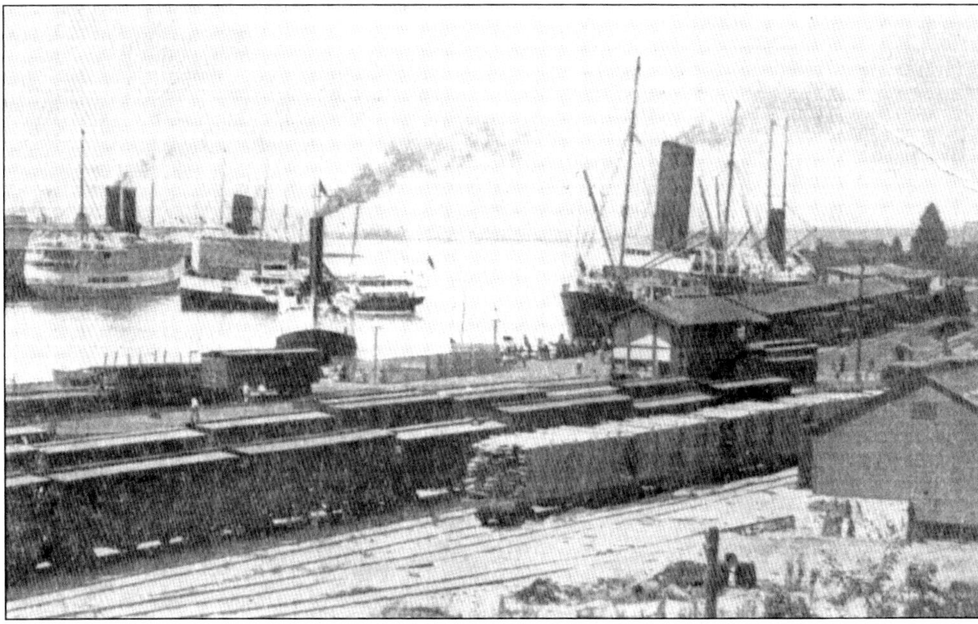

This early postcard was actually a free trip ticket from the real estate offices of the Diemer-Fisher Company at 604 South Spring Street in downtown Los Angeles to tour "the last remnant of waterfront property at Los Angeles Harbor, which is located opposite the big ship yard and adjacent to the five and a half million dollar Union Oil refinery." The property was a subdivision "in the very midst of big activity," according to the card, which also offered a "boat ride and dainty lunch." (Author's collection.)

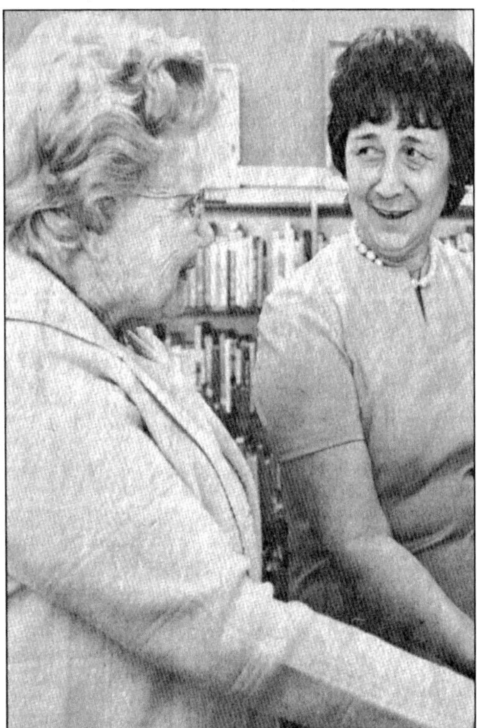

Native Wilmingtonian Angela Erro (right) served 50 years for the Los Angeles City Library Department. Her father came from Spain at age 18 and worked for Phineas Banning. Angela attended Canal Avenue Elementary and Wilmington High School. She started her career as a page in Wilmington in 1922, returned to the local library in 1956, and retired from there in 1972. At Erro's left is Margretta Marshall, head librarian, who established the Wilmington historical photograph collection. (Los Angeles Public Library.)

Two

FAMILY AND FRIENDS

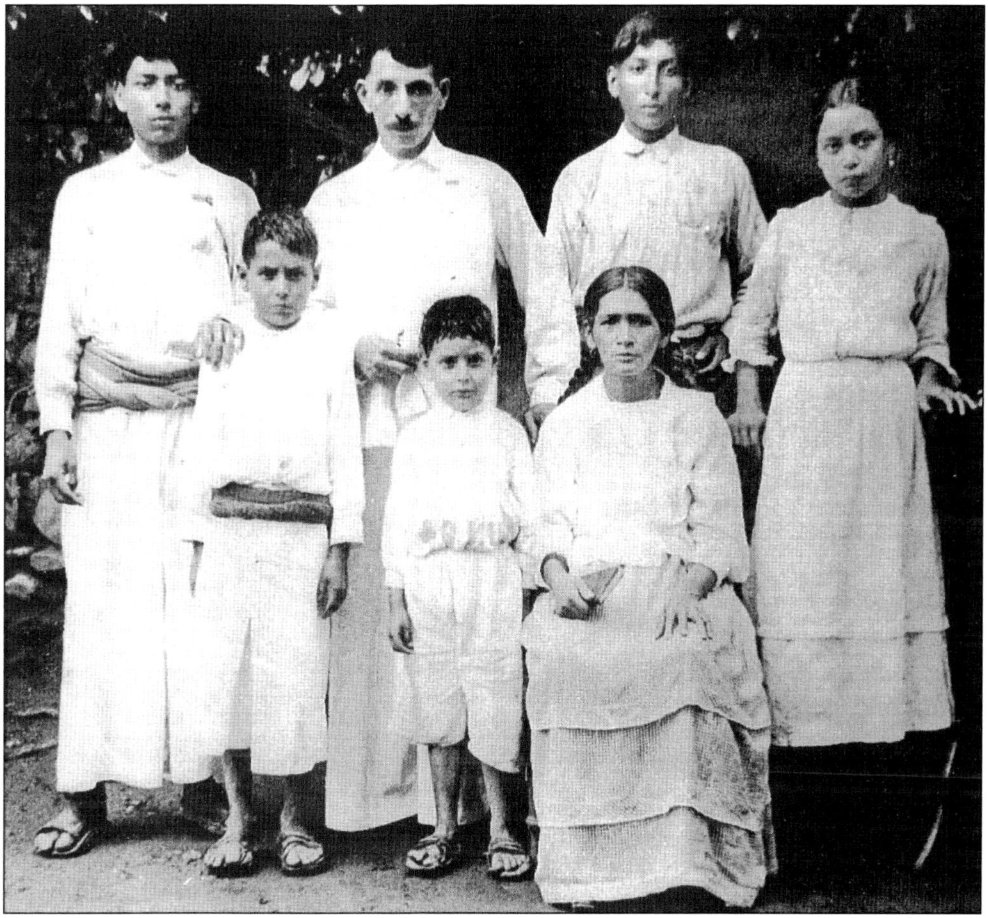

In 1924, Lorenzo Cueva (second row, left) is pictured at age 17 with his parents and siblings before leaving Jalisco, Mexico, to come to Santa Monica. He came to seek his fortune and to help family left behind after unlawful men killed his father. His father was the town sheriff. The family is dressed in the traditional clothes and *huaraches* (sandals) of the countryside. The *ceñidor* is the handmade cloth belt they are wearing, which has many uses. (Author's collection.)

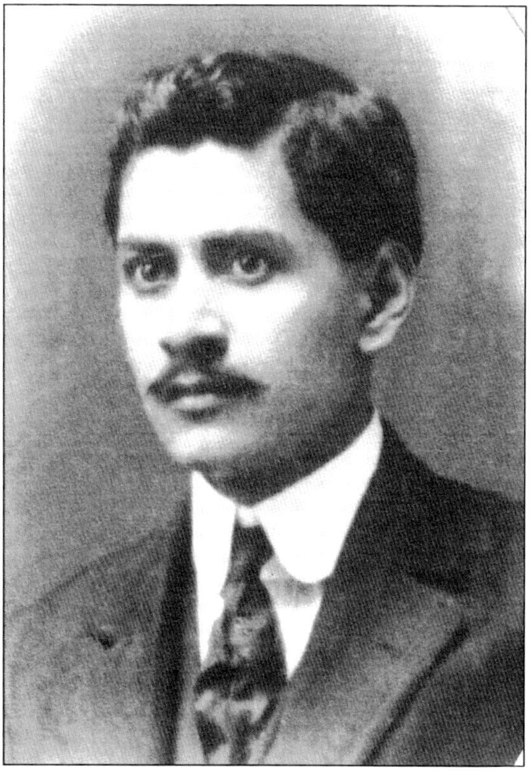

Blas Esparza, an orphan, immigrated in 1906 from San Luis Potosi, Mexico. He worked as a jeweler in San Pedro. He and his wife, Maria Hernandez, had six children: Ray, Alex, David, Robert, Ruben, and Stella. Four sons served during World War II and one in Korea. Ray Esparza was in the Honor Guard for Gen. Douglas MacArthur. (David Esparza.)

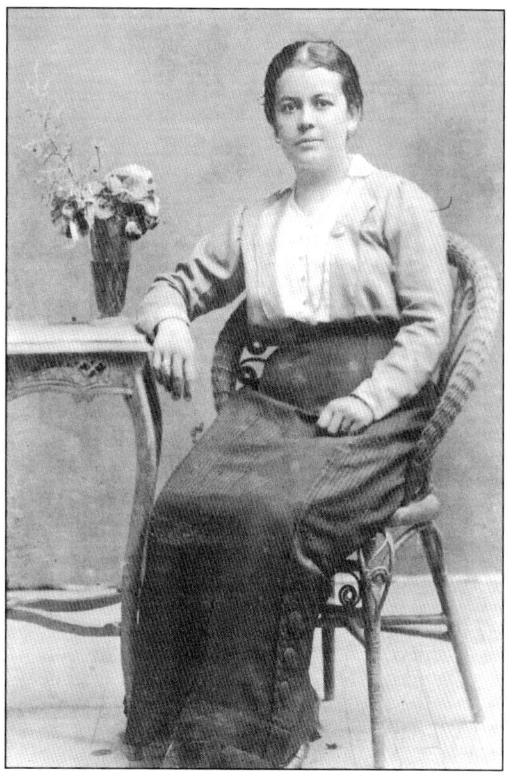

Maria del Carmen Vaca was born in Mexico City in 1890. She married Jesus Gonzalez in Guanajuato in 1905 when she was 15 years old. As landowners in Mexico, it became difficult to live under the reins of revolutionary forces, and, like many others, they left their land. Since there was an open border at the time, for a few cents and proof of vaccination, entrance was granted. Jesus worked for the railroad and traveled to many states. They had 12 children. Their children were born in Mexico, Missouri, and in Wilmington. Maria loved flowers and posed with some for this portrait. (Rita Rosales.)

Maria de Jesus Garcia and Jesus Perez were married in 1918 and came that year to the United States from La Barca, Jalisco, Mexico. Jesus stood beside his wife who was concealing her pregnancy. Jesus worked on a dairy and his wife in fish canneries. They believed in education, and Maria de Jesus, known as "Mama Voo" to her grandchildren, attended adult school while in her 80s. (Vincent D. Perez.)

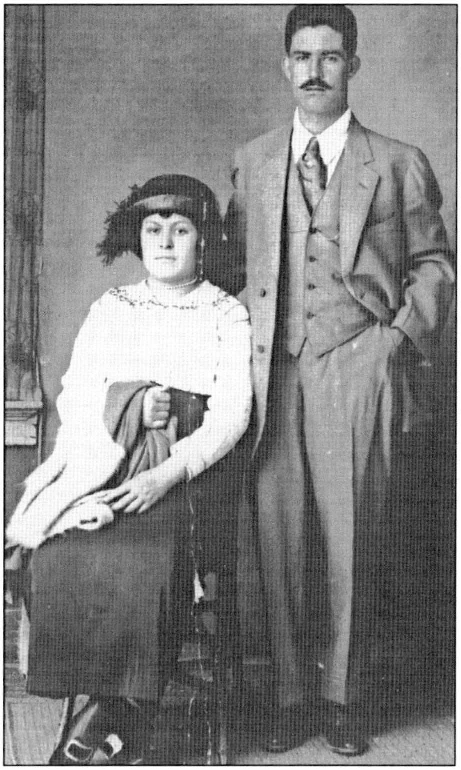

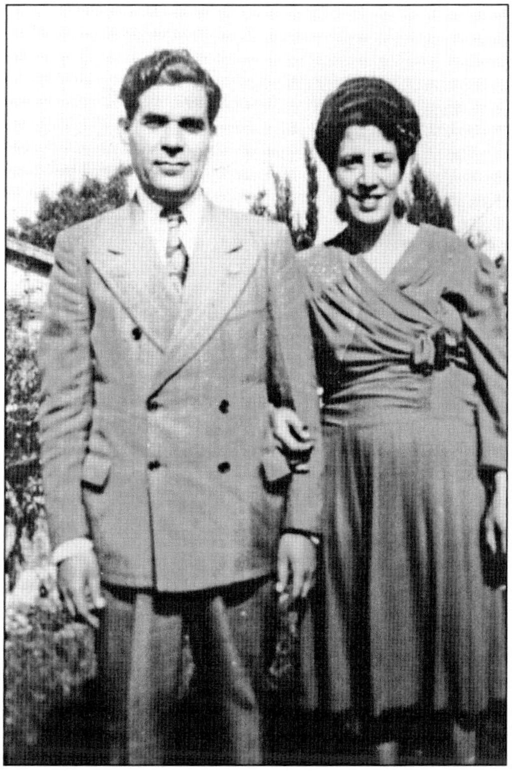

Maria Luisa Ceja and Marcelino Martinez were married for over 50 years. They raised their nine children at 1104 Sanford Avenue in a neighborhood of bungalow-like cottages. The Martinez family was a church-going group, and son Ruben, a priest, presided at their golden wedding anniversary. Maria enjoyed singing in the church choir and whistling. Marcelino worked at the Quaker Oats Company in Wilmington and was in charge of the labels for Skippy dog food. (Carmen Solorzano.)

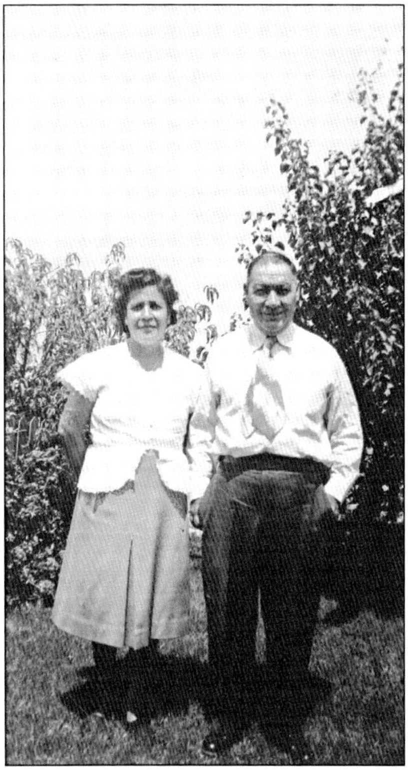

This image of Manuela De La Torre and Felipe Madrigal was taken on Father's Day in 1948. The De La Torre family moved to Wilmington from Terminal Island around 1924, and the Madrigal family had arrived from Watts, California, in 1938. As the De La Torre sisters married, they wanted to be near each other, so they bought homes on East Cruces Street. Madrigal worked in a lumberyard, then a cannery, and retired from the Texaco refinery. He had a farm business, too. During the Depression, he sold groceries to farm workers who paid with chickens, ducks, or other goods. (Eleanor Urrea.)

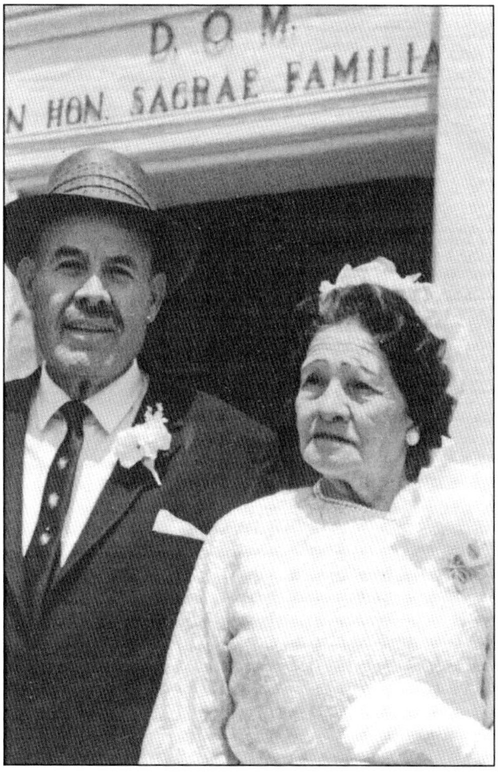

Alvina Marquez and Jose Agustin Villalobos renewed their vows and celebrated their golden wedding anniversary at Holy Family Church in 1963. Villalobos had worked mines in Arizona and in northern California when he became ill. Seeking a better climate and working conditions, he brought his family to Wilmington in 1925. Both found work in the canneries, and they lived with their children on Pioneer Avenue. (Carol Maldonado.)

Standing with two of their children, Ramon (second from left) and Belen, are Gertrudis and Fermin Quesada. The photograph was taken during a Long Beach outing. Quesada was a successful store owner and very active in the community. He was president of La Comisión Honorífica. The organization Sociedad Cívica supported cultural and social functions, including Saturday school for youngsters. (Ramon Quesada.)

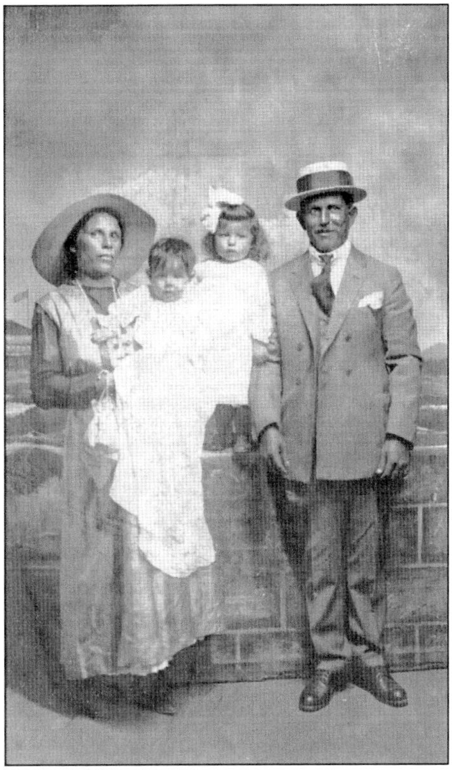

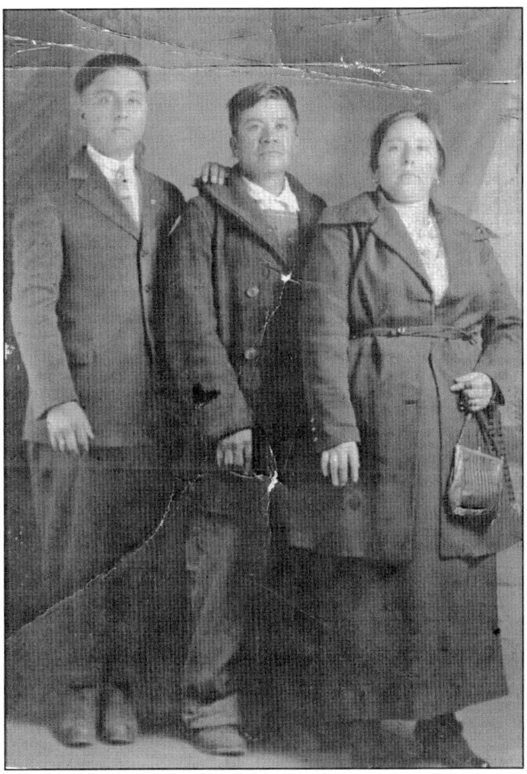

From left to right are Jesus (son), Juan Urrea (born 1851), and Juan's wife, Luisa Valdovino (born 1880). They are preparing to leave Guanajuato, Mexico, for the trip north around 1917. They left Mexico with 8 of their 13 children, 4 were born in Flagstaff, Arizona, and the youngest, Francis, was born in Wilmington in 1926. Juan Urrea worked for the railroad and built a house on Watson Avenue with the help of Jesus Avina. Luisa cared for the children and lived to be 101. (Lino Urrea.)

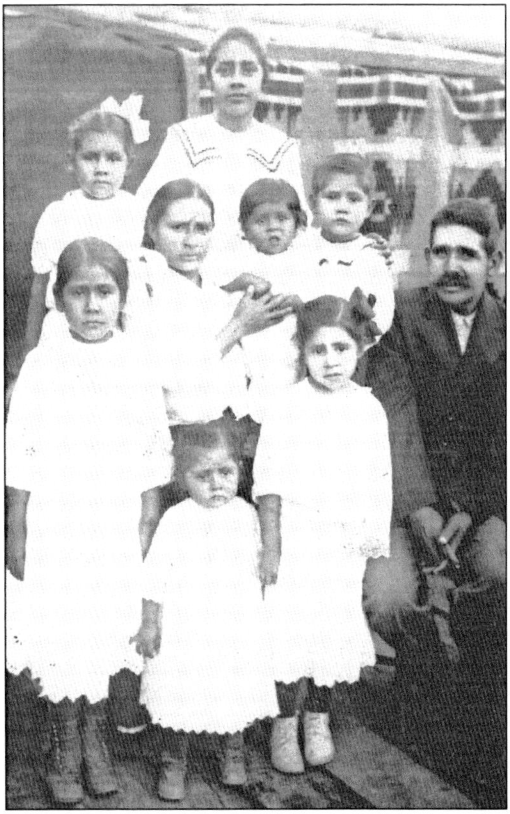

The Sedillo family lived on Mauretania Street. Ruberta (second row, holding child) cared for the children and her husband, Inocencio Sedillo (second row, right), worked in the lumberyards. Ruberta had lived on a reservation in New Mexico before coming to Wilmington. The children are shown wearing white dresses and suits that she sewed for them. (Carmen Galvan.)

Both parents below, Sofia and Cristobal Salcido, were from the state of Chihuahua, Mexico. They married and moved to Arizona in 1919. They moved to the harbor area, living in San Pedro and Terminal Island before coming to Wilmington. Salcido bought property at 526 Banning Boulevard and bought a second lot for $10 in 1936. This second lot made oil history. He worked as a longshoreman, and his sons followed him into dock work. They became union officials, and the youngest son became an attorney. (Anthony Salcido.)

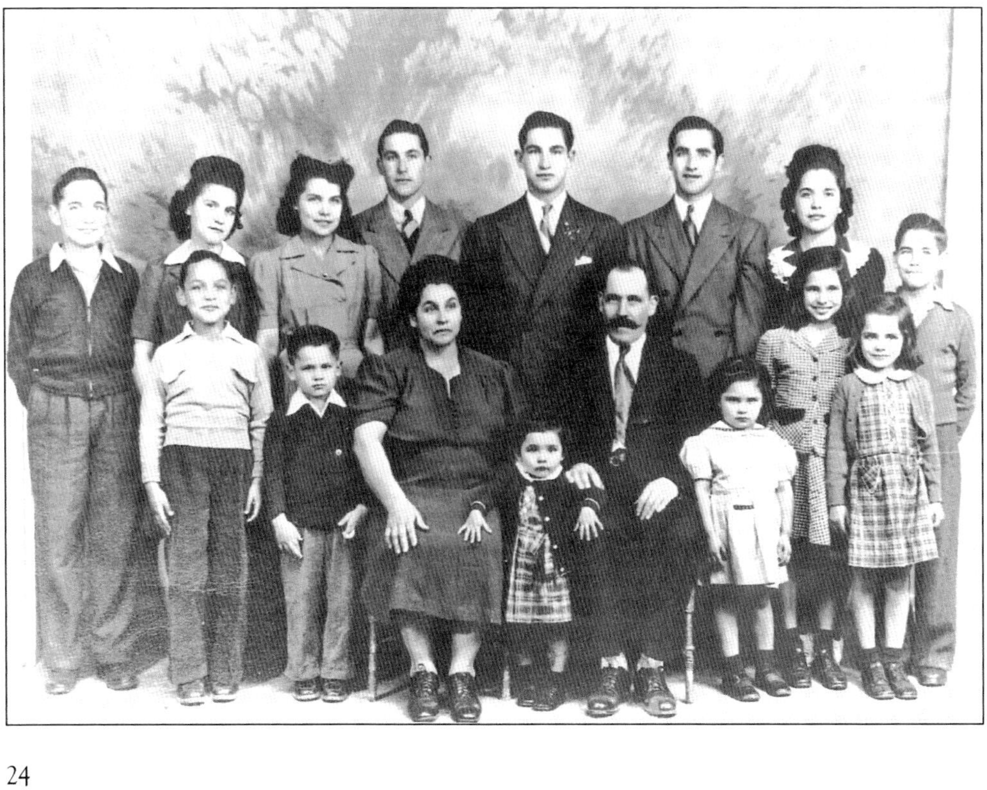

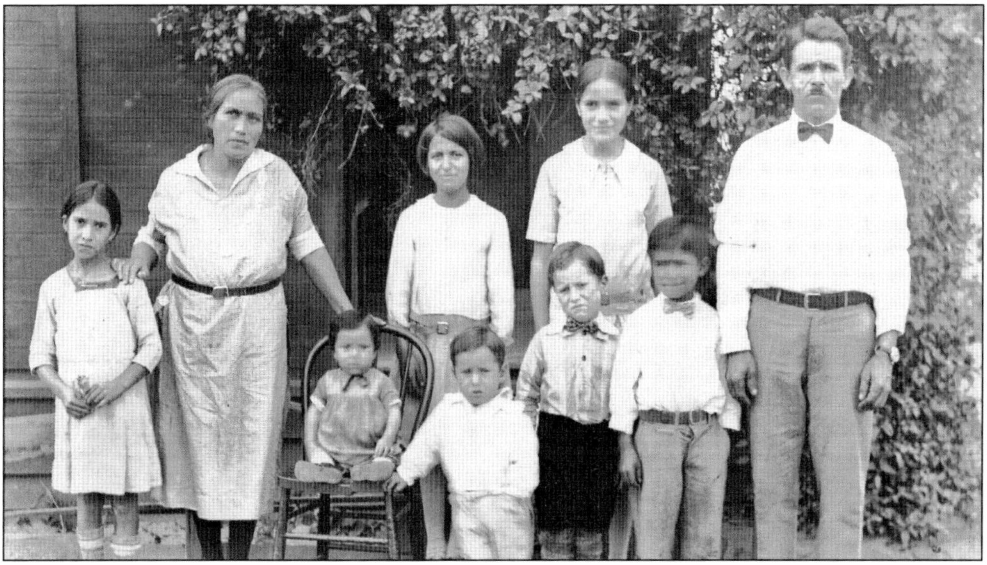

In 1928, Severa Lopez and Marcelino Mota stand with seven of their eight children outside their home on Young Street. The young couple married in Mexico, and since he worked for the Santa Fe Railway, their children were born in Mexico, Brownsville, Texas, and in California (Clovis and Wilmington). Once here, Mota worked at Pacific Coast Borax Company (United States Borax), and his legacy continued with a son and grandson working there, too. The company produced such products as 20 Mule Team, Borateem, and boric acid at the Morman Island location in Wilmington. Pictured from left to right are (first row) Josephine, Severa, Raphael (in chair), Anastacio, Marcial, Pedro, and Marcelino; (second row) Catalina and Dolores; missing is Jose. (Ralph Mota.)

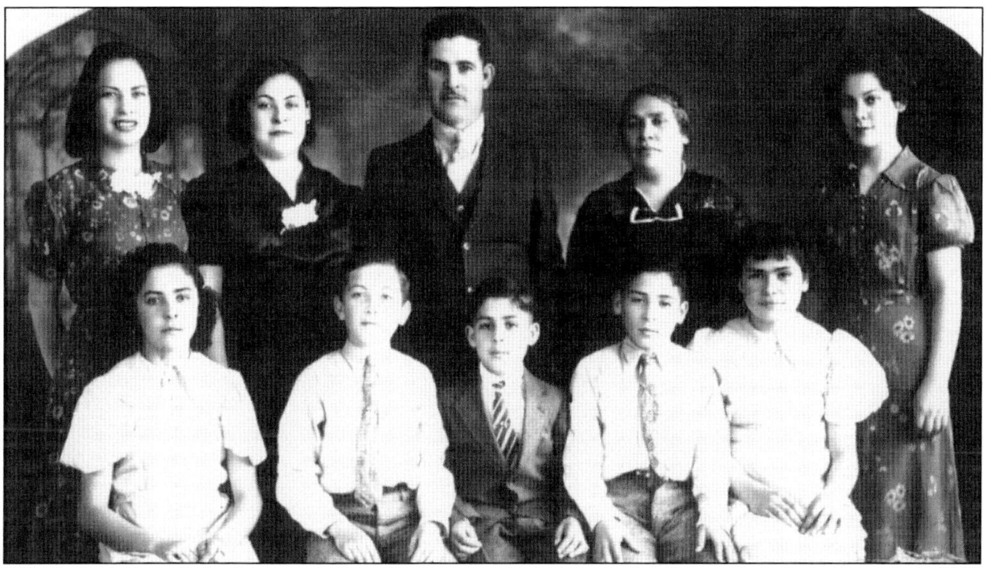

This 1939 Perez family portrait was taken upon the visit of grandmother Guadalupe Ortiz from Mexico. It includes, from left to right, (seated) Rosalie, James, Vincent, Jesus, and Margaret; (standing) Esther, Maria de Jesus, Jesus, Guadalupe (grandmother), and Emma Perez. Emma was born in Arizona, Esther in Mexico, and the younger siblings in California. They attended Banning High School, and worked and married in Wilmington. The family was active in church, community, and in the military. (Vincent D. Perez.)

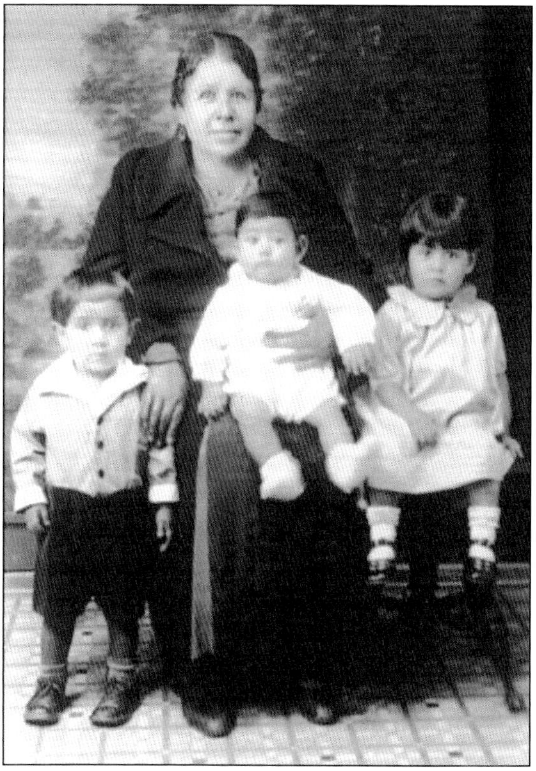

Around 1920, Juanita Medina Macias sits with her son Arthur (standing). Her nephew Alfredo (center), and niece Lupe Fernandez (right) were dressed to join her in the photograph. Macias liked children, and they liked her. She is buried in the Wilmington Cemetery. (Carmen Galvan.)

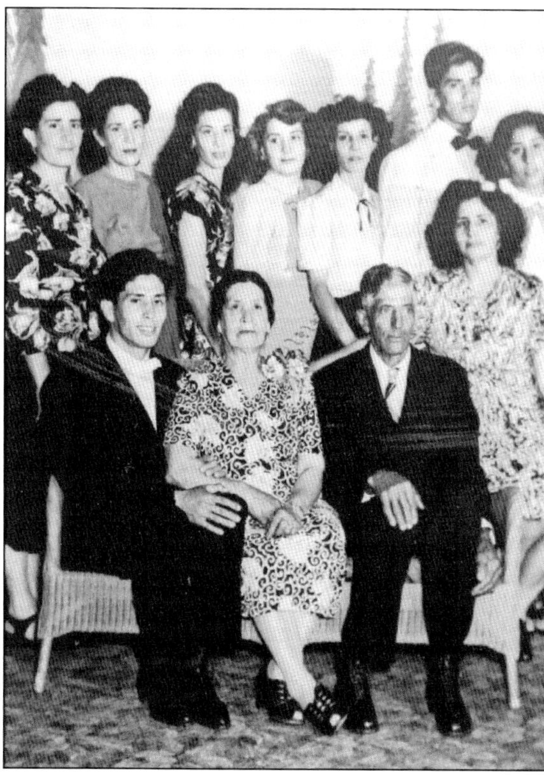

The Ceja family assembles for this 1949 photograph. They came from Michoacan to Wilmington in 1927. Like many families, their faith and hard work were crucial for survival. The women learned domestic responsibilities and worked outside the home, and the men worked to provide basic needs. Both sons, Manuel and Rudy, were outstanding athletes. The Ceja family included, from left to right, (first row) Rodolfo, Isabel (mother), Manuel (father), and Consuelo; (second row) Dolores, Maria Luisa, Esther, Angelina, Victoria, Manuel, and Elisa. (Carmen Solorzano.)

This family picture was taken at a De La Torre family reunion in 1983. Sitting on the far left (first row) with her daughter-in-law, Lila, and son George De La Torre Jr. is Elsie Hamamoto. Her family owned a grocery store on "L" Street, where neighbors could purchase daily necessities. During the war, while most Japanese Americans were sent to detention camps, special arrangements were made to allow Hamamoto to stay at home with her infant child. She was supportive of her husband and son's business, Harbor Canning Company. (Eleanor Urrea.)

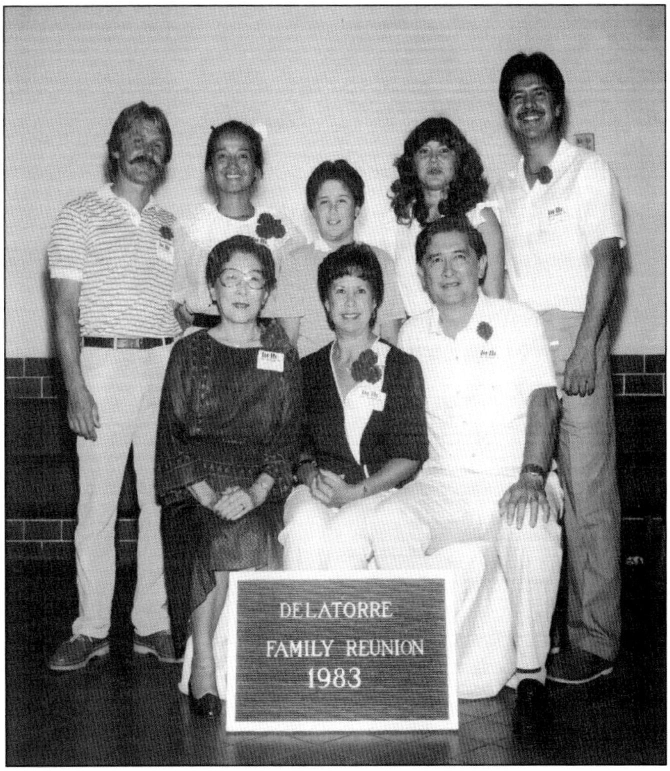

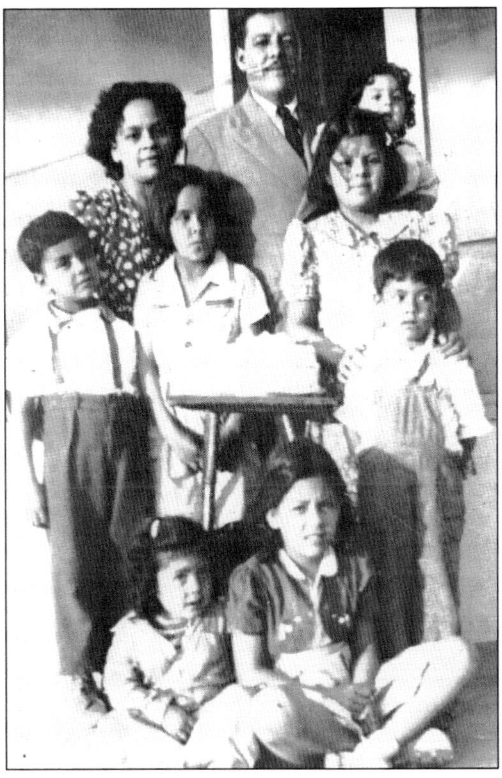

Albert Patino was a baker. He operated a bakery in Watts, and when he moved his family to Wilmington, he opened La Vida Bakery. He was well-known for his bread and cakes. He would deliver to as far away as Watts. Surrounding the cake is the Patino family. They are, from left to right, (first row) Esther and Eugenia; (second row) Richard, Delia, Margie, and Albert; (third row) Carmen (mother), Albert, and Rudy, held in his father's arm. (Eugenia Porras.)

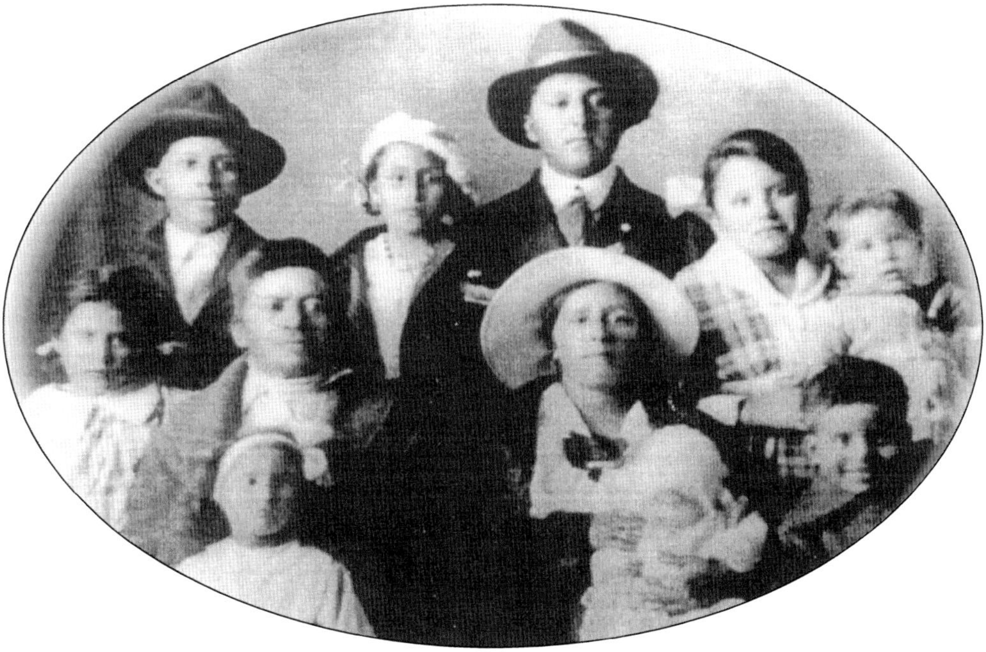

Displayed on the cover of a family reunion booklet on September 30, 2000, is this photograph taken in Arizona in 1922. Juan and Luisa Urrea are shown with 9 of their 13 children. In Wilmington, the family lived at 1028 Watson Avenue. As the children married and left home, they stayed in the community. They remained a close-knit family, helping one another in many endeavors. (Lino Urrea.)

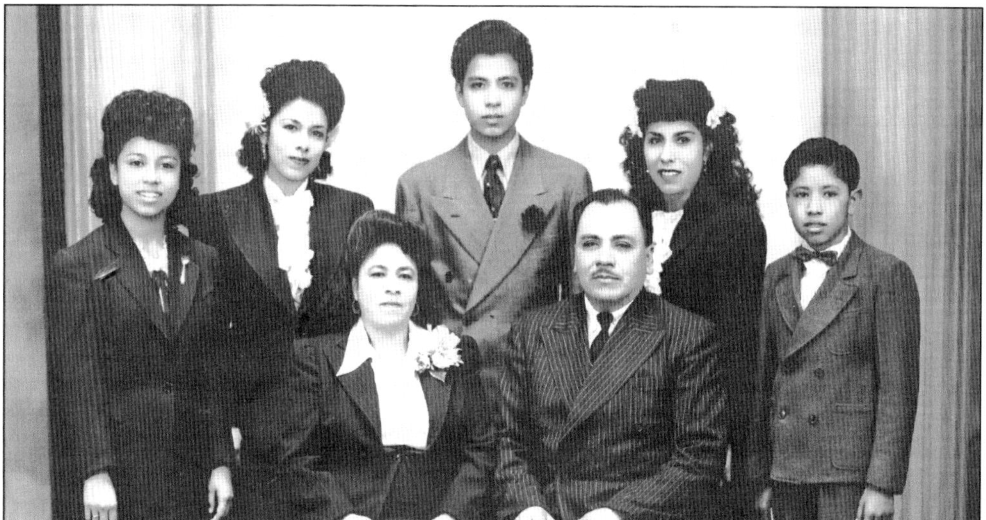

The 1920s brought Mexicans via railroad jobs to the United States. Manuel Calderon worked on the railroad until reaching the border, and there, he changed to being a migrant farm worker. He worked cotton fields, grape vineyards, dairies, and citrus groves to feed and clothe his family, eventually coming to the harbor area. Calderon found employment as a warehouseman and his wife, Julia Palacios, worked in the canneries. The Calderon family members in 1943 are, from left to right, (first row) Julia and Manuel Calderon; (second row) Esther, Jenny, David, Pauline, and Miguel. (Mike Calderon.)

The family of Felix Martinez assembled at the studio in 1944. Martinez had come from Jalisco in the 1920s, escaping from the turmoil of Mexico's revolution. He had his faith and the desire to work. In 1930, he worked for the U.S. Census. The family was, from left to right, (first row) Luis, Felix, Teresa (on lap), Josefina (daughter), and Josefina; (second row) Raul, Jose Manuel, Abigail, and Raquel. (Carmen Solorzano.)

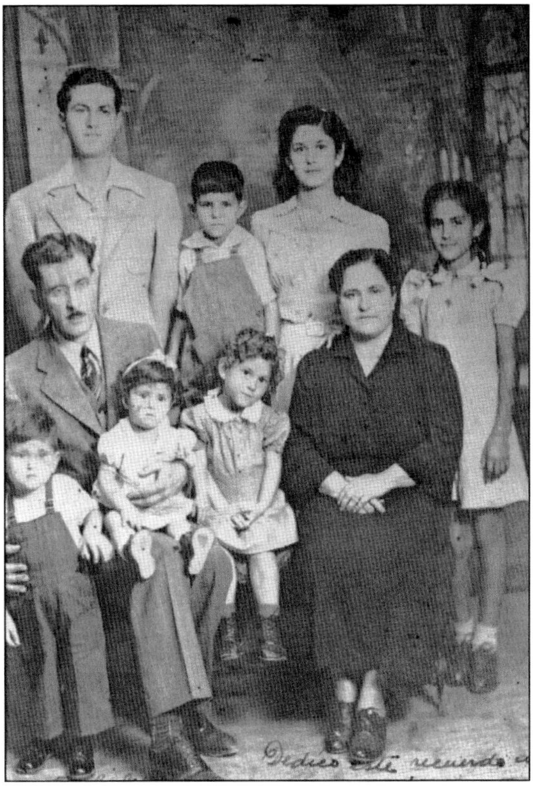

Celebrating *Navidad* (Christmas) meant family, tamales, church, and friends. It was a day to share the closeness of brothers and sisters with whatever might be under the tree. This photograph is dated December 25, 1947, as the children of Alberto and Juanita Macias are ready to share the day's blessings. Seated from left to right are (on laps) Carlos, George, Raquel, and baby Juanita; (on sofa) Carmen, Peter, Alfonso, Arthur, and Alberto. Missing from the picture are Lucy and Paul. (Carmen Galvan.)

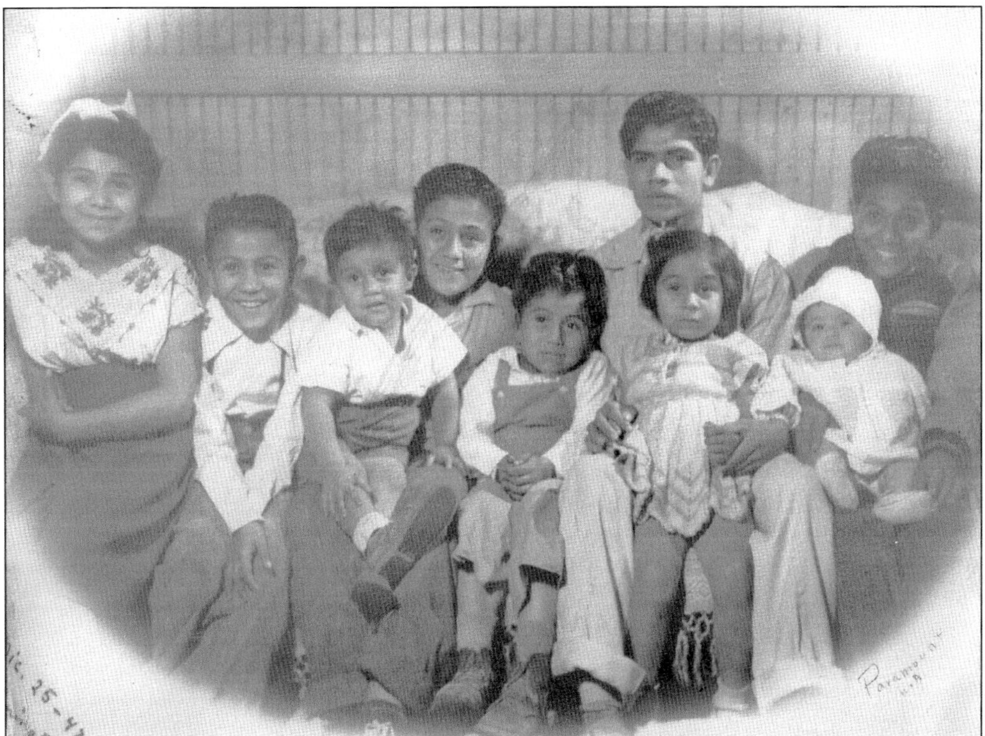

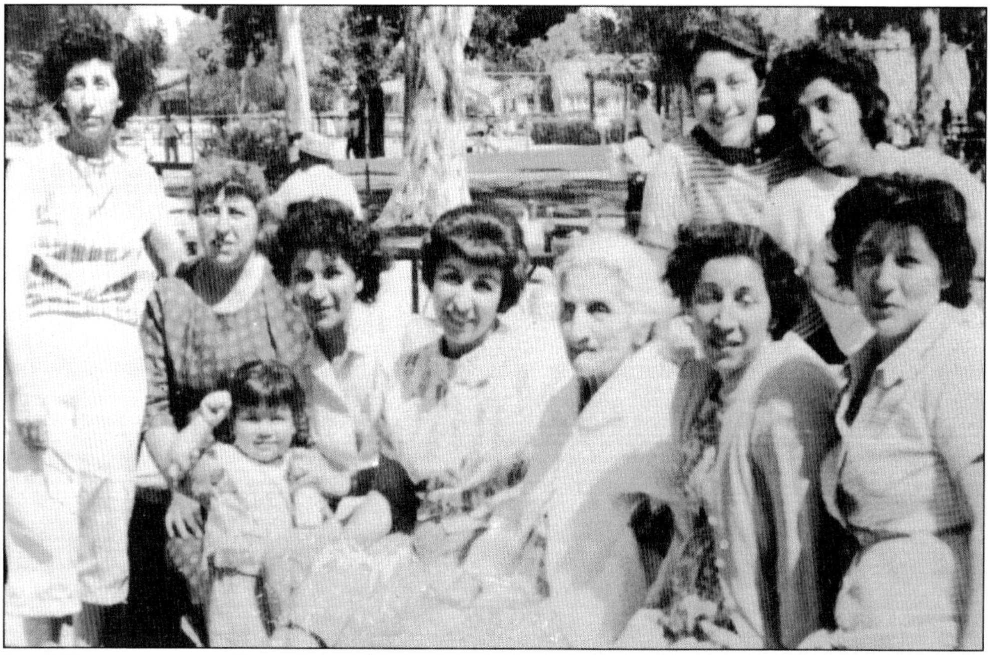

In 1950, at a picnic in Banning Park, the Sanchez sisters joined their mother, Cruz Valenzuela. The Sanchez father, who had served in the army at Fort McArthur during World War I, was deceased. The widowed Sanchez raised her eight daughters and son on East Cruces Street by ironing and working the cotton fields. Her only son, Nick, who was an airplane mechanic, was killed in World War II, three days after the war ended. The Sanchez family members are, from left to right, (first row) Margaret, Frances, Evelyn (holding Sandra Solorzano), Rosie, Cruz (mother), Jessie, and Tillie; (second row) Mary, and Carmen. (Dolores Marquez.)

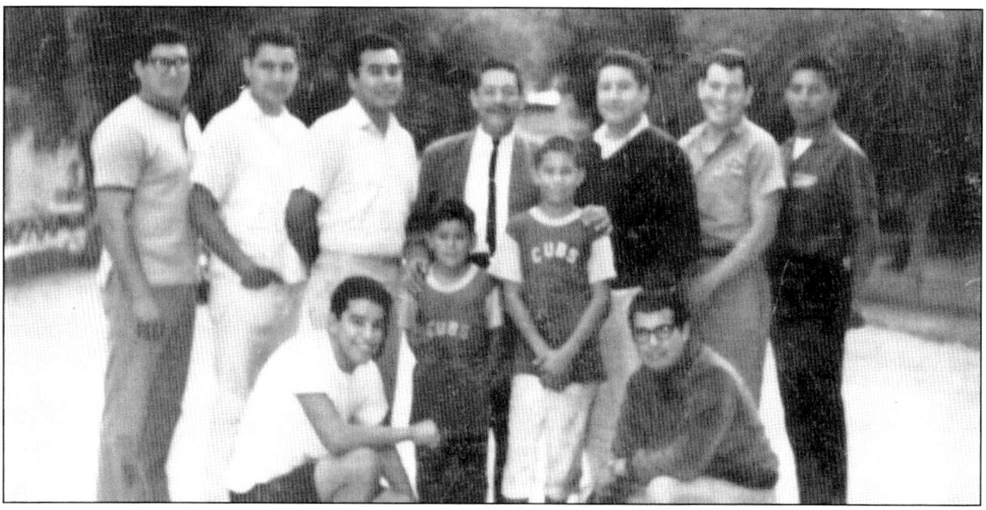

Banning Park is the venue for the only photograph of David Pacheco Sr. and his 10 sons. The Pachecos were athletes and student body leaders in high school. They became musicians, artists, firemen, police officers, teachers, and served in the military. They are, from left to right, (first row) Manuel, Richard, Robert, and Ruben; (second row) Saul, Alfredo, Francisco, David Sr., David Jr., Alfonso, and Henry. In 1964, Teodora (mother) and daughters Rachel, Barbara, and Sofia were observing this special moment. (Saul Pacheco.)

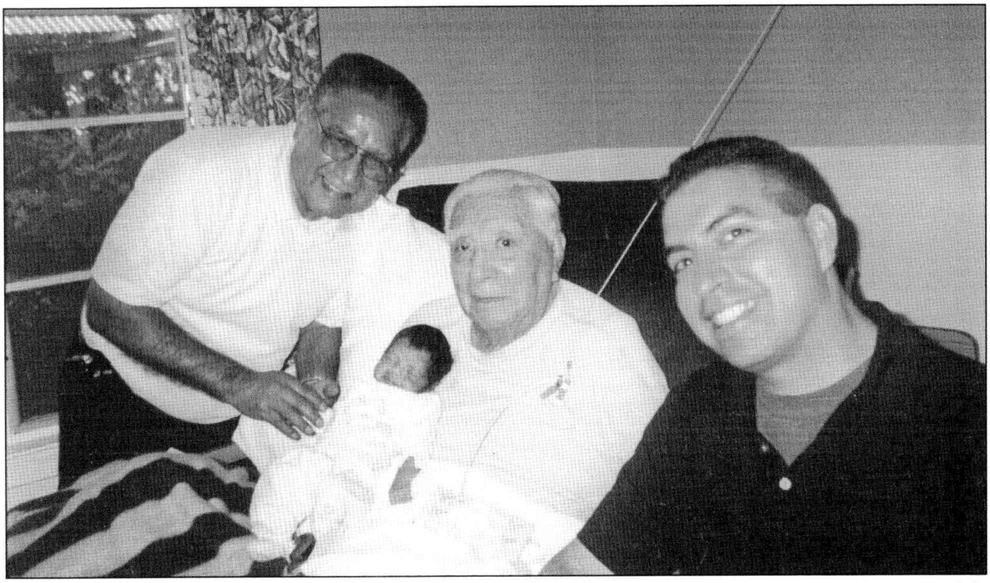

Four generations gathered in 1985. They were David (son), Benito (holding great-grandson Gerado), and grandson David E. Esparza. Having contracted polio after the birth of his first child, Benito H. Esparza never allowed his disability to limit community involvement or his family obligations. He served on the first Mahar House Board of Directors and helped found the Harbor Area Scholarship Committee. He was an honorary mayor of Wilmington, Citizen of the Year in 1958, and worked as an immigration counselor and accountant on Watson Avenue with wife, Paula Escudero. The couple was active in the voting process and Democratic Party. (David Esparza.)

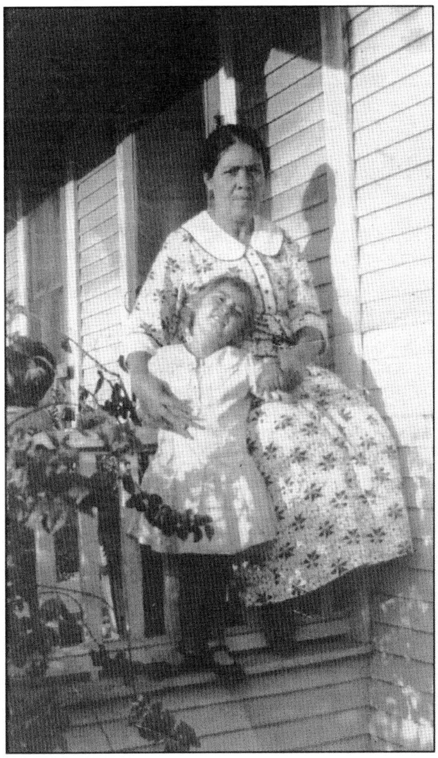

Maura Flores sits on the front porch of her house on Sanford Avenue around 1943. At her side is a grandchild, Mary Angel Flores. The child's grandfather, Tomas Flores, worked at Consolidated Lumber Company at Anaheim and Alameda Streets. It was a huge lumberyard that employed local men. Many workers constructed their homes with lumber bought from the yard and with the help of neighbors. A good number of those homes still stand today. The wood siding of many old homes has been covered by plaster. (Esther Pacheco.)

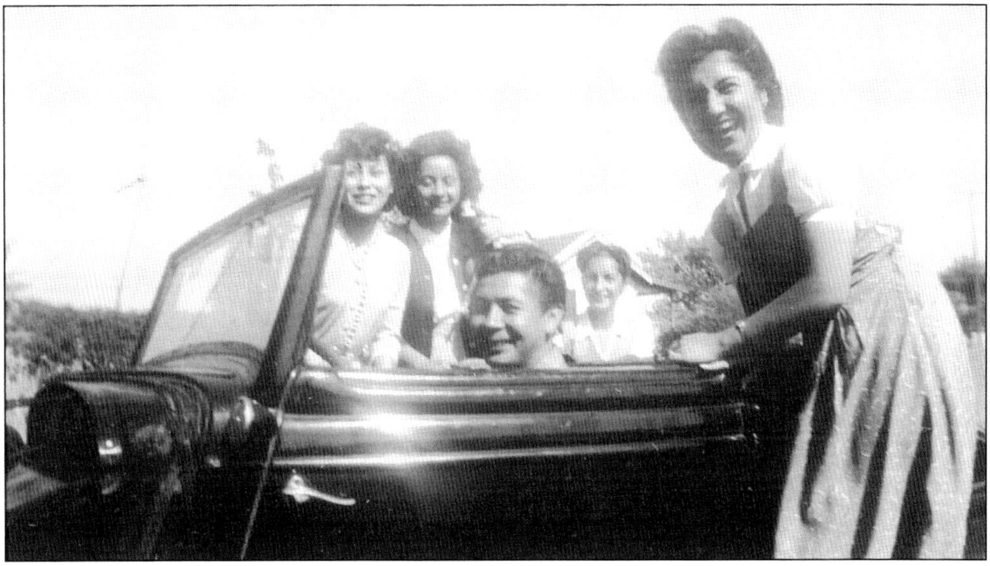

A ride with Paul Madrigal (driver) is a treat. It is 1942, and Madrigal is showing his sisters and cousins his first car, a 1934 Ford convertible. Passengers are, from left to right, Eleanor and Vera Madrigal and Antonia and Catalina Fernandez. Madrigal was a merchant marine and worked as a machinist. (Eleanor Urrea.)

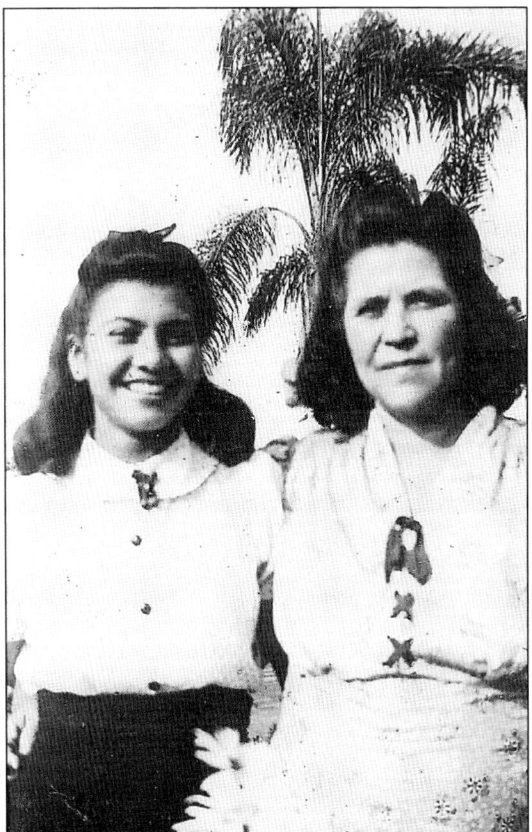

Teenage daughter Emma smiled and embraced her mother, Jesse Olmos, as they enjoyed an afternoon together. Emma's mother was born in Zacatecas and her father, Juan Gonzales, was from Jalisco. He fled from the revolution and worked in Arizona mines. In Wilmington, in 1920, he found work at a refinery but lost his job during the Depression because of prevailing layoff practices. Gonzales then worked on Japanese farms in Palos Verdes, and in empty fields near their home on Sanford Avenue, he planted and sold corn, tomatoes, and chilies to support the family. (Raul Gonzales.)

The Native Americans of Mexico regarded corn as a gift from the gods. Corn was introduced to Europe by Columbus, who took it to Spain. Corn was a staple in the diet and homes in Wilmington. Cornfields also served as a playground for the children. Standing between rows of corn are brother and sister Tony and Esther Vargas. They knew that the summer crop would grow taller and that it would provide delicious meals. (Esther Pacheco.)

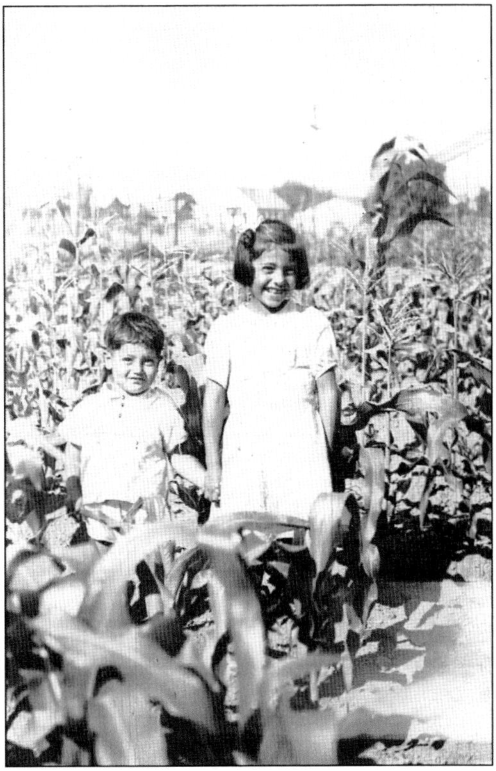

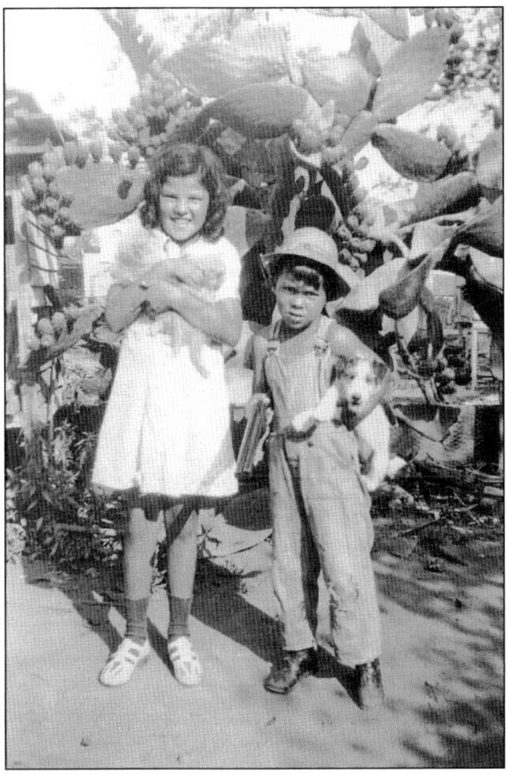

Cousins Lilien Teran and Richard Machado stand with pets in their arms as they pose in front of a large cactus plant. Homes often had a nopal plant and families shared its edible leaves or paddles with neighbors. Many favorite dishes were made from this vegetable. Visible on the left side of the plant are *tunas* (prickly pears), the fruit of the cactus. (Anna Mendez.)

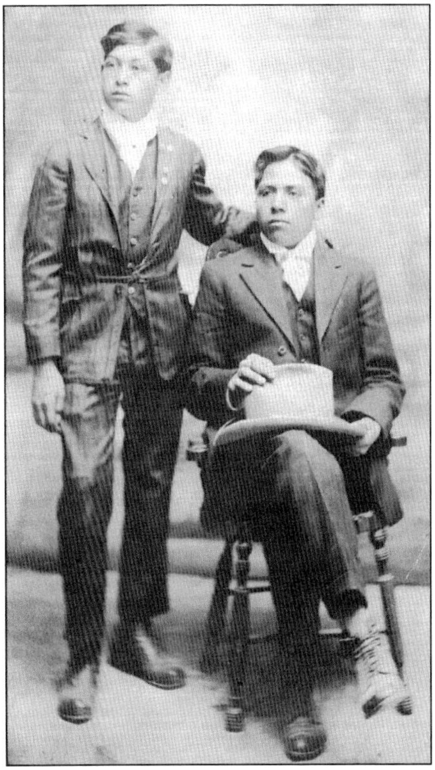

In 1920, Manuel Calderon (seated) and Antonio Guerrero, his *padrino* (godfather), took this picture in Mexicali, Baja California, where they worked for the railroad. They had gone there from Guanajuato, Mexico. Once in California, Calderon worked the fields before working at the Los Angeles harbor. Interestingly, Mexican workers formed a major part of the labor force in the construction and maintenance of the Pacific Electric Railroad Line in Los Angeles. (Mike Calderon.)

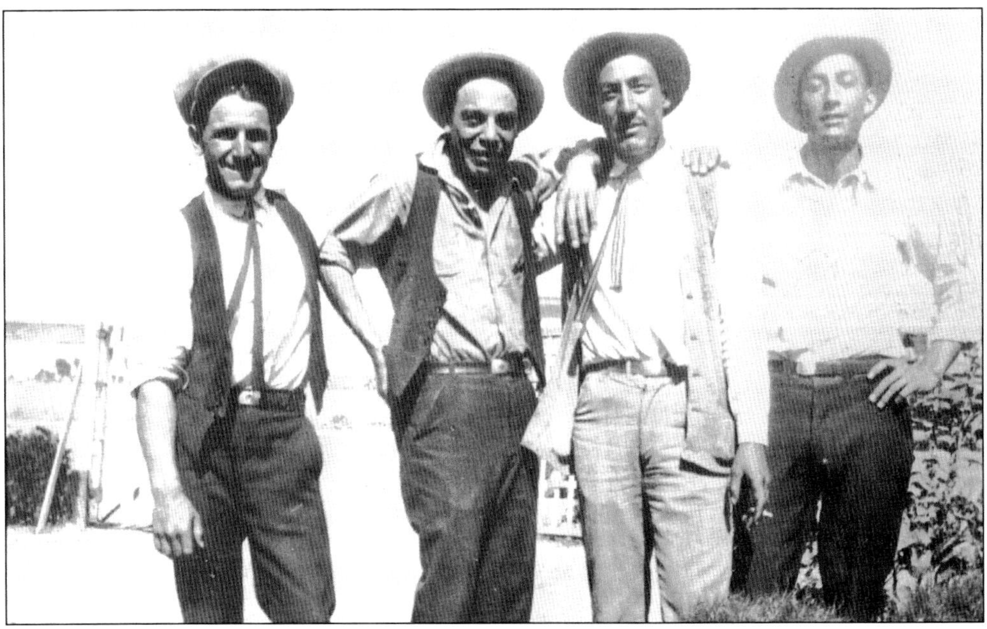

Brothers, from left to right, Andres (second) and Guillermo Garcia (fourth), are with friends in nearby La Rambla in San Pedro. The brothers worked at Todd Shipyard and enjoyed playing baseball in community self-made fields. The fields were maintained by volunteers and were mostly used by young men on business-sponsored teams. Some of the fields were known as Tortilla Flats, Rancho Grande, and Skipper's Field. (Carlos Rico.)

It is December 25, 1966, and Holy Family ushers are stylishly attired and prepared to perform their assigned duties for the day. With friendship and cooperation, the small group of volunteer ushers was responsible for four services on Sunday. When the Spanish Mass and more services were provided for the growing parish population, the ushers group recruited more volunteers. (Jess Marquez.)

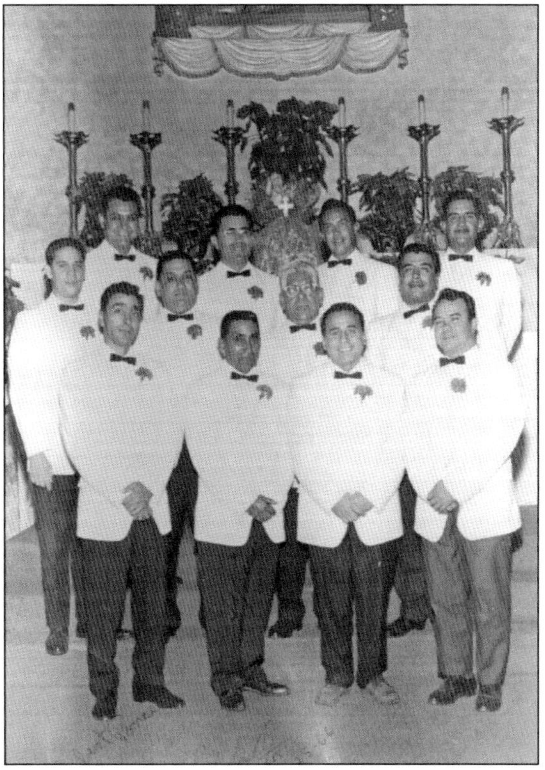

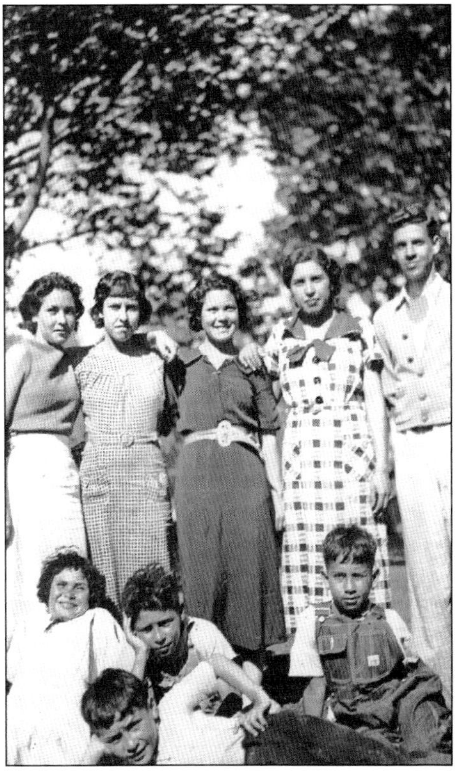

Strong lifetime bonds were formed in the neighborhood. Close friends became *compadres* through marriage, religious occasions, or through informal friendships and activities. Pictured at Banning Park in 1935 were the Perez and Violante families, who lived next door to each other on Pioneer Avenue. They were in each other's weddings, they baptized and were sponsors for first communions and confirmations, they were classmates, and they worked and socialized together. They became an extended family. (Author's collection.)

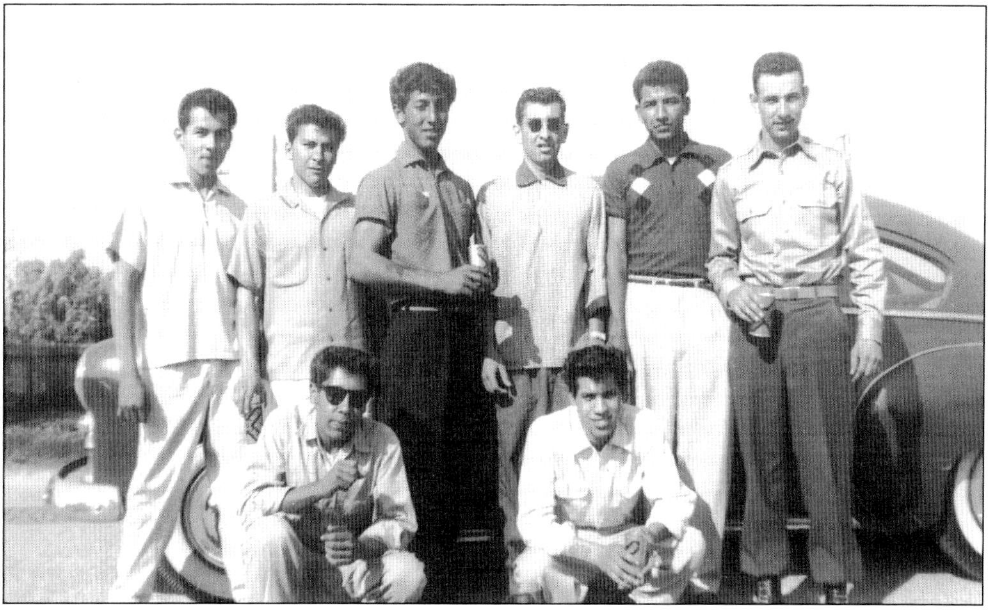

Ramon Cruz (second row, far right) was greeted by his brother and childhood friends in 1955. On leave before being sent to Germany, they gathered at his parents' home at 1210 East Cruces Street and alongside his brother John's 1949 Chevrolet. His mother was Ventura and his father, Rafael Cruz, worked at White King Company. Friends pictured are, from left to right, (first row) Peter Gonzales and Henry Hernandez; (second row) Jim Cruz, Ruben Garcia, Tony Vargas, John Cruz, Gregory Flores, and Cruz. (Ramon Cruz.)

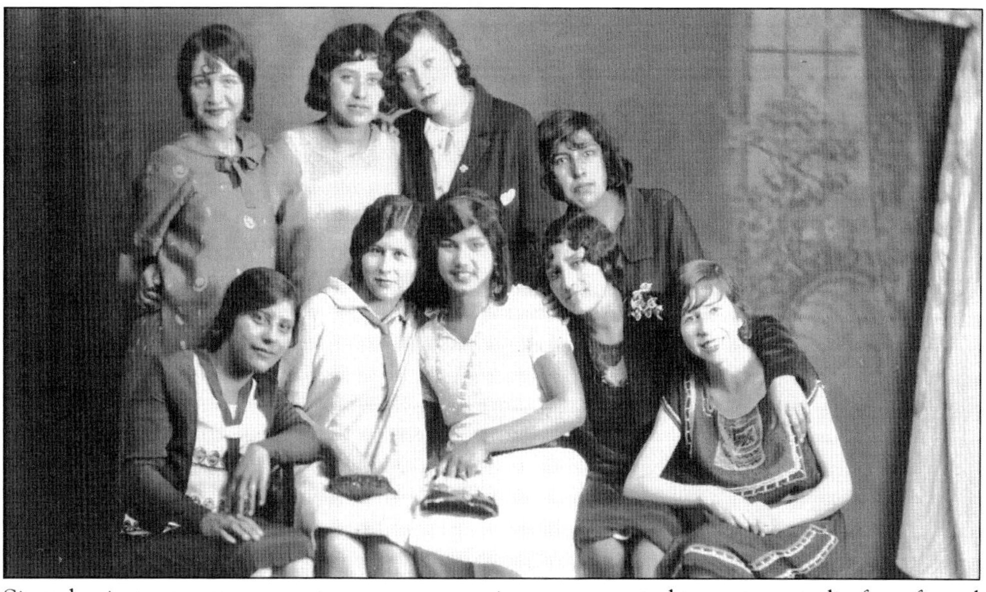

Since having a camera was not common, occasions were created to go to a studio for a formal portrait. This group of single women decided to get together at a studio before they began to get married. Relaxed and in fashion with hair, dress, and shoes, they gathered in 1932. They are, from left to right, (first row) unidentified, Elvira Gonzalez, and three unidentified; (second row) unidentified, Jacoba Urrea, Consuelo Garcia, and Esperanza Violante. Most of these young women worked in the canneries. (Author's collection.)

These young women were out for adventure and fun on a Saturday afternoon. Once a month, Javier Ponce took his family to Irvine Park. His children would always invite friends to join them. It was 1941 and his daughter Esther Ponce (far right) invited friends Connie Violante (left) and unidentified. They are prepared for a ride on their rented bicycles. Also, the Mutualistas de San José had yearly picnics at the park on Labor Day. Food, games, bicycles, horses, and rowboats kept everyone entertained. (Author's collection.)

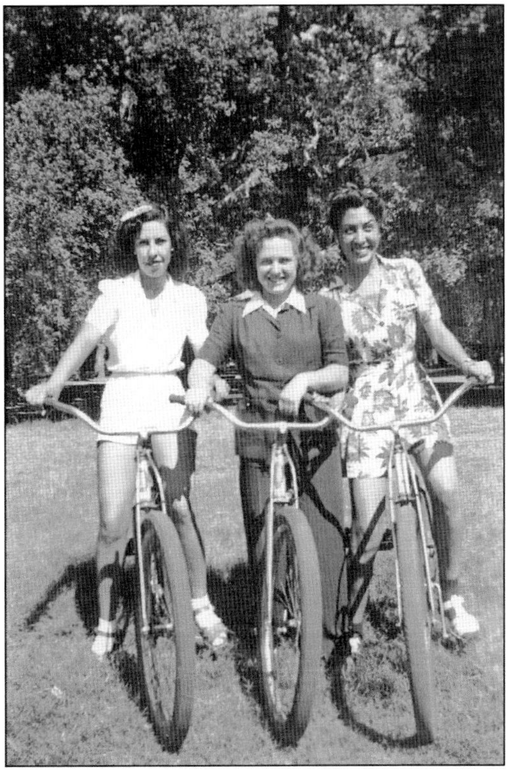

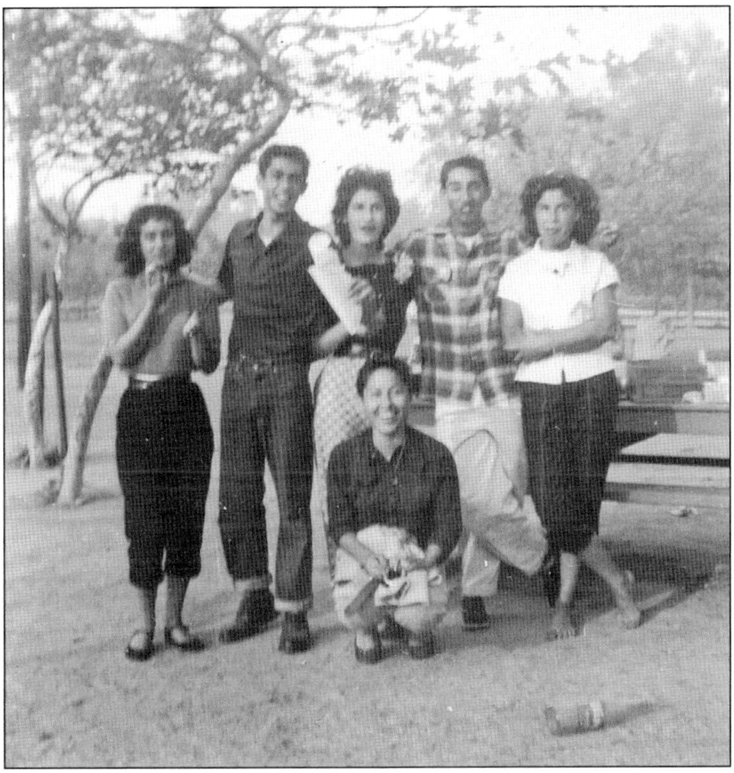

The 1957 Phineas Banning Senior Picnic was held at Griffith Park in Los Angeles. Classmates were taken on school buses to this favorite spot. The trip was an annual tradition held by combined summer and winter seniors. Pictured after lunch are, from left to right, (kneeling) Yolanda Flores; (standing) Rose Marie Alvarado, Manuel Jesolva, Ofelia Sedano, Theodore Robles, and Erlinda Medina. (Author's collection.)

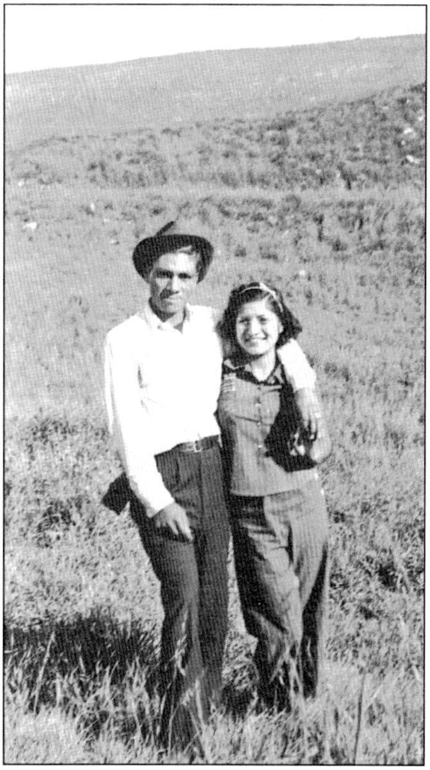

The photograph at left shows the Palos Verdes hillside landscape as it was in 1940. Celia Rivas and Ruben Martinez had been with a group of friends on an afternoon excursion when they stopped to admire the view. They married and raised their family in Wilmington. She graduated from Banning High in 1937 and worked as a school clerk at San Pedro High School. Martinez worked at Consolidated Lumber and retired from Sun Lumber. (Ralph Violante.)

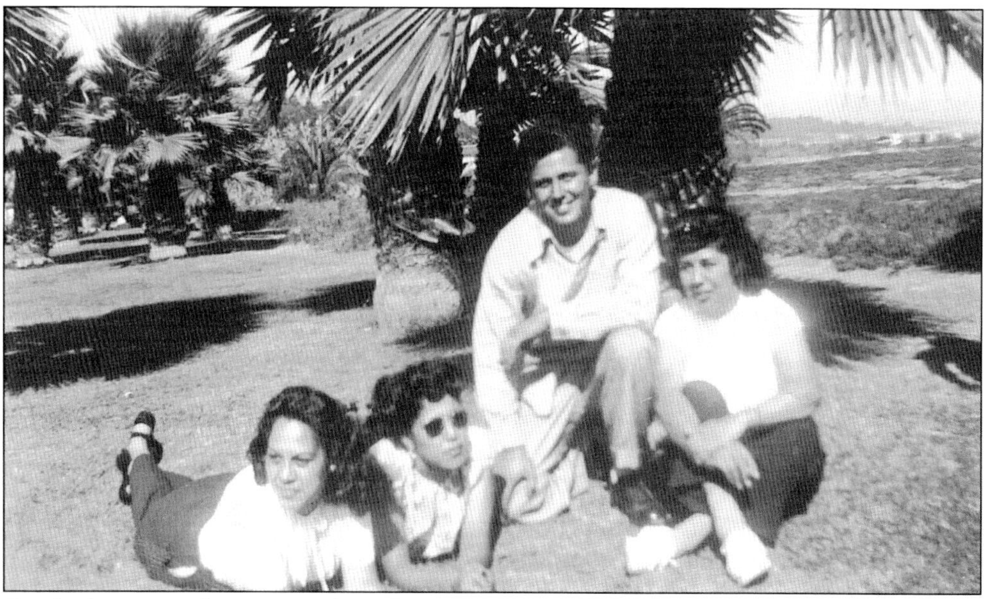

On the horizon, oil storage tanks are seen from a San Pedro park. In the foreground are the Monge sisters, from left to right, Alice, Stella, and Rose. Their friend is Luis Rodriguez. Rose was a "Rosie the Riveter" at an aircraft plant, having learned welding and soldering. Fred Monge, a brother, was an outstanding athlete at Banning High School. At a special assembly in 1943, he and Raul Dominguez received a standing ovation and cheers before leaving for the armed forces. (Author's collection.)

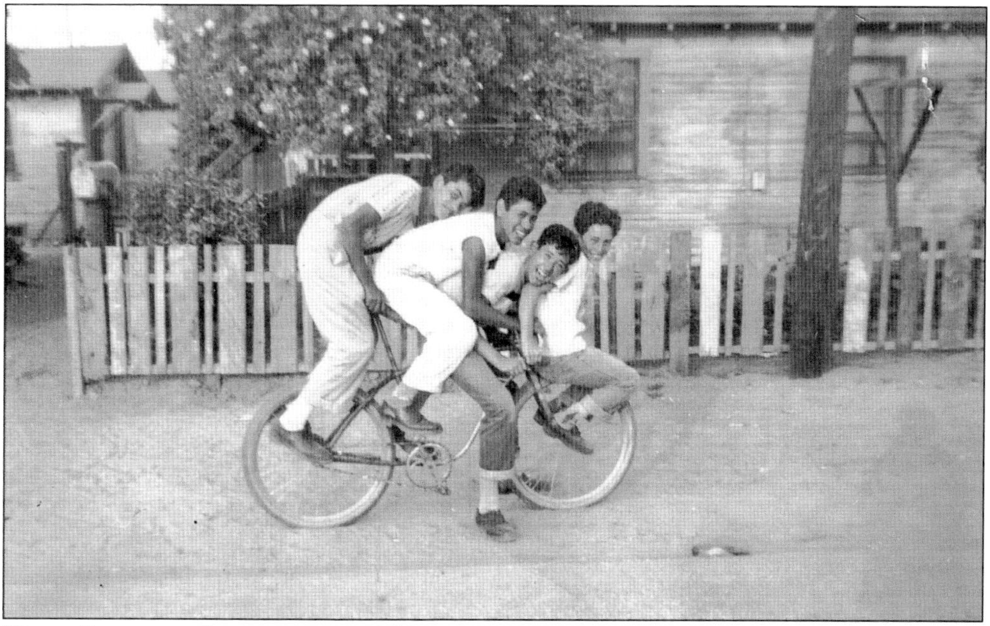

"Courts" or cottage housing was available in many areas of Wilmington. Each house or structure was usually small in size, but families large and small rented until they were able to buy or build their own home. This group of homes was near the corner of Watson Avenue and "L" Street, and this older section of town still did not have paved streets in 1949. Four friends passing by were, from left to right, Agustin Magdaleno, Eddie Martin, Raul De La Vara, and Edward "Wedo" Mendoza. (Gabriel Mendoza.)

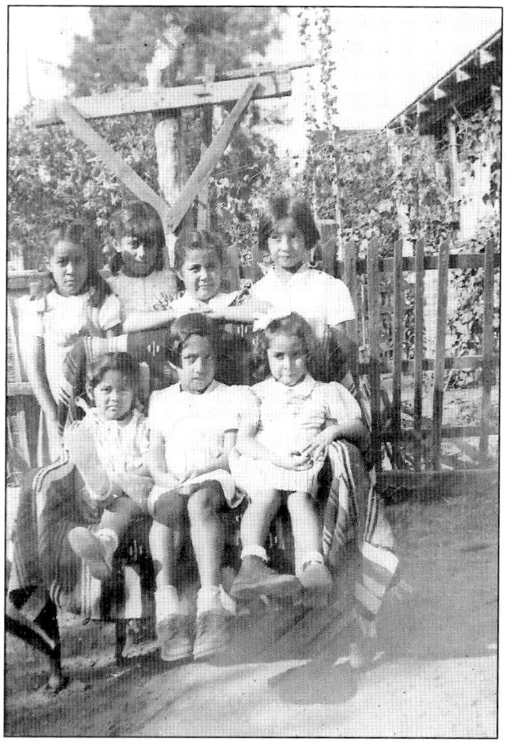

At a birthday party on Watson Avenue, the five-year-old birthday girl, Irene McKenna, was with her guests. The attendees were gathered at a large serape-covered chair with a homemade clothesline behind them. The yard was full of plants common in homes, both for beauty and for food and remedy sources. The girls were, from left to right, (first row) Trinidad Arroyo, Esther Robles, and Irene McKenna; (second row) Nani ?, unidentified, Amelia McKenna, and Rosie Robles. (Amelia McKenna.)

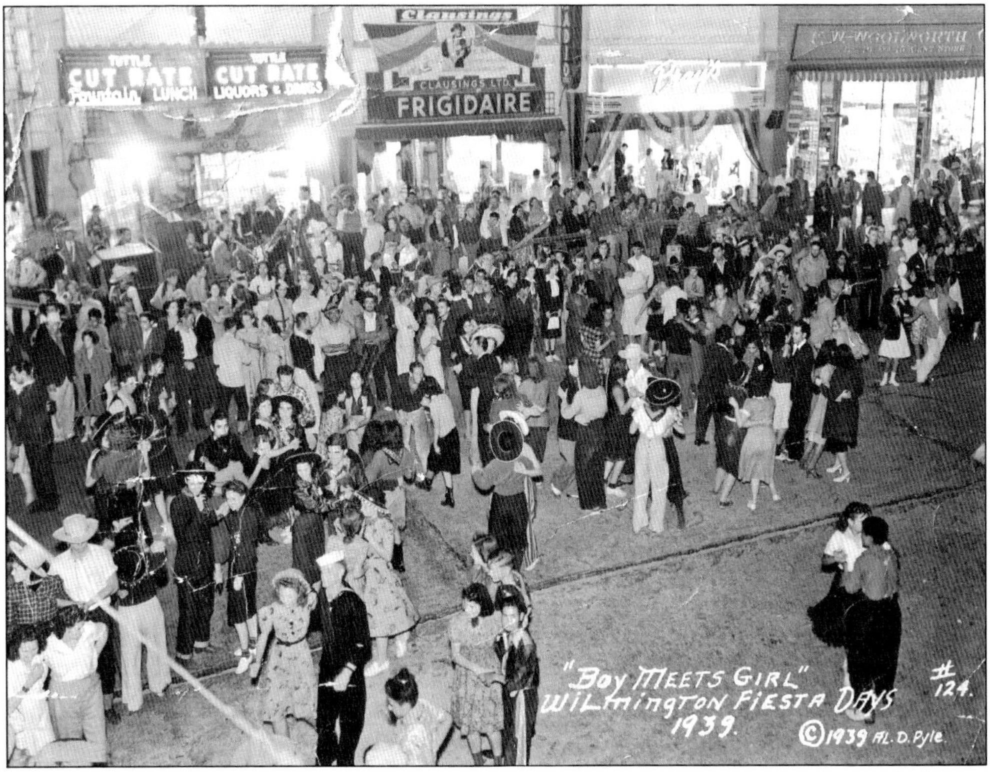

Both of these late-1930s group photographs demonstrate the type of celebrations that took place in the community, often necessitating street closures to allow dancing. Everyone enjoyed themselves in themed costumes or dress. Above is the "Boy Meets Girl" Wilmington Fiesta Days event on the downtown section of Avalon Boulevard. The live band played in front of the Tuttle store. The picture below shows a group on stage for the annual September 16 celebration at the Honorífica on "L" Street. In the *charro* (cowboy) outfit at the center of the picture is Jesus Urrea. Next to him is Rod Gonzalez (right), and other participants are John Urrea, Maria Urrea, Bertha Ortega, and sisters Angie, Carmen, and Esther Gonzalez. (Above, Anna Mendez; below, Cecilia Jacinto.)

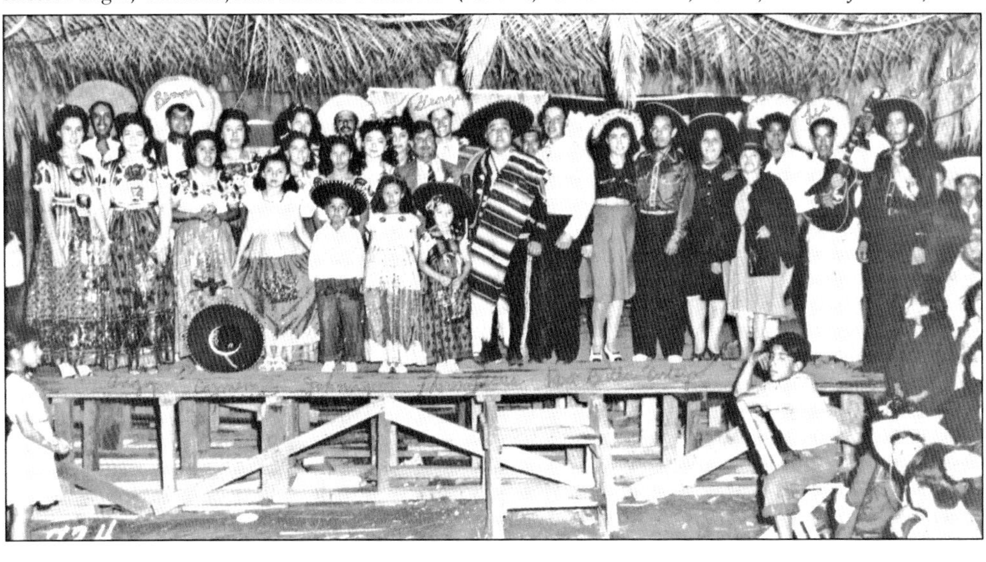

Three

School and Church

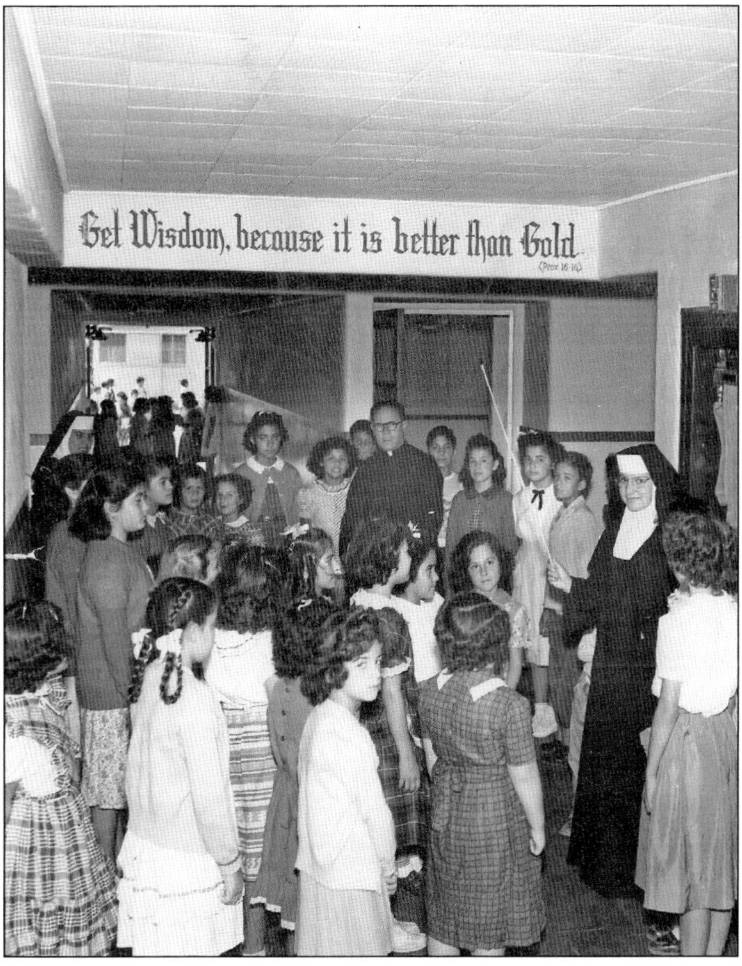

Principal Sister Josephine points to the opening day banner at Holy Family School on September 11, 1950. Fr. Manuel Canseco, the driving force in building both the church and school, stands among children, and by 1953, the school offered a K–8 program. Carmelite Sisters of the Sacred Heart staffed the school until 1996. The nuns' first home was on Avalon Boulevard, and they moved to the present convent on Robidoux Street when it was completed in 1951. (Amelia McKenna.)

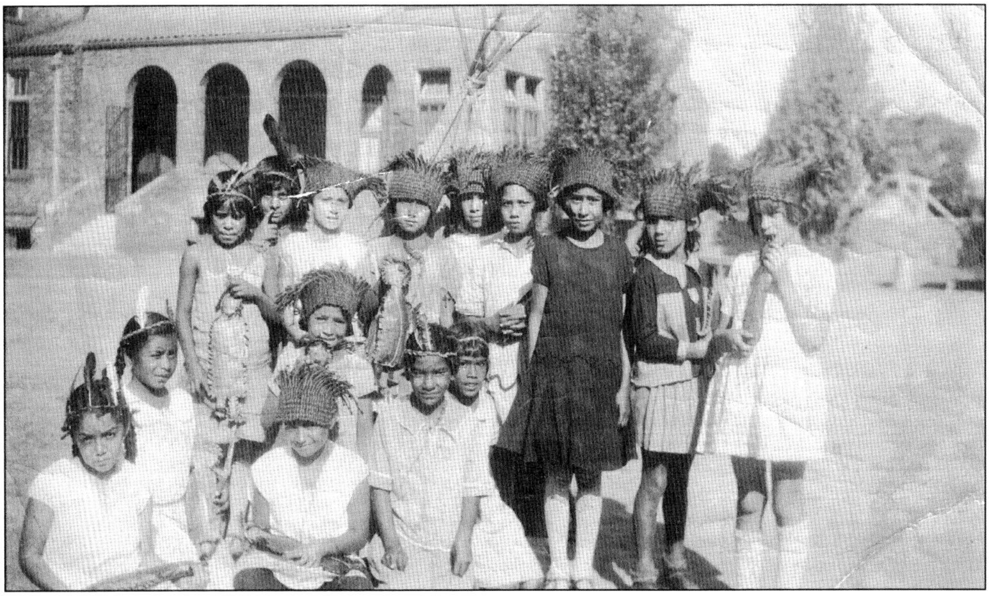

These students are in front of a teepee at Wilmington Park Elementary School in 1930. They had participated in a Thanksgiving program. Martina Lazos, in the dark dress, stood with her classmates while some of them held paper puppets, which had helped tell the story of the holiday. She was born in Texas, attended Phineas Banning High School, and worked in the fish canneries. (Henrietta Perez.)

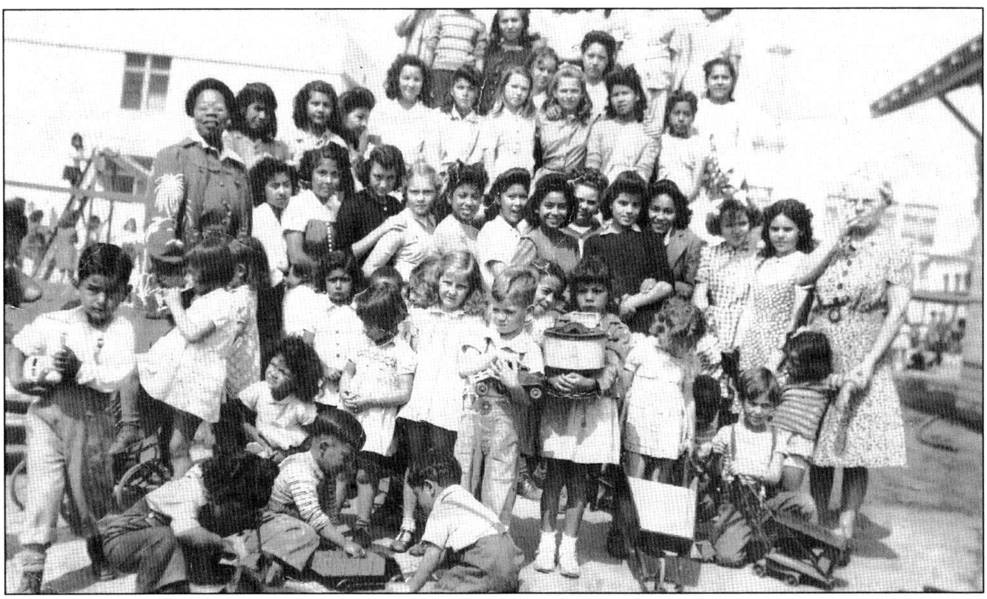

This is a day care class at Wilmington Park School in 1943. Poised and smiling are some sixth-grade girls who were allowed to volunteer in the classroom. They were given the privilege because they had maintained good grades in their class work. Most of the children appeared to be more interested in the toys rather than the photographer's camera. The bungalow (right) housed the day care class and toy loan that was extremely popular with all the neighborhood youngsters. (Dolores Marquez.)

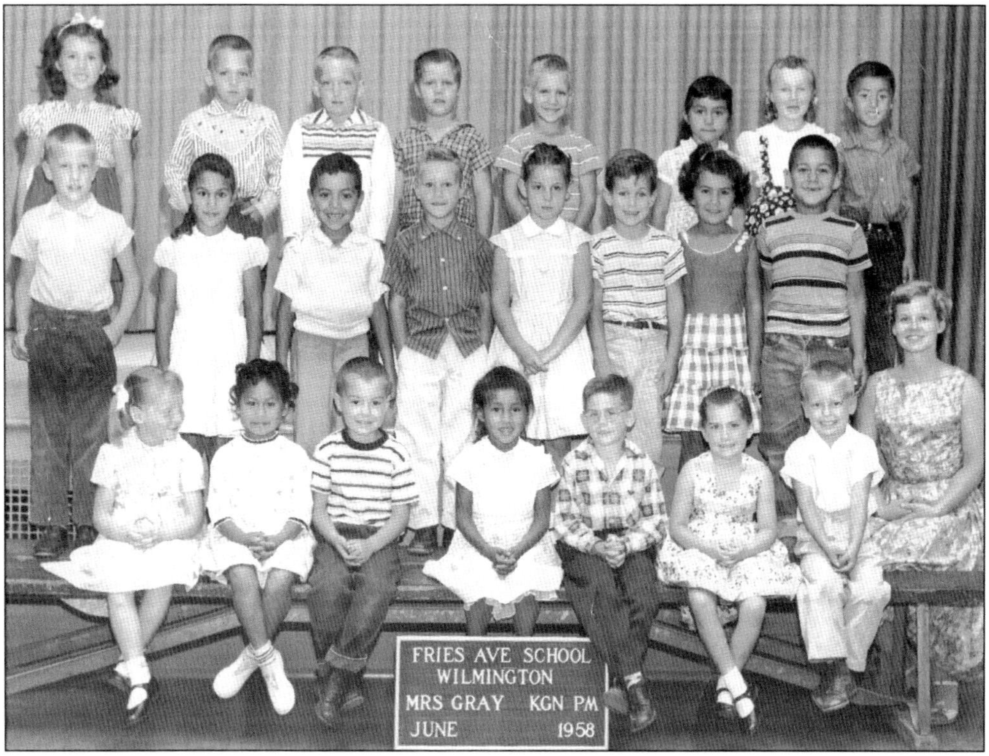

In June 1958, twenty-three kindergarteners sat smiling with their teacher at Fries Avenue School. Standing in the second row is Cynthia Estrada (second from left), who continued her education at St. Peter and St. Paul School and graduated from St. Anthony's in Long Beach. Estrada used the Wilmington Branch Library at Opp Street and Fries Avenue to complement her studies. The library was opened on March 18, 1927, a few months after Fries Avenue School opened its doors. (Cynthia Pratt.)

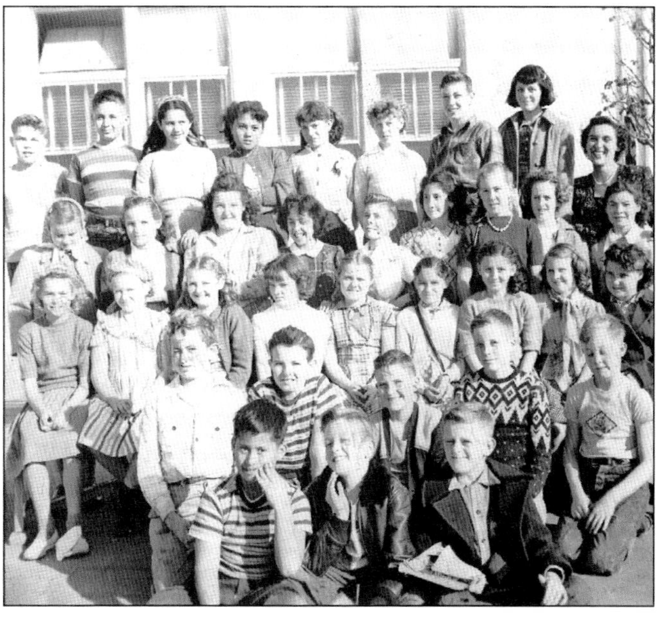

In 1950, Marguerite Guidinger was with her fifth-grade class at Fries Avenue School. Several years before, there had been an attempt to change the school's eastern boundary. All but one of the eight second-generation Mexican American students in this class lived east of the school on Eubank and Hyatt Avenues. Margaret Estrada, a parent, led a campaign against the proposed change, because the affected students would have to cross two separate sets of railroad lines at Watson and at McFarland Avenues. (Author's collection.)

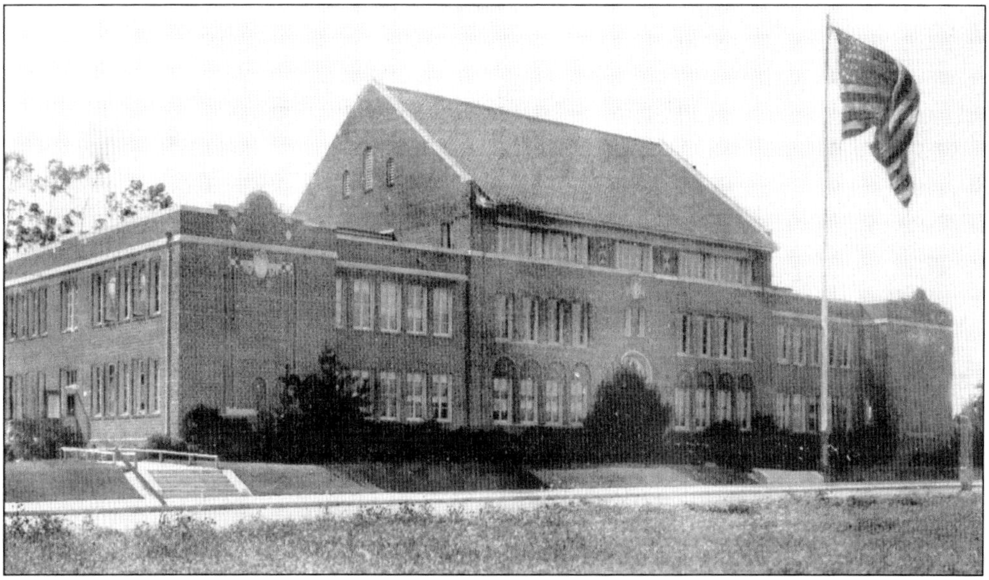

Wilmington High School (first called Canal Street School), built in 1912, was located at Anaheim Street and Avalon Boulevard. In 1920, its girls' glee club listed Antonia Hernandez, Angela Erro, and Lola Varela as members. In 1921, the senior class consisted of 11 students, having grown from one in 1912; the alumni list includes George Garcia, a dentist from the class of 1915. The school was replaced in 1925 by Phineas Banning High School at 1500 Avalon Boulevard. (Glenn French.)

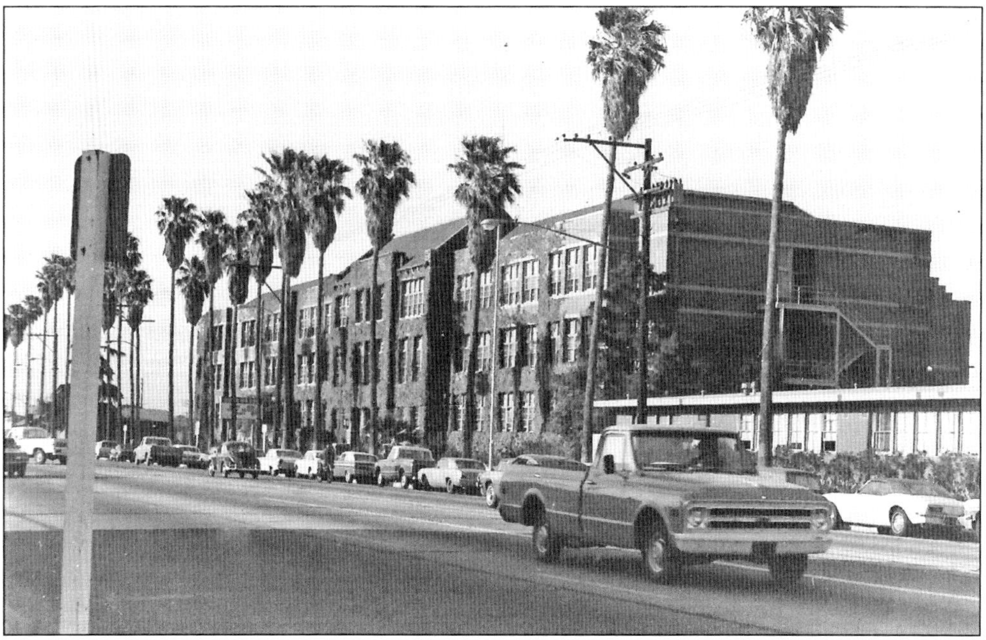

Phineas Banning High School was the nucleus of educational endeavors. It offered academic, social, athletic, and leadership opportunities, and its vine-covered facade was attractive and inviting. Those who attended or graduated from the school have fond memories of their days there. The ivy-covered building was torn down (1971) and replaced (1975). This 1958 photograph also shows the Wrigley palm trees lining Avalon Boulevard. They are the last reminders of the prior brick building's frontage. (Amelia McKenna.)

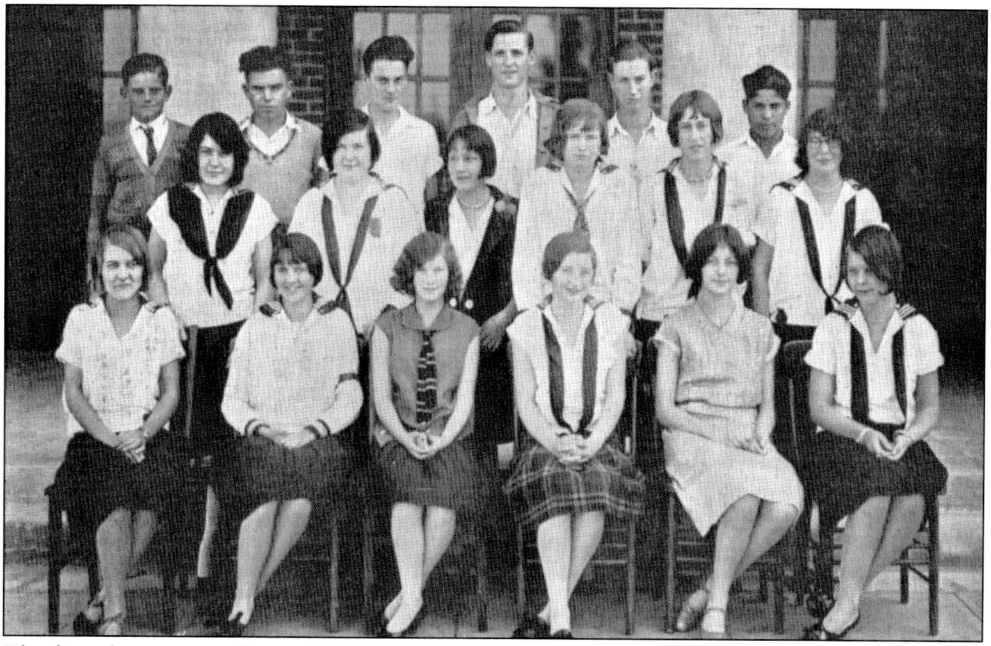

The first class to enter Banning High as freshmen are pictured here as juniors. One third of the class was boys, and Charles Gonzales (third row, far right) was one of them. He became active in sports, clubs, and government. An all-around athlete, he soon earned his varsity letter, the "B." He excelled in his courses, and Gonzales went on to work as a surveyor-contractor. One of the projects he worked on was the Grand Central Market, later known as Foodman on Pacific Coast Highway. (Raul Gonzales.)

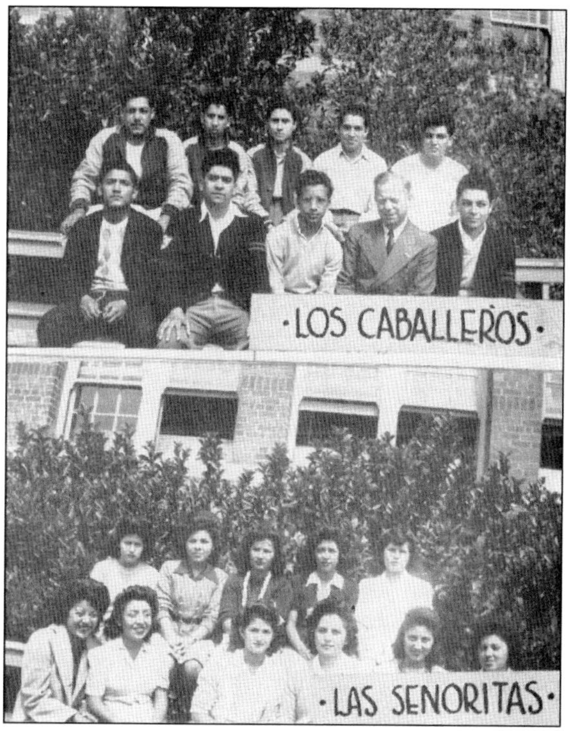

The 1943 Banning High School annual (*Pilot Wheel*) showed Los Caballeros as a school club. The April 15, 1943, issue of the *Portlight* (school newspaper) reported officers for the ensuing term had been elected as follows: Tony Manzo, president; Charles Rico, vice president; "Chief" Camarillo, secretary; and Elizardo Flores, treasurer. It explained the club as an honor society. Not only were these future club officers leaders, but they were also outstanding athletes. Las Senoritas appeared in the yearbook, too. (Glenn French.)

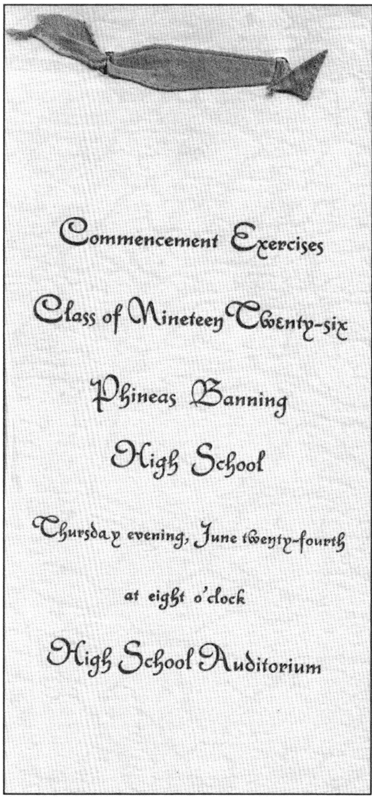

Commencement Exercises

Class of Nineteen Twenty-six

Phineas Banning

High School

Thursday evening, June twenty-fourth

at eight o'clock

High School Auditorium

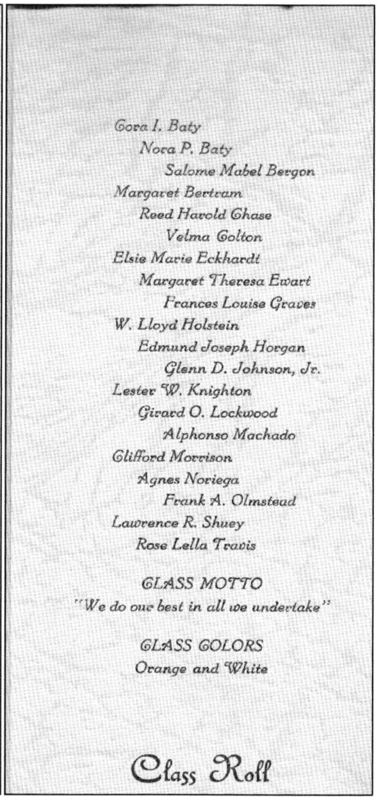

Cora I. Baty
Nora P. Baty
Salome Mabel Bergon
Margaret Bertram
Reed Harold Chase
Velma Colton
Elsie Marie Eckhardt
Margaret Theresa Ewart
Frances Louise Graves
W. Lloyd Holstein
Edmund Joseph Horgan
Glenn D. Johnson, Jr.
Lester W. Knighton
Girard O. Lockwood
Alphonso Machado
Clifford Morrison
Agnes Noriega
Frank A. Olmstead
Lawrence R. Shuey
Rose Lella Travis

CLASS MOTTO
"We do our best in all we undertake"

CLASS COLORS
Orange and White

Class Roll

The roll of the first graduating class of Phineas Banning High School appears on the June 24, 1926, commencement program. Below, graduates are dressed for their class picture in attire typically worn by students in the 1920s. Alphonso Machado is kneeling in the first row, fourth from the left. He obtained an engineering degree and manufactured farm equipment. His living and working on the family farm paid off. (Both, Anna Mendez.)

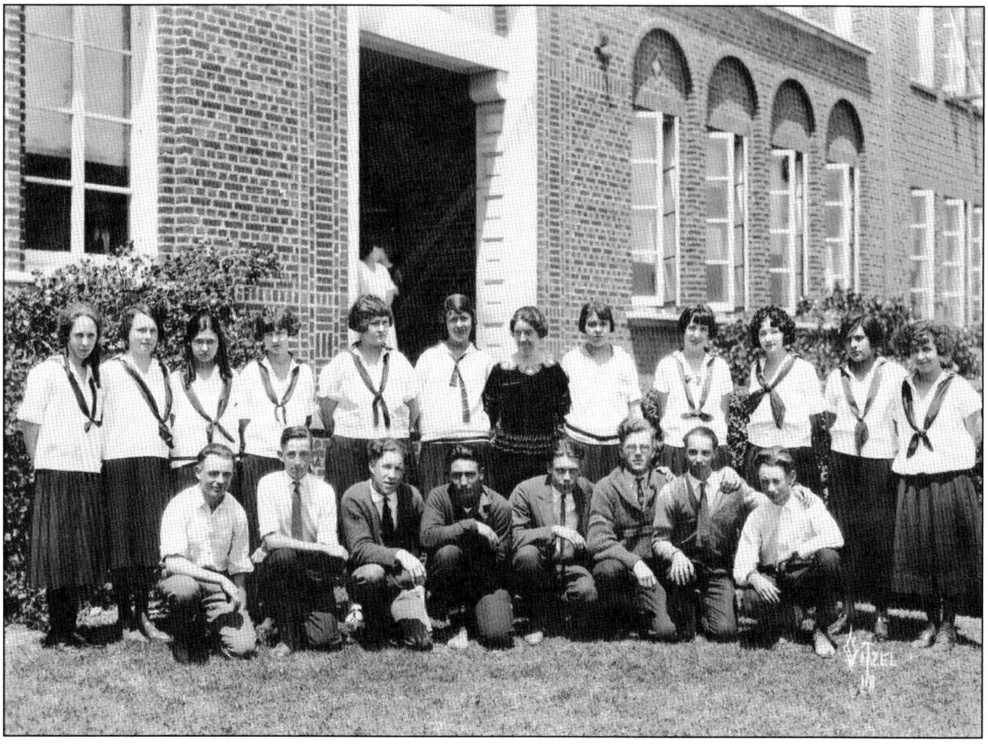

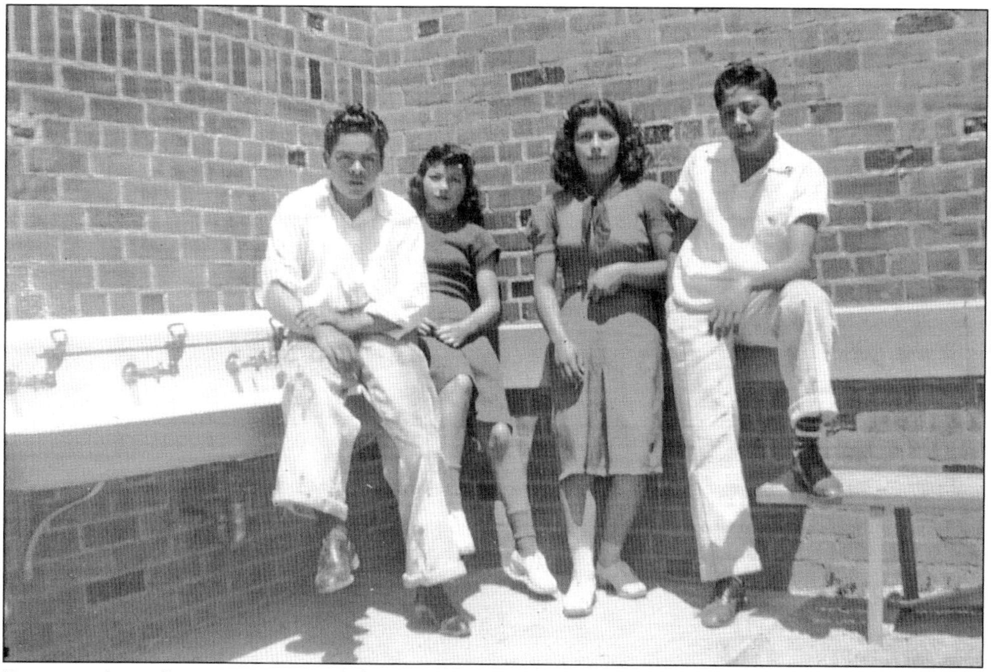

Between the girls gymnasium and the main building, Phineas Banning High School was a social gathering place during recess and lunch. The tennis courts and main gymnasium were no deterrents for passing the time of day. On May 26, 1939, near the fountain, from left to right are Leonard Rodriguez, Maggie de la Torre, ? Fematt, and Mike Ramirez. (Anna Mendez.)

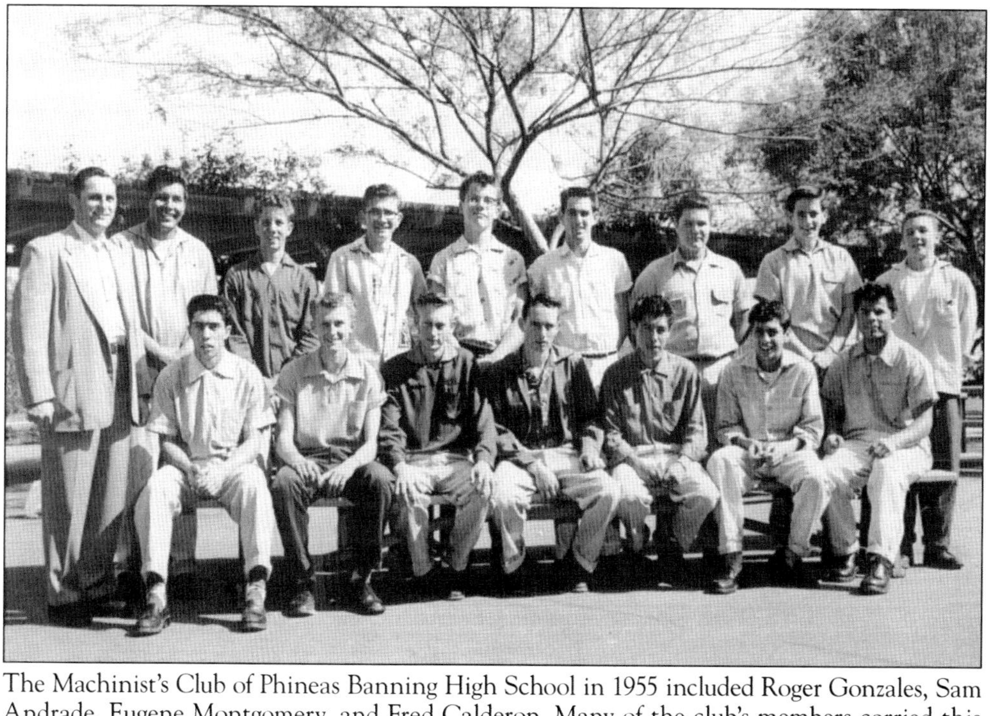

The Machinist's Club of Phineas Banning High School in 1955 included Roger Gonzales, Sam Andrade, Eugene Montgomery, and Fred Calderon. Many of the club's members carried this interest into future hobbies or employment. (Roger Gonzales.)

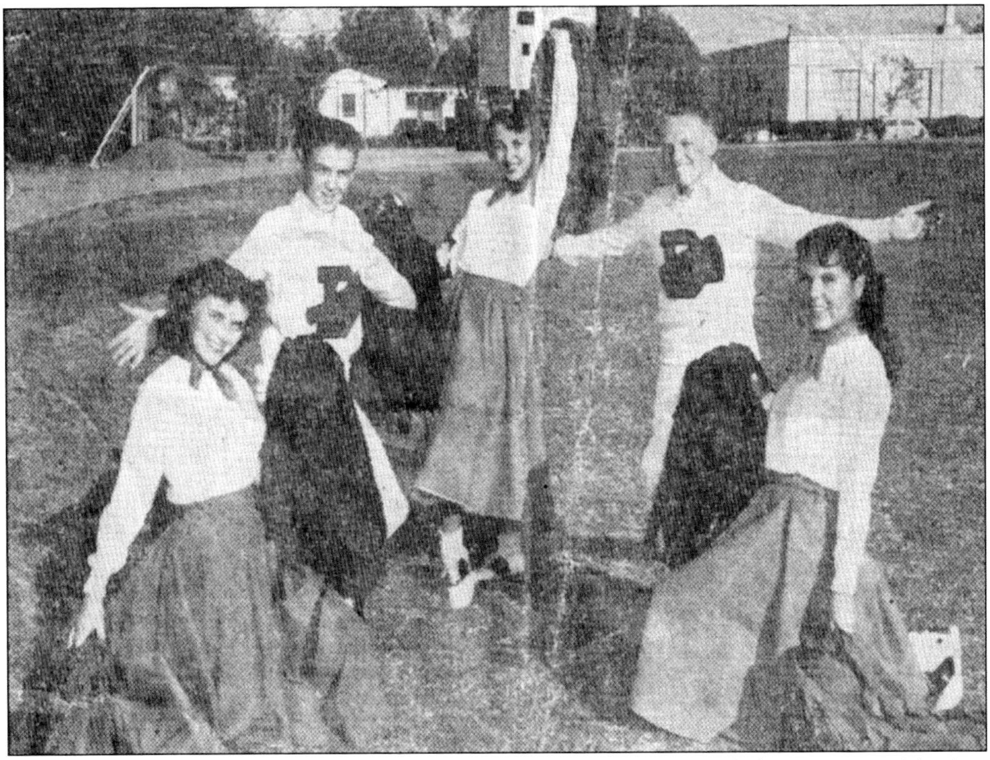

The newspaper article shows Henrietta Espinoza (far right), who not only became one of the first women to lead the Pilots in cheers but also the first Mexican American to do so. She graduated from Phineas Banning High School in 1954. The cheerleading squad is posing at the school's all-sports field, Travis Field, at Avalon Boulevard and Pacific Coast Highway. The large building in the background is the Pacific Bell Telephone Company on Broad Avenue. The following year, Sofia Salcido became a school cheerleader. (Henrietta Perez.)

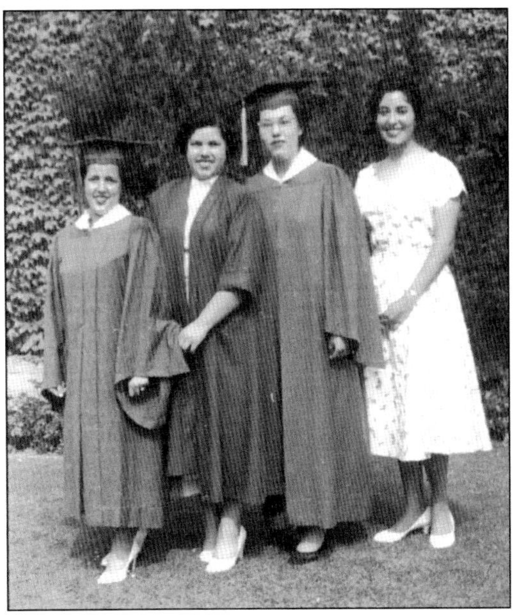

It was graduation for the summer 1954 class. The ceremony was held in the school's auditorium. The motto over the stage read, "Education is learning to use the tools that man finds indispensable." It is the same motto that graces Royce Hall at UCLA. Classmates were, from left to right, Maria Gallegos, Sylvia Martinez, Olga Kavathas, and Stella Nieto. Martinez and Nieto were honor guards for this class and graduated in winter 1955. (Author's collection.)

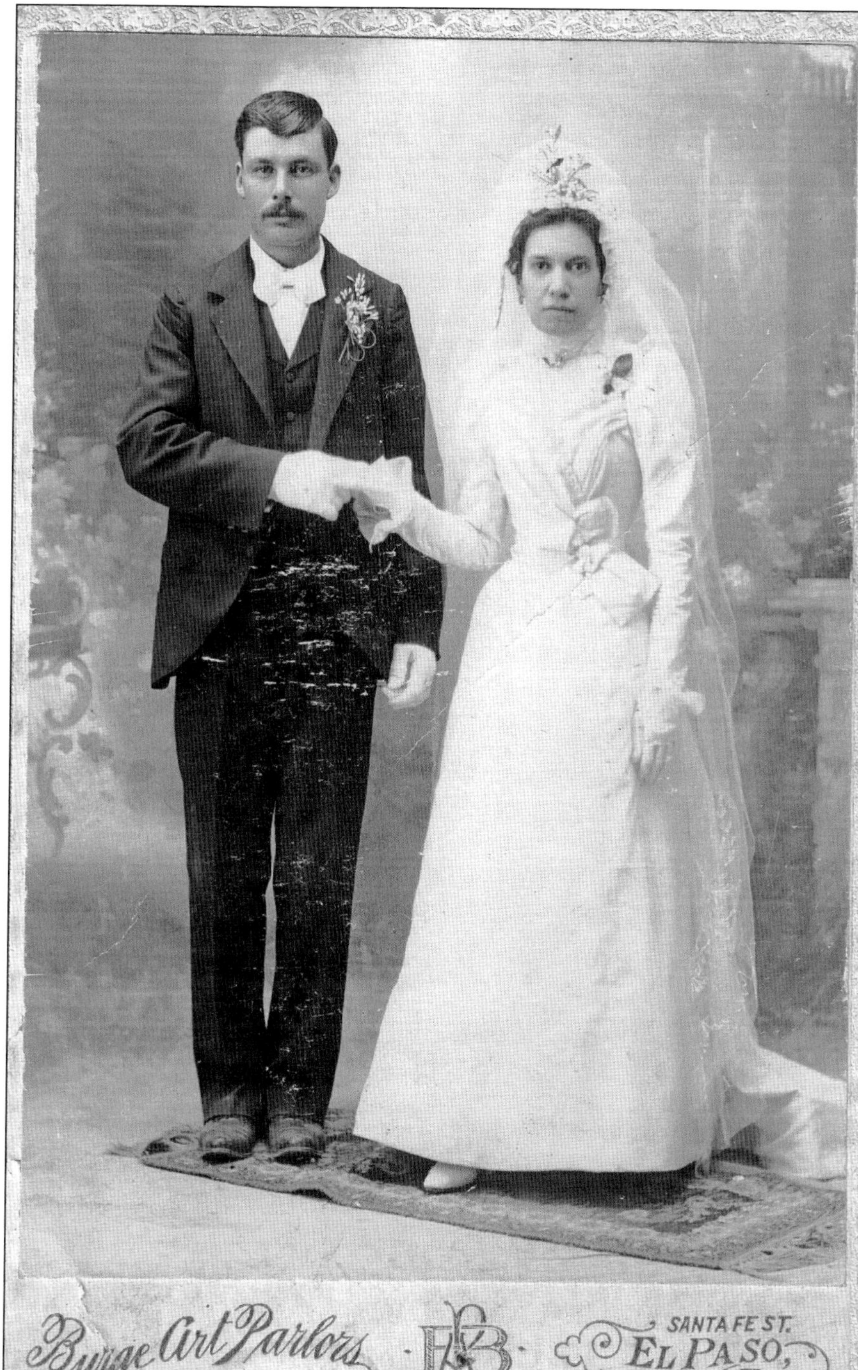

This delightful postcard wedding portrait of Valentina Rico and Pedro M. Garcia was taken before the 20th century dawned. They were married in El Paso, Texas, and are wearing the wedding fashion of the period. The postcard was addressed to their family as a loving memento of their marriage, and the date inscribed was October 12, 1899. They came to the harbor area soon after. (Carlos Rico.)

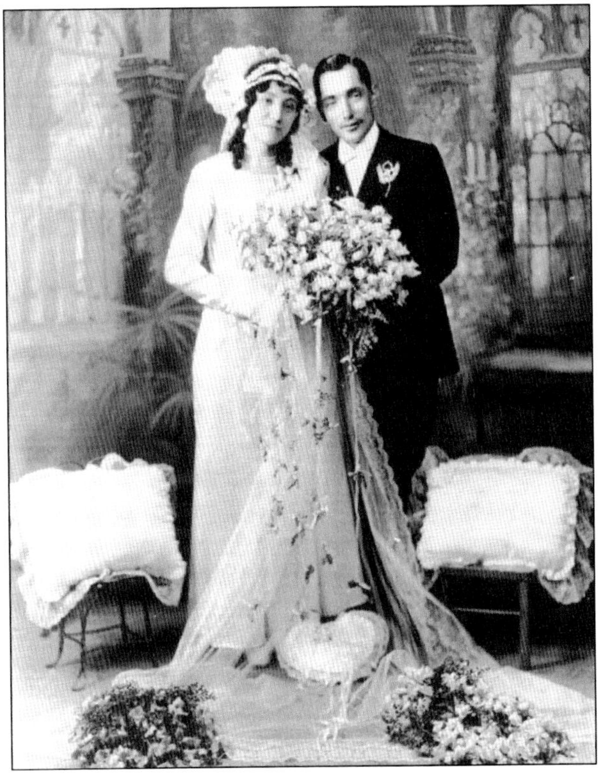

Eliseo Vargas, born in 1899, came from Jalisco, Mexico. At a picnic in Los Angeles, he and his friends met a priest from their hometown who helped them found Holy Family Church. He helped in the construction of the church and retired from U.S. Borax. At age 12, Rafaela and her parents, Tomas Perez and Maura Flores, came from Michoacan seeking a better life. Eliseo and Rafaela were married on May 1, 1932. They had five children: Esther, Josephine, Tony, Robert, and Maggie. (Esther Pacheco.)

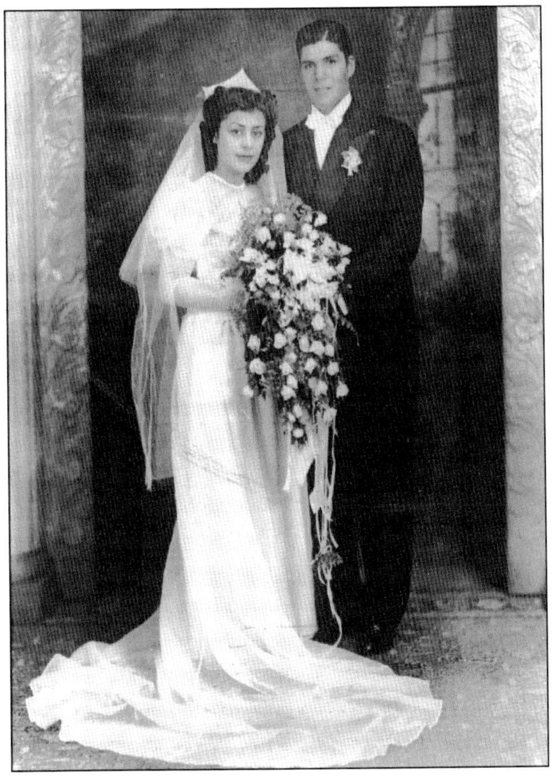

Guadalupe Gonzalez married Henry Teran before World War II. It was a difficult time for families. Mexican Americans suffered discrimination in housing, employment, at school, and in the military, but their sons served the country. Teran joined the Marines and was killed in action, becoming a Purple Heart recipient. He had a daughter Martha, and his pregnant wife delivered their second daughter, Suzanne, without him. (Rita Rosales.)

In 1945, Juana Gonzales and Ramon Suarez stand proudly on Pioneer Avenue with their newly baptized daughter, Rita. She was baptized at Holy Family Church. The Suarez baby is dressed in a long gown made of fine batiste, which she still treasures today. A baby's godparents become its protectors, assuring safekeeping and practice of the faith. Godparents are called *padrinos* and become *compadres* of the couple. The first recorded baptism at the Holy Family parish took place on February 14, 1929, for Maria Raquel Acosta. (Rita Rosales.)

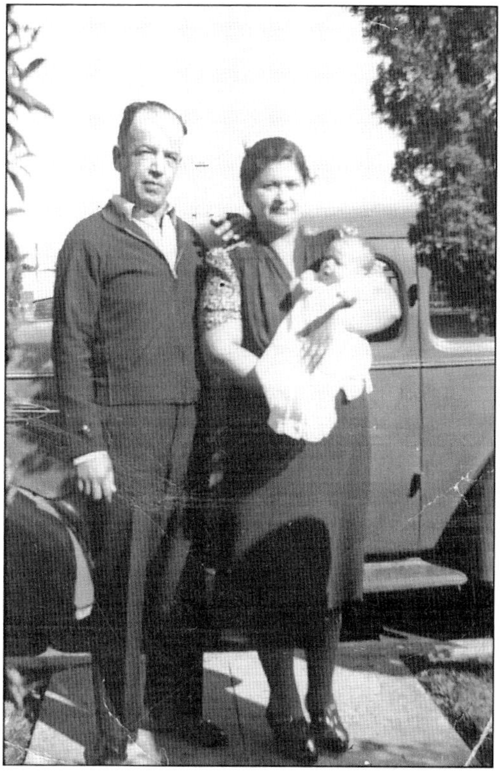

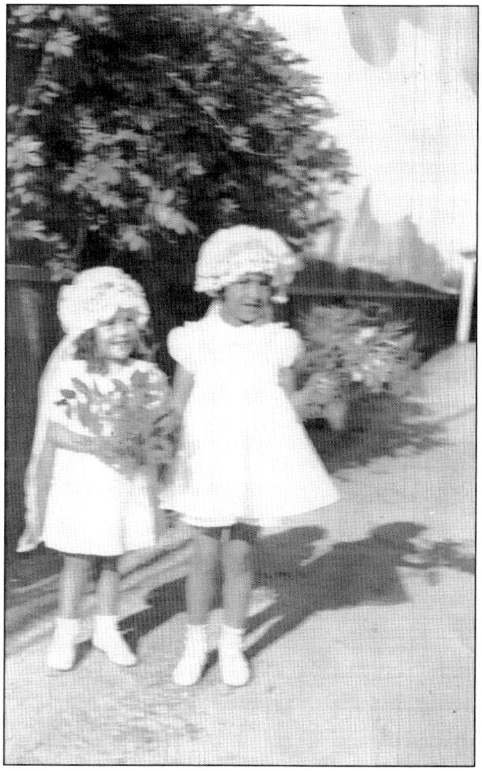

During May, it was the custom for children to offer flowers to the Blessed Virgin during the rosary service. All the little girls wore white dresses and veils and walked down the aisle to place flowers at the altar. Josephine (left) and Esther Vargas are shown in the dresses and head coverings made by their mother, Rafaela Vargas. (Esther Pacheco.)

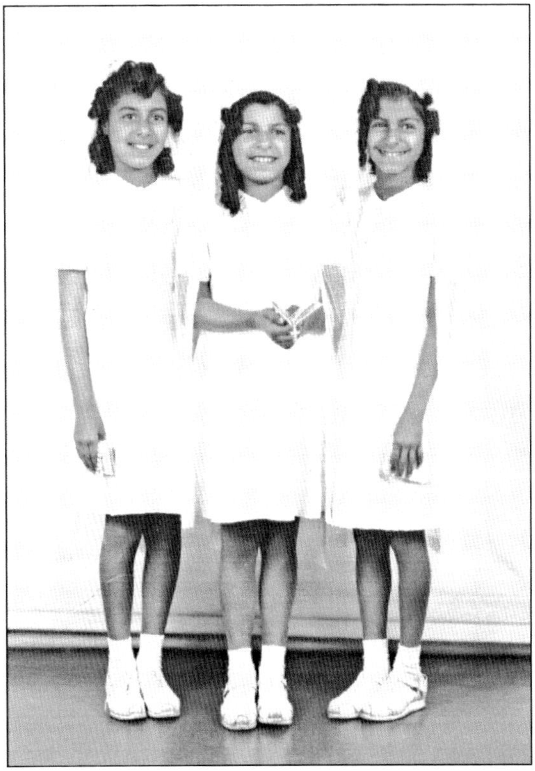

Three Sanchez sisters (from left to right), Margaret, Mary, and Carmen, made their First Communion together. They are holding their prayer books and rosaries. They are wearing fashionable and popular curls and are attired in the required short white dress. No long dresses were permitted to avoid the bride look. Years later, when men were in the service, the sisters worked what people called a man's job at local gas stations wearing unladylike pants, a fashion that came to stay. They grew up on Cruces Street, across from an army camp, and recall the roosters, bugles, and marching drills on the dusty streets of the neighborhood. (Dolores Marquez.)

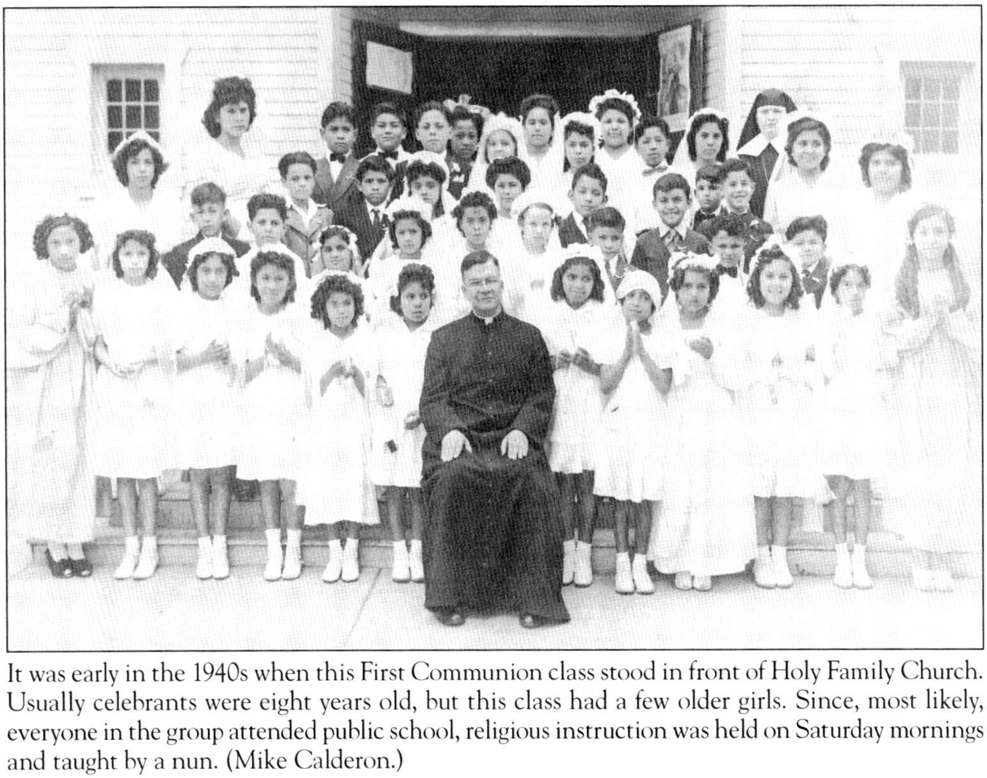

It was early in the 1940s when this First Communion class stood in front of Holy Family Church. Usually celebrants were eight years old, but this class had a few older girls. Since, most likely, everyone in the group attended public school, religious instruction was held on Saturday mornings and taught by a nun. (Mike Calderon.)

To become eligible for the sacrament of First Communion in the Catholic Church, children learn prayers and basic principles of the church. On that occasion, they receive communion for the first time. Their sponsors, called *padrino* (godfather) or *madrina* (godmother), become important persons in the life of the child and family. Raphael Mota, the *ahijado* (godchild), stood proudly with his godfather Joseph Palumbo in this 1934 photograph. Mota is holding religious articles he received. (Ralph Mota.)

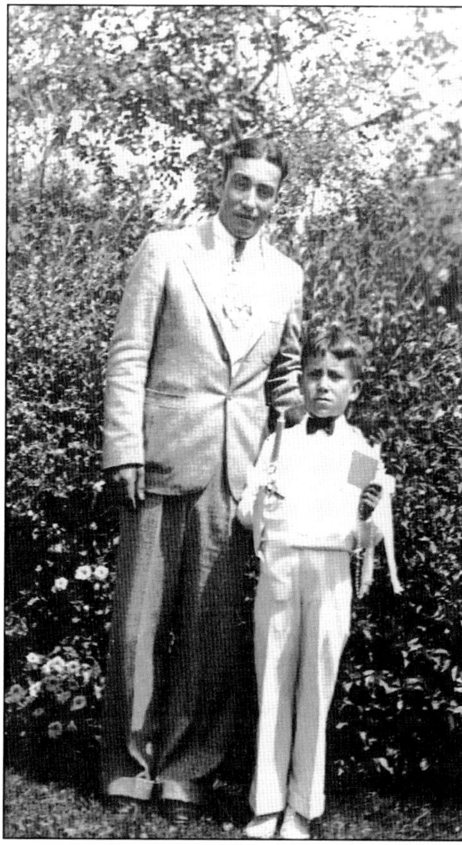

This 1947 First Communion group stood with Fr. Jose Veloz in front of the Holy Family Church parish hall. The hall served many purposes, but a favorite activity was the *loteria* (Mexican bingo) game. Prizes were displayed on different levels with players seated in an outer circle. The caller eloquently chanted a prose or rhyme indicating the drawn card. The parish hall was replaced in 1965, and the equipment and kitchen utensils were purchased with donated books of blue and green chip stamps. (Henrietta Perez.)

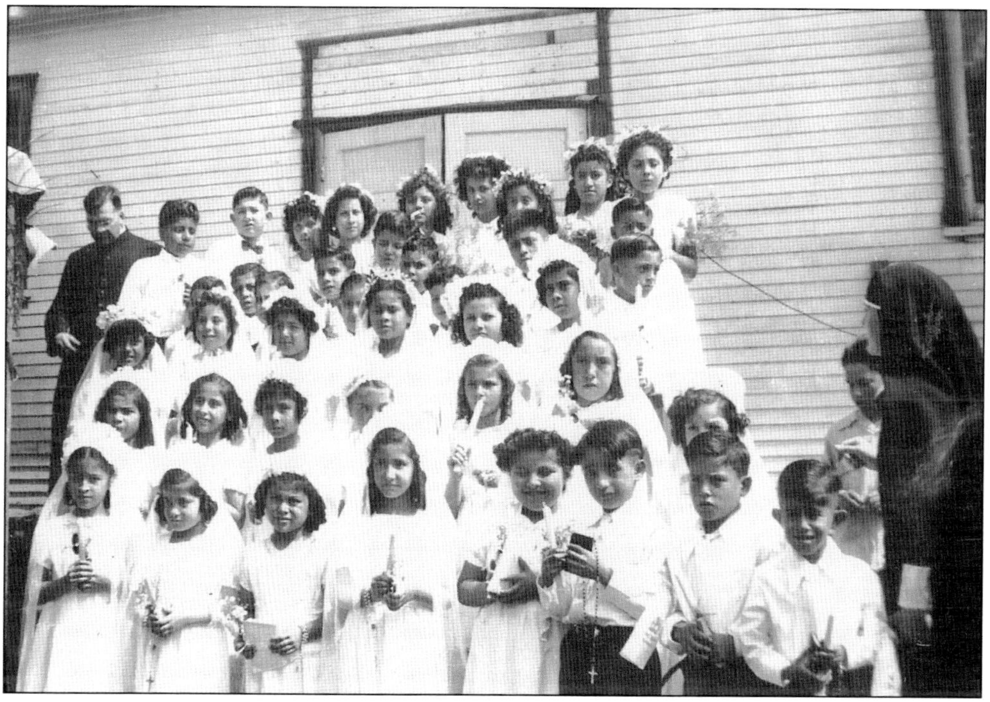

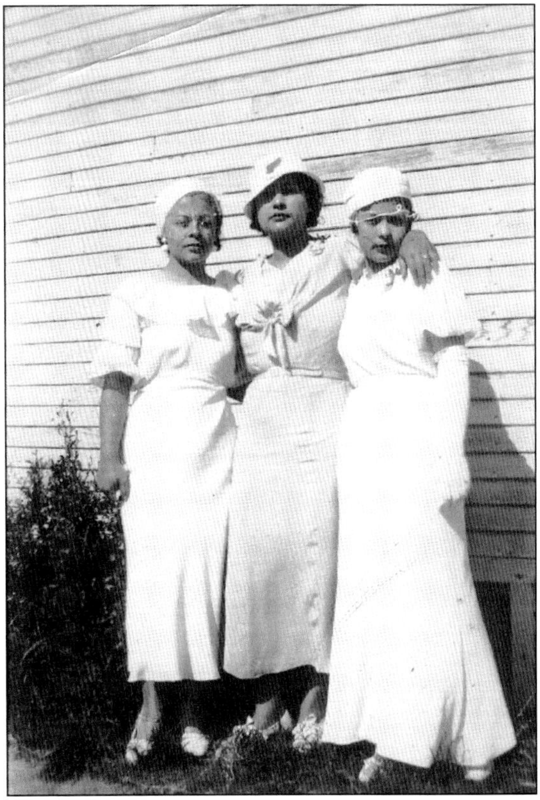

Always fashionable women, from left to right sisters Sara, Maria, and Evangelina Gonzalez made their confirmation at Holy Family Church around 1930. Sara and Maria were born in Mexico and Evangelina in Missouri. They married, raised their families, and worked outside the home. Sara and husband, Roberto Garcia, lived on Terminal Island when the war broke out and endured hardships when he contracted tuberculosis. Maria's husband, Jesus Urrea, was an air raid warden during the war and later owned the Tijuana Restaurant. Angie worked at Douglas Aircraft and married Ralph Johnson who was stationed at Fort MacArthur. (Cecilia Jacinto)

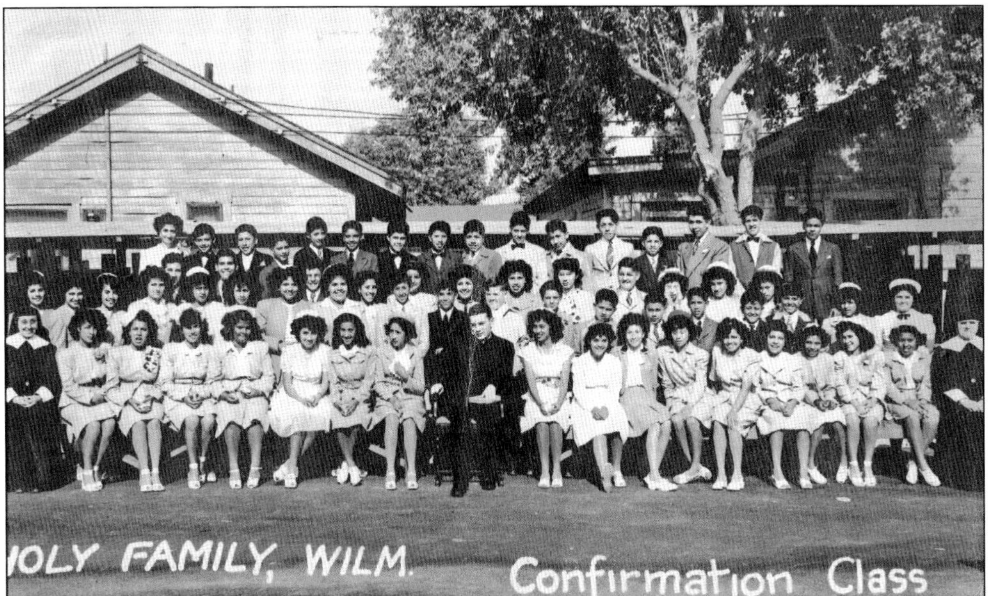

The confirmation class of 1947 sat for the photograph on the church grounds where the *jamaicas* (bazaars) were held. The 14 to 16 year olds had now completed another sacrament. They had made a mature commitment. On this occasion, participants may choose another name to identify their personal decision of faith. (Alfonso Macias.)

This Holy Family Church bulletin of June 20, 1948, features five altar boys wearing the traditional cassocks. They are, from left to right, (first row) Edward Arroyo and Ben Mauricio; (second row) John Cruz, Raymond Arroyo, and Ramon Cruz. They learned the Latin responses and were prepared to assist at Sunday and weekday Mass, funerals, weddings, and at other special observances. (Raymond Cruz.)

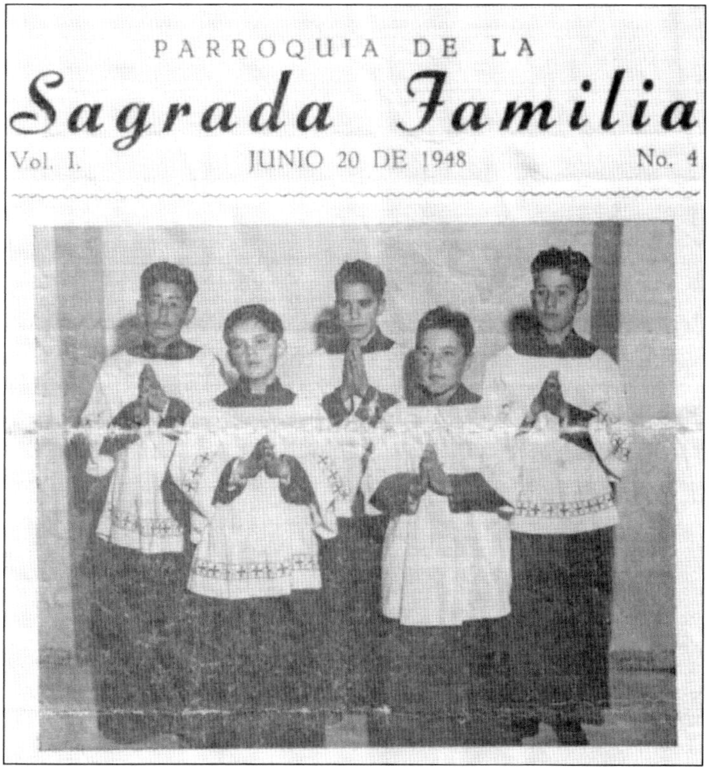

PARROQUIA DE LA

Sagrada Familia

Vol. I. JUNIO 20 DE 1948 No. 4

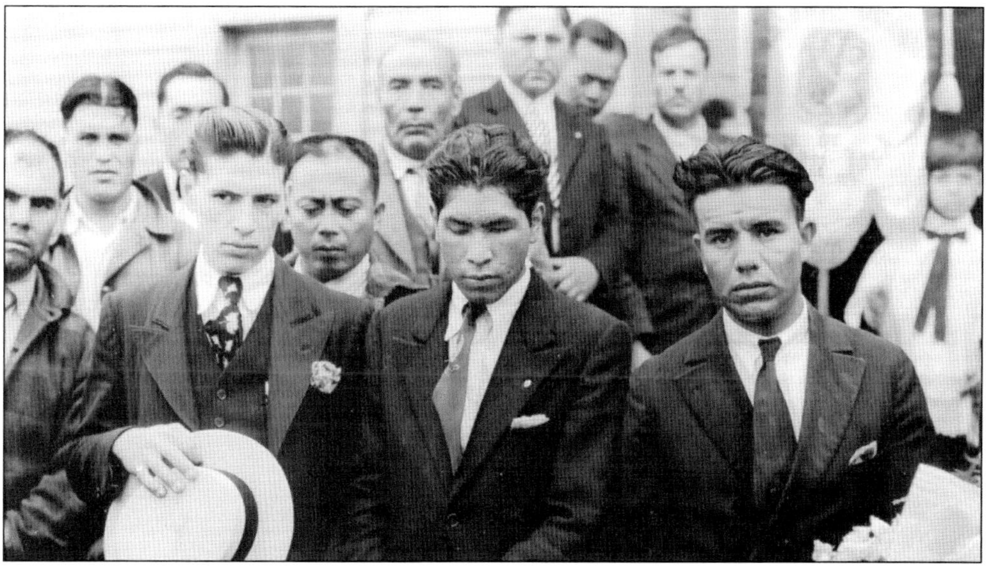

In a solemn moment, friends of a deceased church member are reflecting and praying on his passing. They are before his open casket. They are, from left to right, an unidentified man holding his hat, Benigno Orona, and Alberto Macias. Others in the picture are Eliseo Vargas and Juan Urrea. (Ralph Mota.)

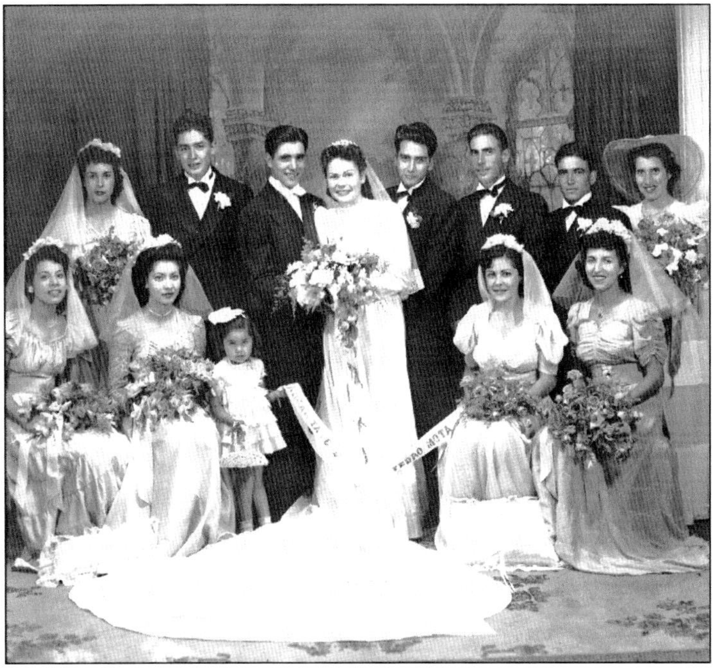

The bride and groom are Margaret Perez and Peter Mota. They were married on August 9, 1942. A few months later, the bride took her first train ride to join him. For 27 years, she volunteered as secretary at Holy Family School, and after 40 years, he retired from Shell Oil Company. They will celebrate 68 years of marriage in 2010. The flower girl is the book's author. (Author's collection.)

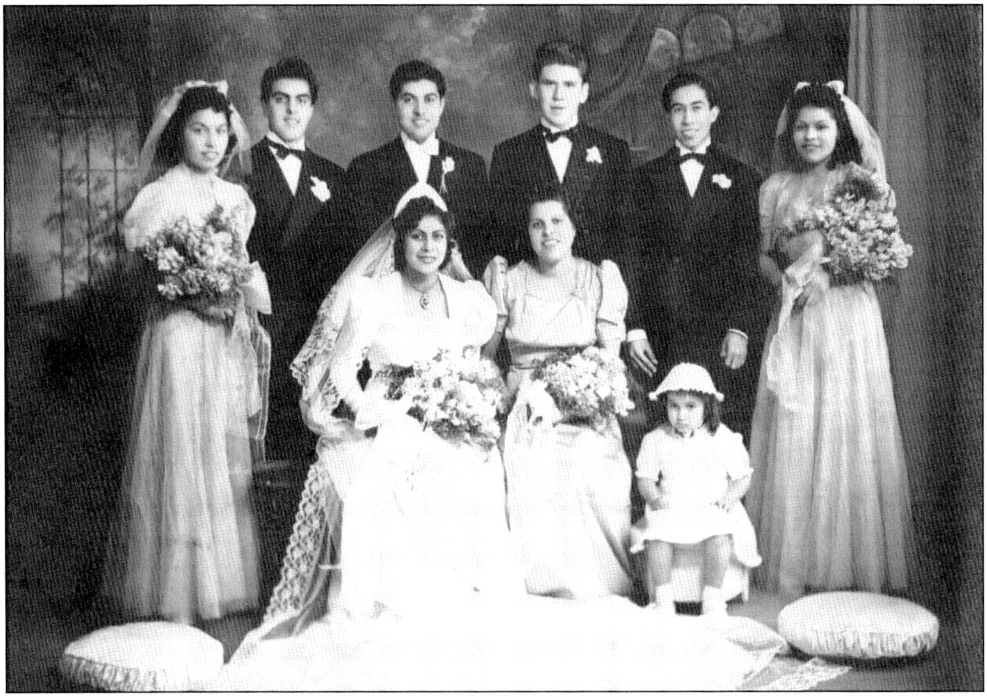

The wedding of Rose McKenna and Salvador Hernandez joined a Wilmington family with one from Watts. She graduated from Banning High in 1937, and he attended Jordan High School. Her roots were always in Wilmington, but they lived and raised their two sons in Los Angeles. He worked for American Can Company. The two communities were joined by the streetcars, which provided rapid transportation. Watts residents often participated in events at the Honorífica, Banning Park, and at the Holy Family Church. (Amelia McKenna.)

Wedding bells rang at Holy Family Church on November 8, 1943, for Fanny McKenna and Ray Madrigal. The wedding party represented the Aldape, Montana, Madrigal, Cabrera, Cardona, and McKenna families. The flower girl was Irene McKenna and ring bearer was Robert McKenna. The newly married couple made their home on Mauretania Street where they raised their three children. (Amelia McKenna.)

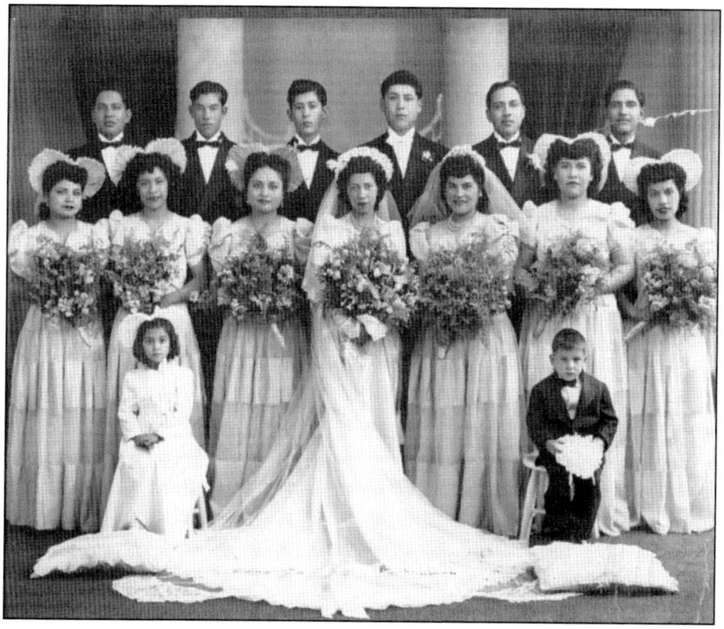

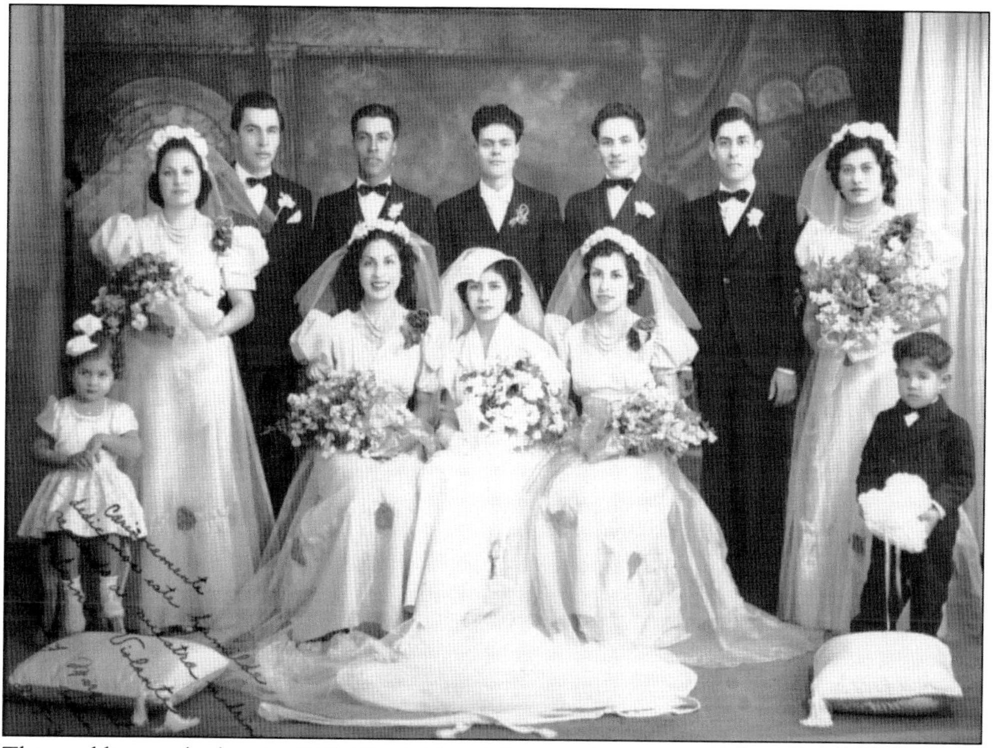

This wedding took place in 1939. The bride is Margaret Ponce and the groom is Jesus Medina, standing in the center of the photograph behind the bride. The four bridesmaids are, from left to right, Antonia Medina, Esther Ponce, Connie Violante, and Amparo Valdez. They wore orange dresses with stylish puffy sleeves. On the floor in front of the bride is the traditional *lazo* (rope), which symbolizes the union. The *lazo* is usually a white silk cord, but often is a wide white ribbon with the couple's names on it. (Maria Enriquez.)

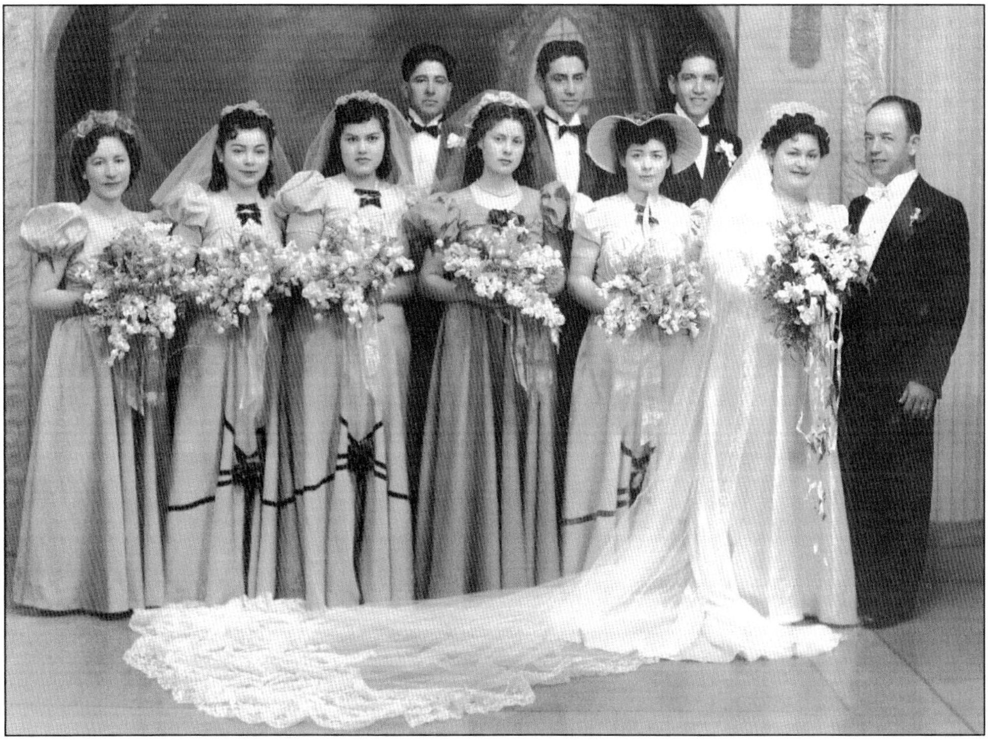

The wedding portrait was taken in 1941 at the marriage of Juana Gonzalez to Ramon Suarez. Two of her sisters, Esther (second from left) and Evangeline (standing next to bride), are in the party. Her long trailing veil with exquisite lace on its end is spread before the bridesmaids. She was a housewife, and he worked in the fish canneries. Their children were Rita, Esther, and Alfred. (Rita Rosales.)

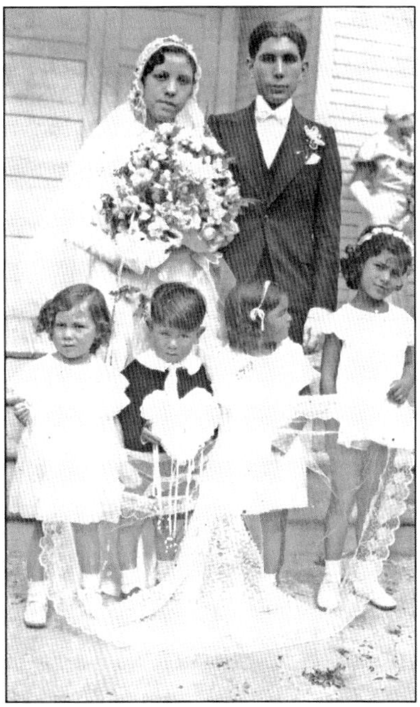

Soledad Oropeza and Pedro Espinoza were married at Holy Family Church in 1934. They are shown with four young attendants. In 1918, her father, who worked for Union Pacific railroad, and his family, originally from Chihuahua, migrated from Texas to Wilmington. The Espinoza family had come from Michoacan in 1909, and Pedro Espinoza was born in Signal Hill in 1914. He worked the family's vegetable farm near Dominguez Hills, and during the Depression he went to work for the Work Projects Administration (WPA). Afterwards, he worked at Terminal Island canneries for 28 years and retired from the Texaco refinery. The couple raised two daughters and two sons while active at the church. (Henrietta Perez.)

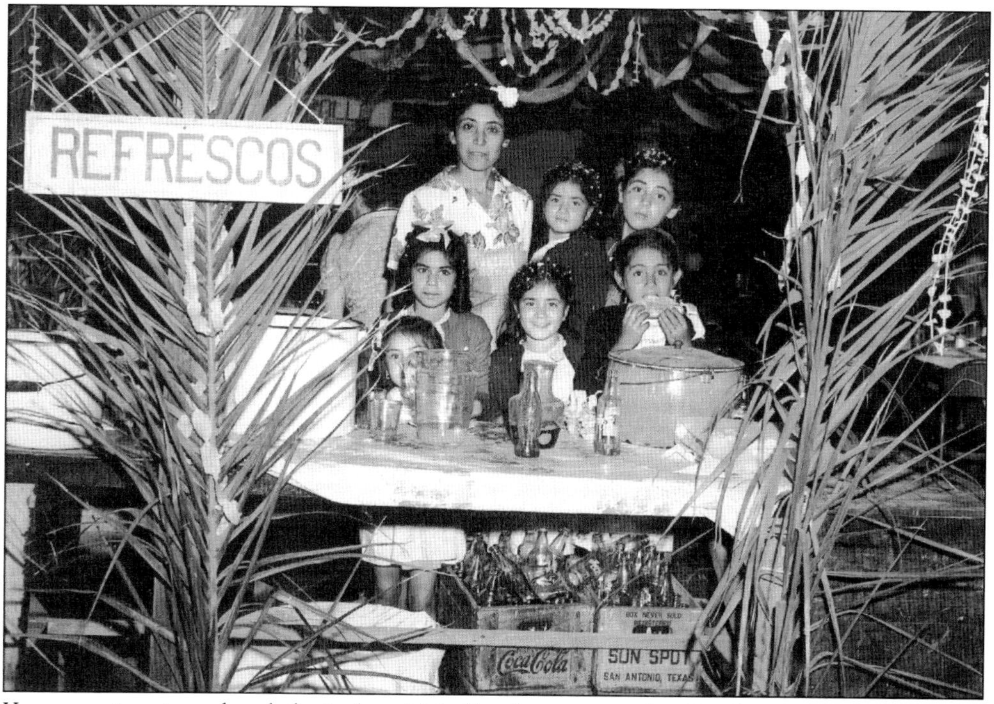

Known as *jamaicas*, church festivals at Holy Family were popular. Parishioners gathered to eat, socialize, listen to music, and play games. Teenagers bought *cascarones* (egg shells filled with confetti) to crack on the heads of special friends. This refreshment booth shows Rafaela Vargas and her daughters Maggie (first row, far right) and Josephine (second row, far right) with Barbosa and Estrada girls. (Esther Pacheco.)

A fun booth at Holy Family fiestas was the jail. Standing outside the jail in 1947 are Ruth Barbosa and Henrietta Espinoza. They are pretending to be jailed, and on this day, beardless men were being detained. There was a fee to get out of jail. Families sponsored the particular booths that sold *raspadas* (snow cones), *palomitas* (popcorn), cotton candy, candies, tostadas, tacos, and other food items. The profits went to the church building fund. (Henrietta Perez.)

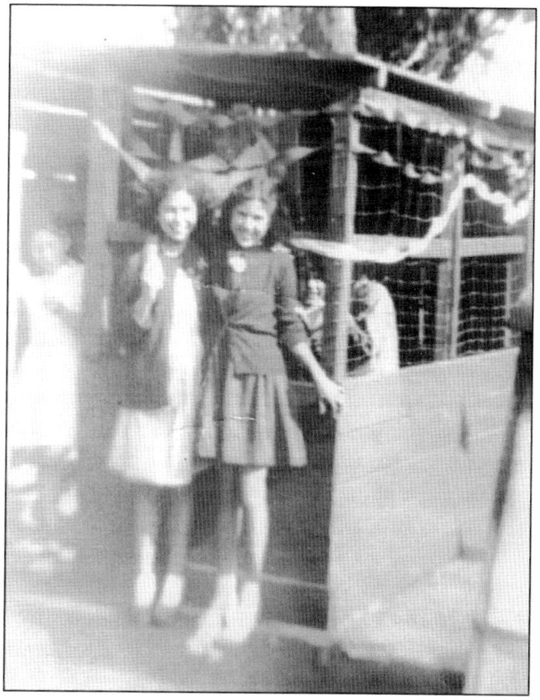

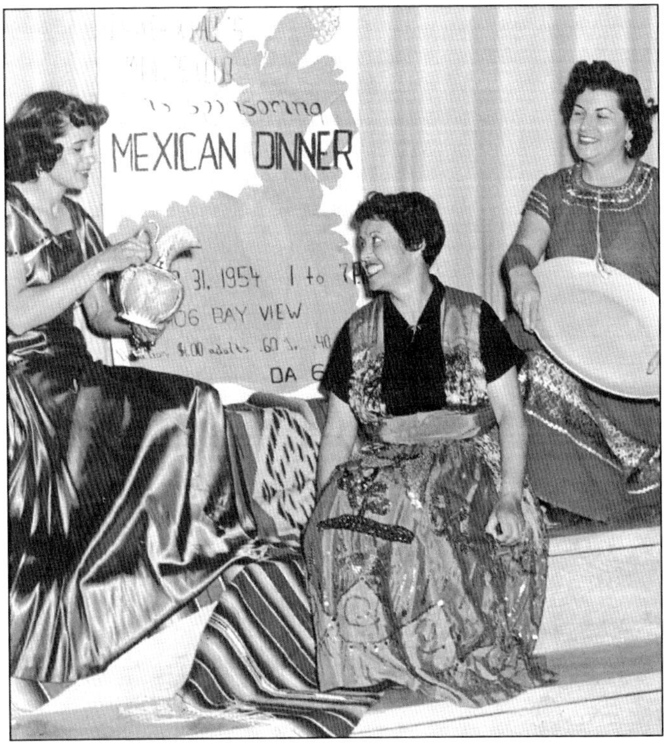

Records show that in 1824 there was a Mexican Free Methodist Church located at 1305 Watson Avenue, but most people of Mexican heritage were Catholic. On November 29, 1865, the first Mass in the harbor area was celebrated at St. Peter and St. Paul Church. Gov. John Downey had donated the land, and the first and oldest Altar Society in Southern California was established. In 1951, Maria Dolores Dominguez de Watson donated $60,000 to build the eight-room school. The mother's club sponsored a Mexican dinner for the school. Seated from left to right are unidentified, Emma Guzman, and Estella Picasso Rubio. (Wilmington Historical Society.)

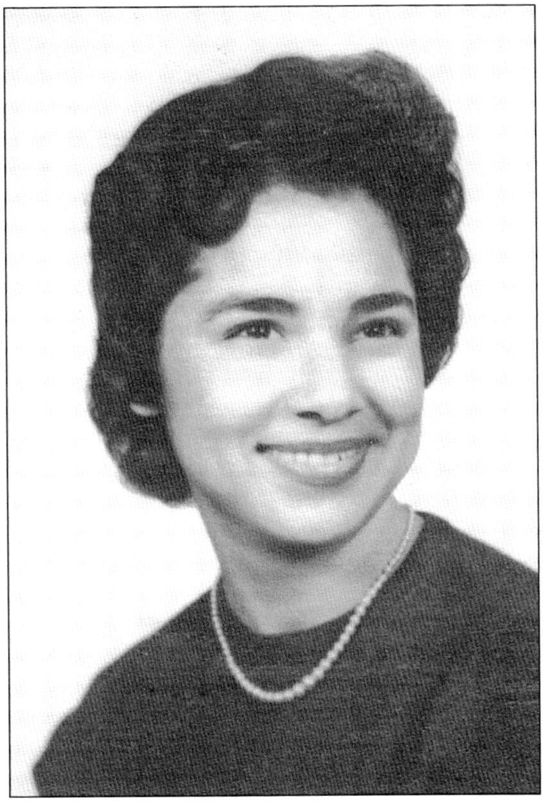

Maria Guadalupe Arroyo entered the religious community of Immaculate Heart of Mary (IHM) in 1959. She became a golden jubilarian of the Catholic order in 2009. After she attended Holy Family School and St. Anthony's High School, she earned a degree in nursing and is licensed as a nurse practitioner. Arroyo's parents were Ramon and Elvira Arroyo. Her cousin Elena Barbosa became a Carmelite nun. Several other women from Wilmington chose a religious vocation and among them were Lupe Sedillo and Sylvia Esparza. Esparza is presently assigned to the Vatican. (Ed Arroyo.)

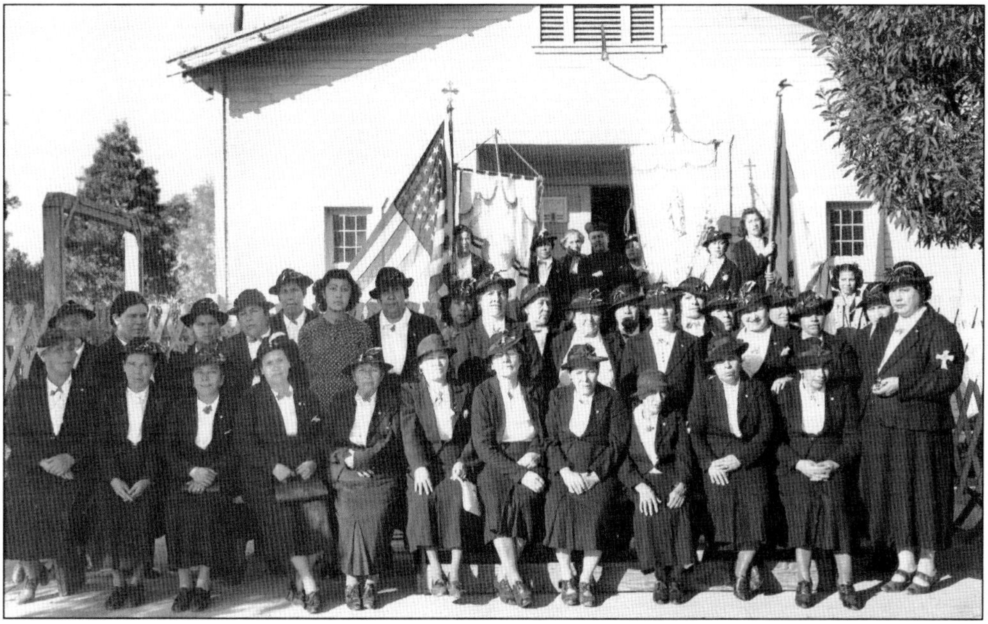

In 1937, the Guadalupana Society, *las Guadalupanas*, was photographed in front of the small wooden-framed Holy Family Church that served for 18 years at Sanford and "L" Streets. The Guadalupanas were devotees of the Virgin of Guadalupe and participated in all church events. Members are shown wearing the Guadalupe Medal, which acknowledged their commitment to Our Lady of Guadalupe. (Ralph Mota.)

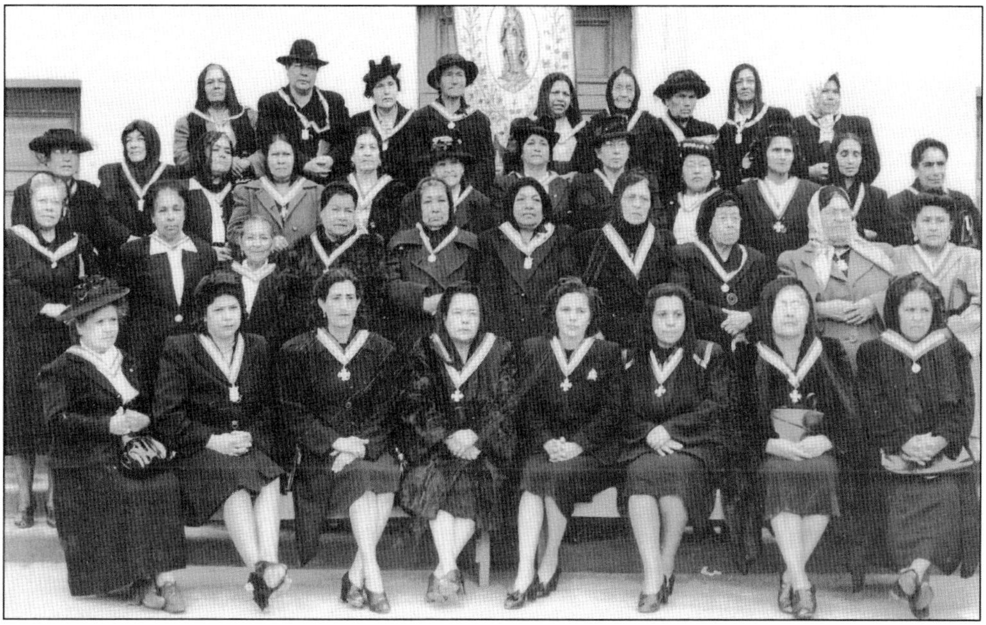

In this later picture, around the late 1940s, the Guadalupanas are gathered in front of the new church. They are now wearing *mantillas* more than hats, but they continue to support church activities. The group consists of younger women, some being mother and daughter members. The church was dedicated on December 12, 1947, the feast day of Our Lady of Guadalupe. (Carmen Galvan.)

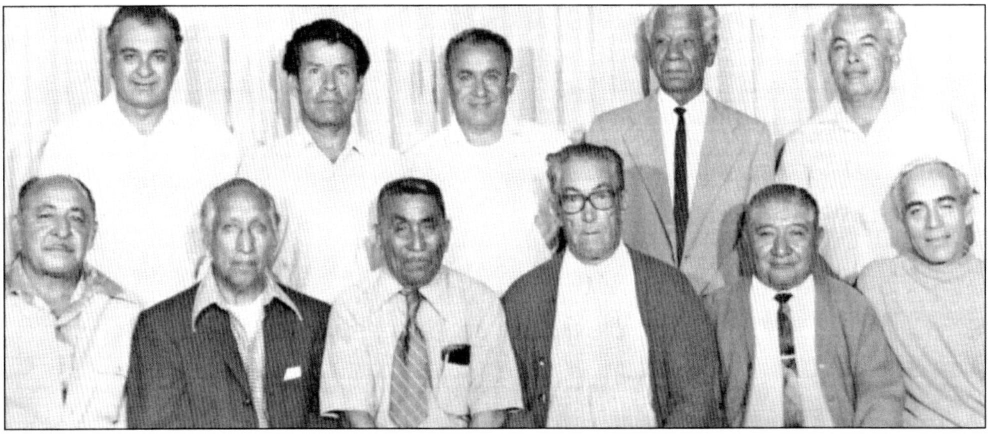

Mutualistas de San José was a community-based mutual aid society. It fostered cooperation and benevolence. The group was involved in church and civic activities, and its hall on Henry Ford Avenue became a venue for dances, receptions, and meetings. Above, in 1976, its civic committee joined with Wilmington's Hispanic Bicentennial Committee to celebrate this country's bicentennial. The group included, from left to right, (first row) ? Sandez, Louis Sapien, Frank Sapien, Mike Mazon, Cruz Hernandez, and Lupe Delgado; (second row) Oscar Schmerber, Serafin Rodriguez, Alix Valdilles, Benito Cabrera, and Gregorio Garcia. Below, in 1949, are the founding members of the Mutualistas de San José. (Above, Jess Marquez; below, Carmen Galvan.)

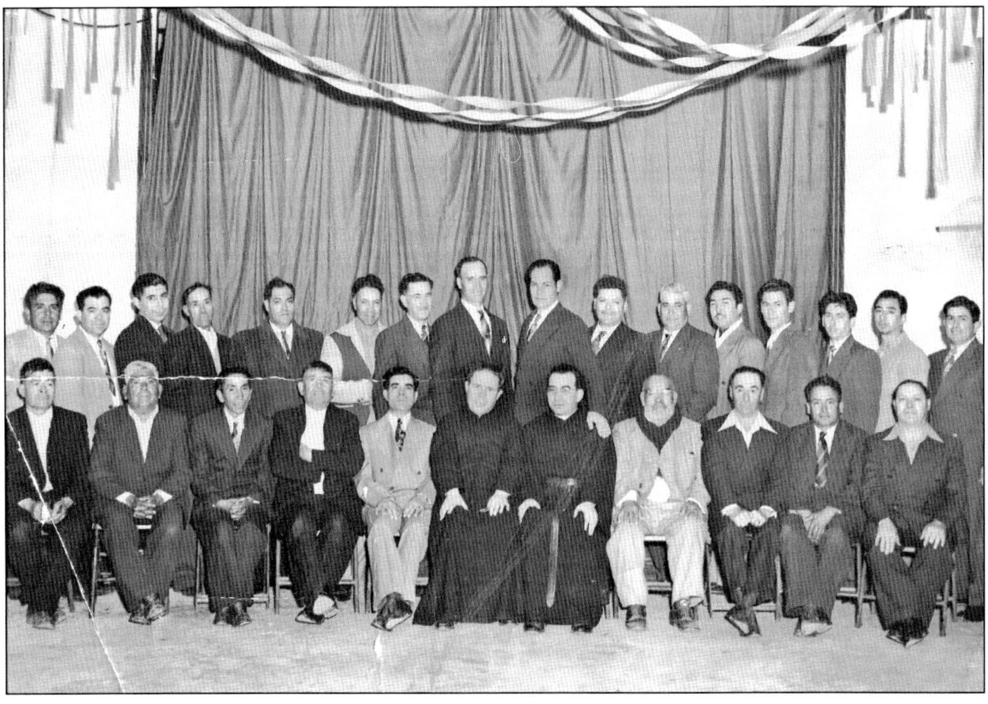

Four

PLACES AND EVENTS

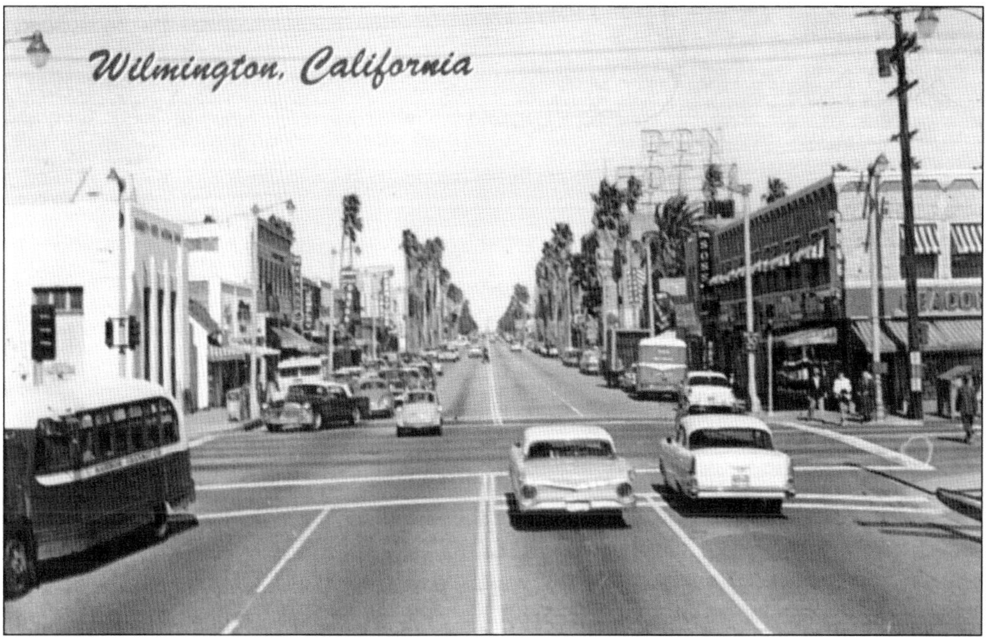

This is a postcard view of downtown Wilmington at North Avalon Boulevard and Anaheim Street in 1957. The skyline shows the Don Hotel where prominent guests stayed for voyages on Matson Line ships or to go 26 miles across the sea to Catalina Island. The hotel is appropriately named from the Spanish use of "Don," meaning gentleman. A rare find is a picture of the "Red Bus" (left) that transported eastside Wilmington residents through the neighborhood to downtown and to work. (Ingmar Sorenseene.)

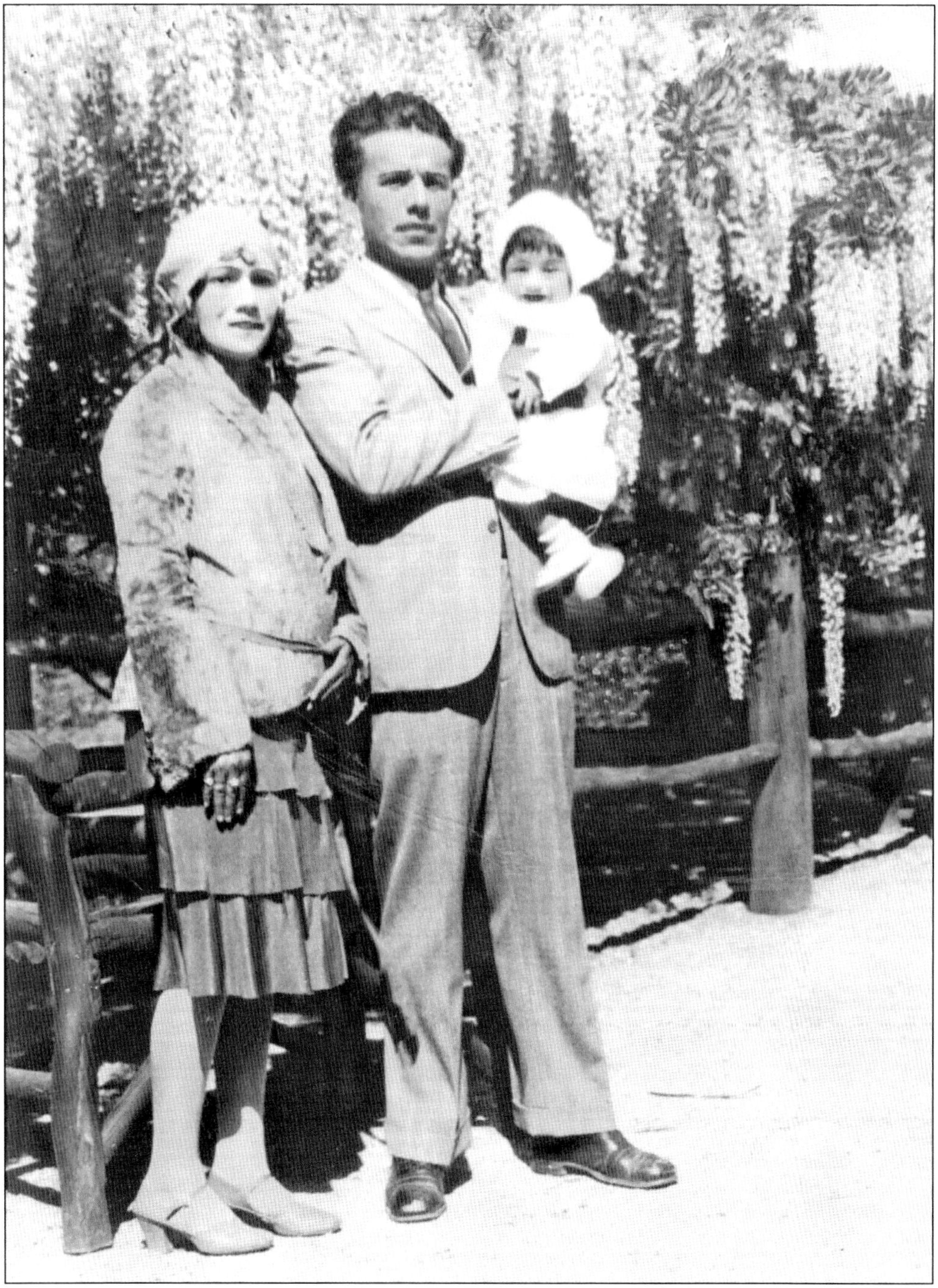

As a young woman, Juanita Vargas came from Guadalajara, Jalisco, to spend the summer vacation with an aunt and uncle. She worked at the canneries to earn money before returning home, but met her future husband, Alberto Macias, and stayed. They married in 1930 and lived on Terminal Island. He worked in the lumber industry and canneries. They used a rowboat to go to San Pedro and Wilmington. They are pictured near the wisteria at Banning Park with their firstborn, Arturo. (Carmen Galvan.)

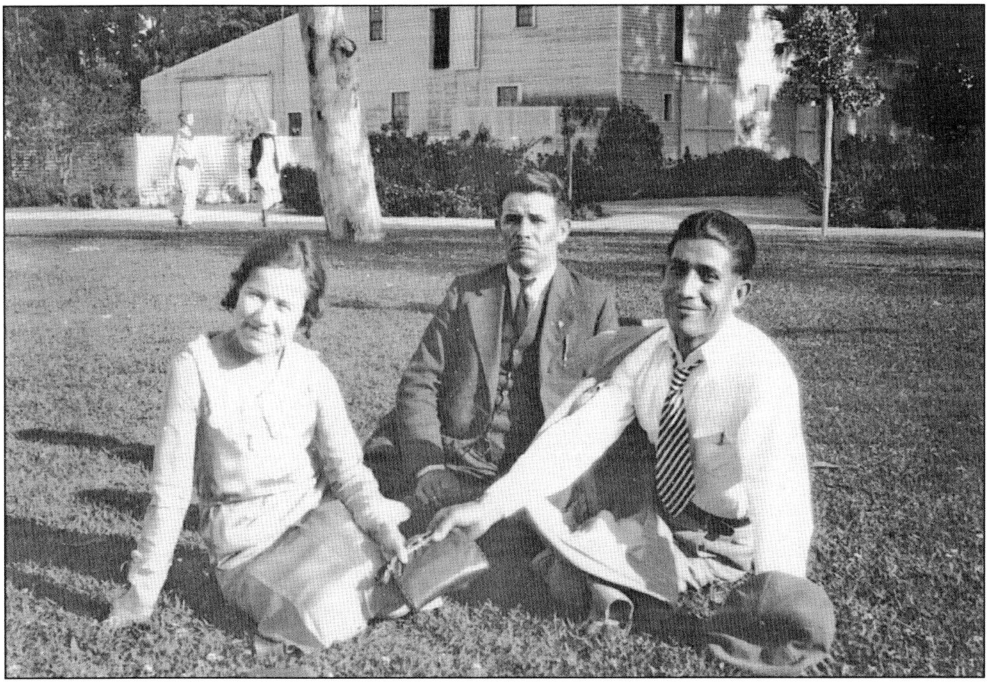

With the Banning Park carriage barn in the background, Concha Islas and Frank Cantu sat in front of Marcelino Mota. They were relaxed and smiling. Undoubtedly, Mota, dressed in a three-piece suit, was serious about his role as chaperone. The couple married and was active in the community. (Ralph Mota.)

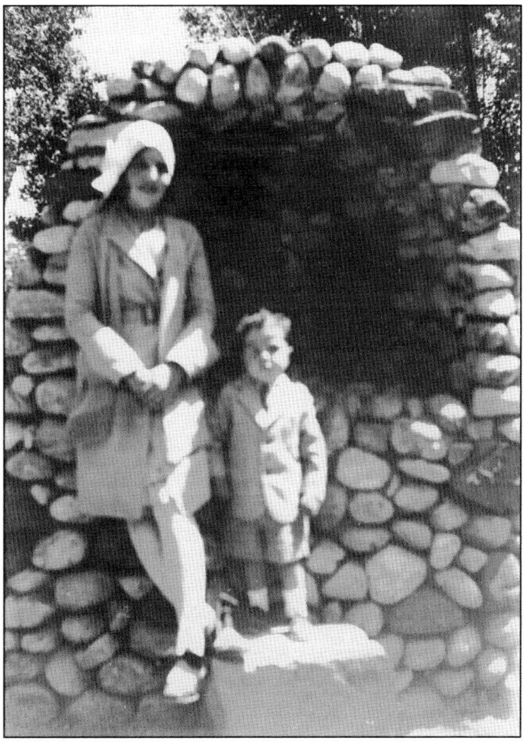

Two-year-old Carlos Rico stands beside his mother at Banning Park's wishing well in 1929. The wishing well added a special touch to a visit to the park, and like the creek and other features of the park, it too was removed. Rico's mother, Mary Garcia, would dress him in shorts and high-top shoes for a favorite afternoon pastime. (Carlos Rico.)

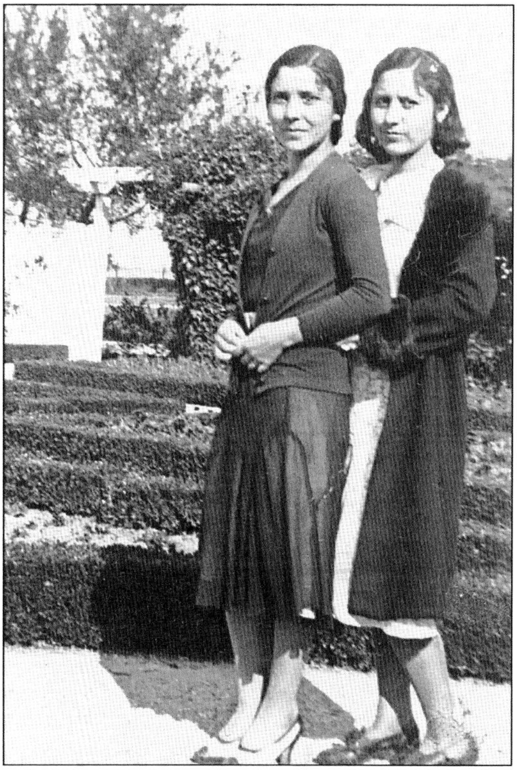

Eleuteria Navarro (left) and friend Trinidad de la Torre share a moment of friendship in 1932 as they pose in the rose garden of the Phineas Banning residence. Throughout the year, young men and women dressed up to stroll at the park on Sundays, chaperoned or with friends. This was an important social event. (Joe Manzo.)

These young women made crepe paper dresses and hats for a festival in Banning Park around 1935. They are, from left to right, (first row) unidentified; (second row) Trinidad Caracoza, Santos Robles, unidentified, Jacoba Urrea, Serafina Urrea, Elvira Gonzalez, and Esperanza Violante. Presently, this image appears in a mural at Wells Fargo Bank in Wilmington. Wells Fargo was established in the community in 1883. Business between California and Mexico was expedited with Letter Express in the 1800s and money orders after 1883. (Author's collection.)

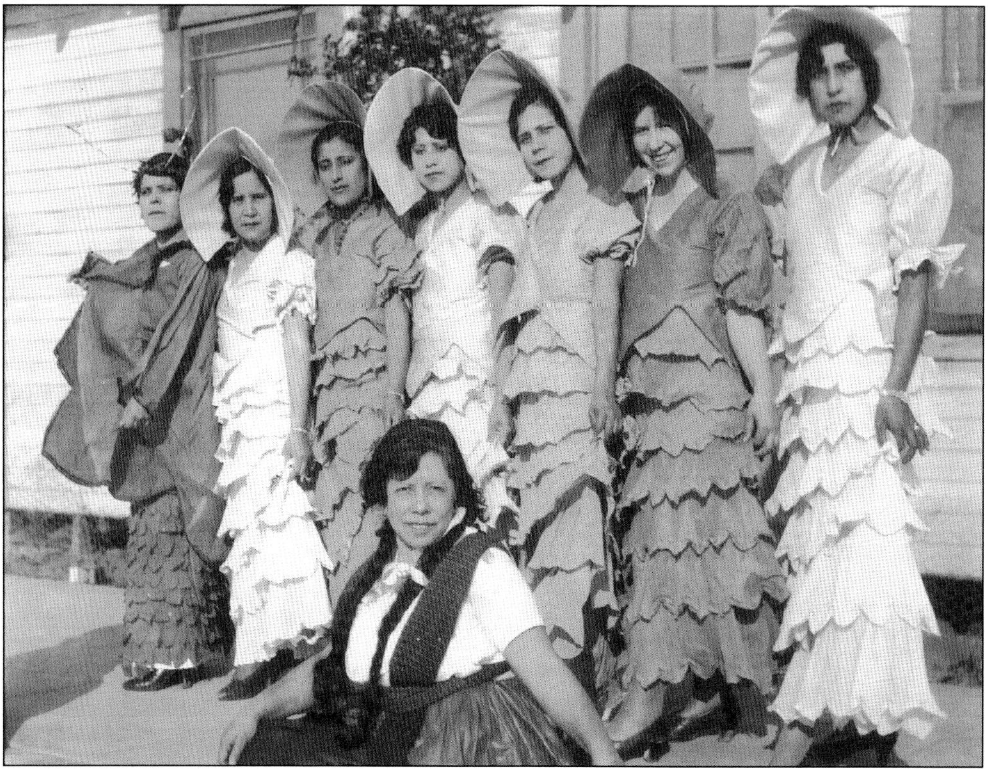

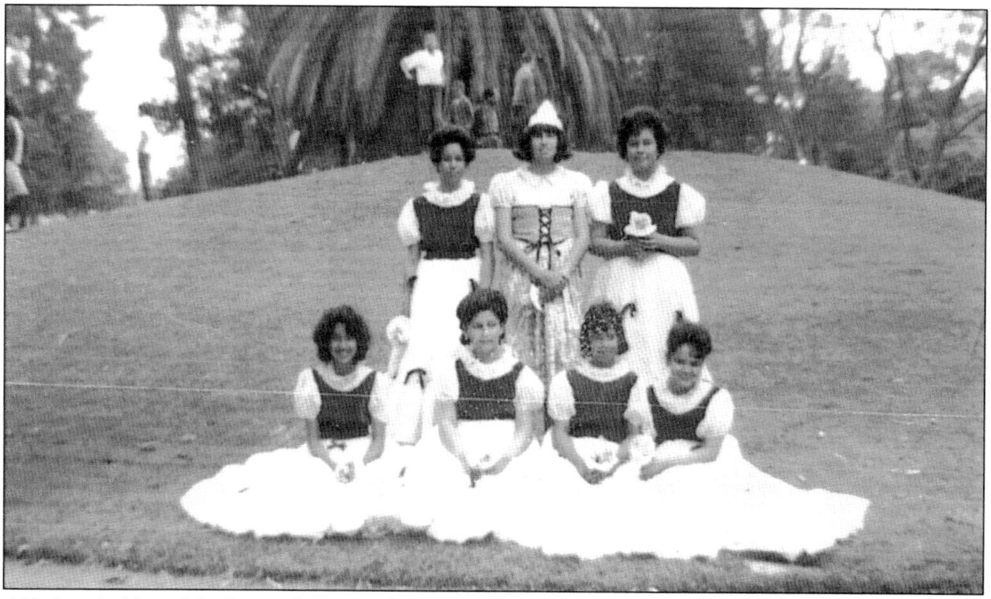

All the children liked to roll down the hill at Banning Park. The hill was called Katherine's Hill. It was made for Katherine Banning as a reminder of her roots back East. These costumed girls were sitting pretty because they were the 1961 May Day festival court. The queen and her attendants were, from left to right, (first row) Maria Cueva, Carol Villalobos, unidentified, and Guadalupe Islas; (second row) Rosalie Dominguez, Carmen Dominguez (queen), and Shirley Atencio. (Carol Maldonado.)

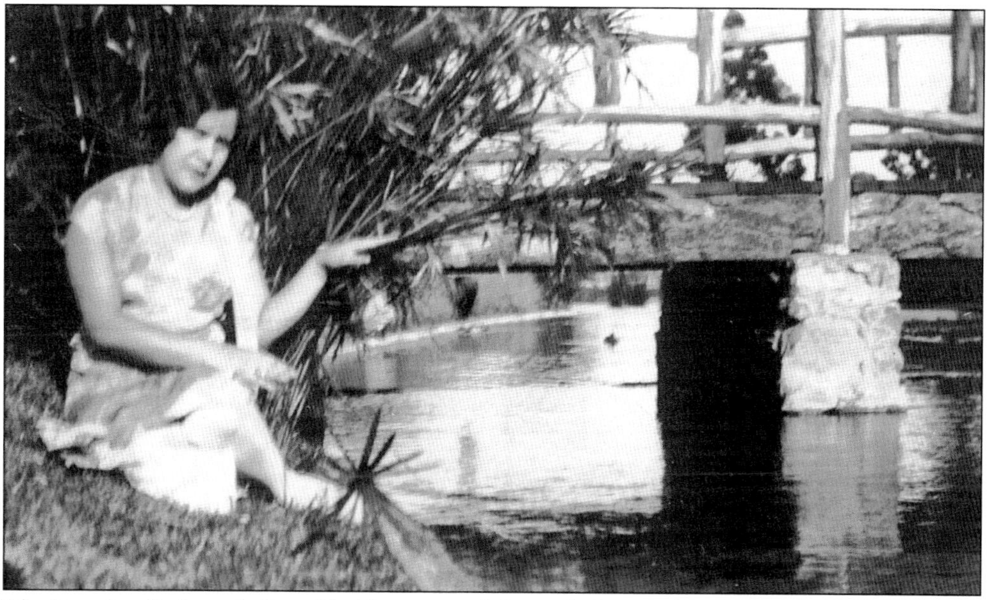

The Banning Park creek flowed halfway around the park. It passed under quaint wooden bridges and rippled through and over stepping stones. The creek had ducks, frogs, crayfish, and koi. It was a passive, but beautiful, water feature. Santos Robles sat for this snapshot taken around 1937. She worked in the canneries and was married to Ralph Carrasco. He owned the "Red Bus" business and hired local men to drive the route, which included making late-night runs when the cannery whistle had summoned the workers. (Cecilia Jacinto.)

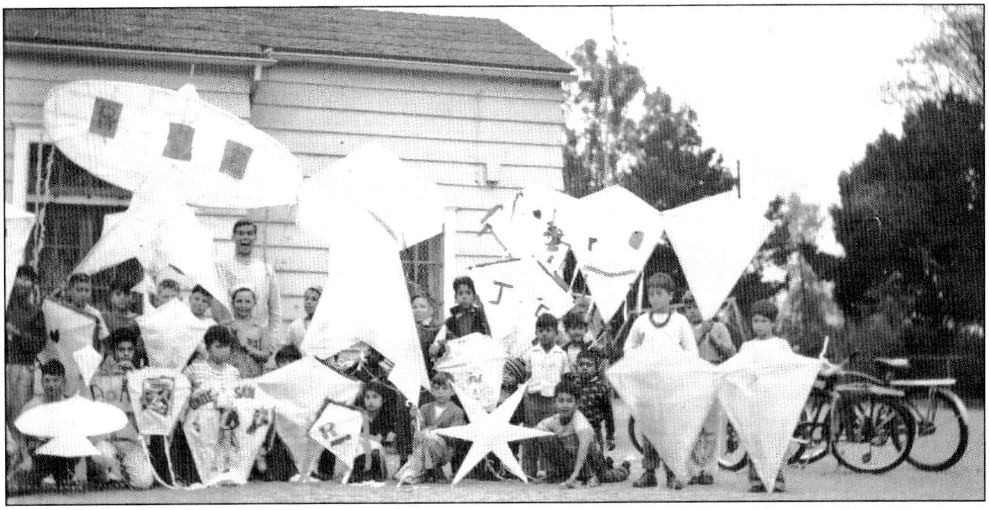

Leonard Estrada (first row, sixth from left) was kneeling to the right of his star kite that won second place for "Prettiest Kite" in the annual kite contest at Banning Park playground on March 23, 1946. Among the contest participants was Rachel Nuno, the only girl (first row, fifth from left). Standing in the back row was assistant park coach John Pohlman. Some of the boys had newspaper routes, and their Schwinn bicycles can be seen close by. (Leonard Estrada.)

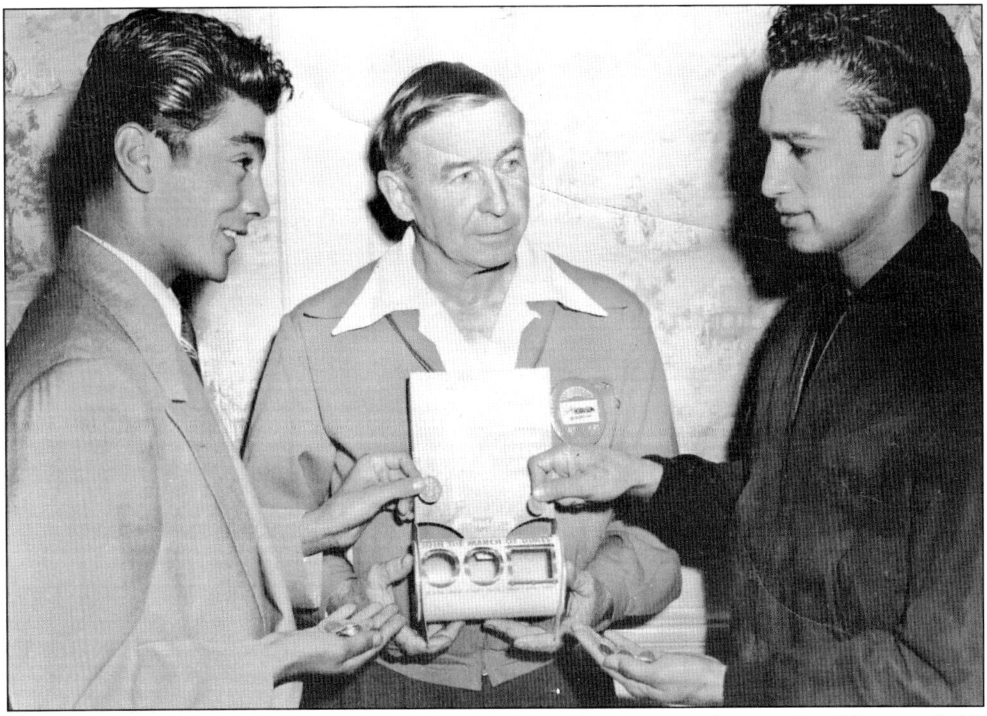

Early in 1950, Ray W. Hudgson (center), the Banning Park recreation director; Jess Marquez (left), president of the park's Boy's and Girl's Club; and Gilbert Lopez (right) campaigned for the March of Dimes. Former park participants credit Hudgson for their personal successes. Marquez was a merchant marine for eight years and worked at Borax for nearly 40 years. His family came from Wyoming to visit his dad's cousin, Father Lopez, at Holy Family Church. They liked the weather, found work, and stayed. (Jess Marquez.)

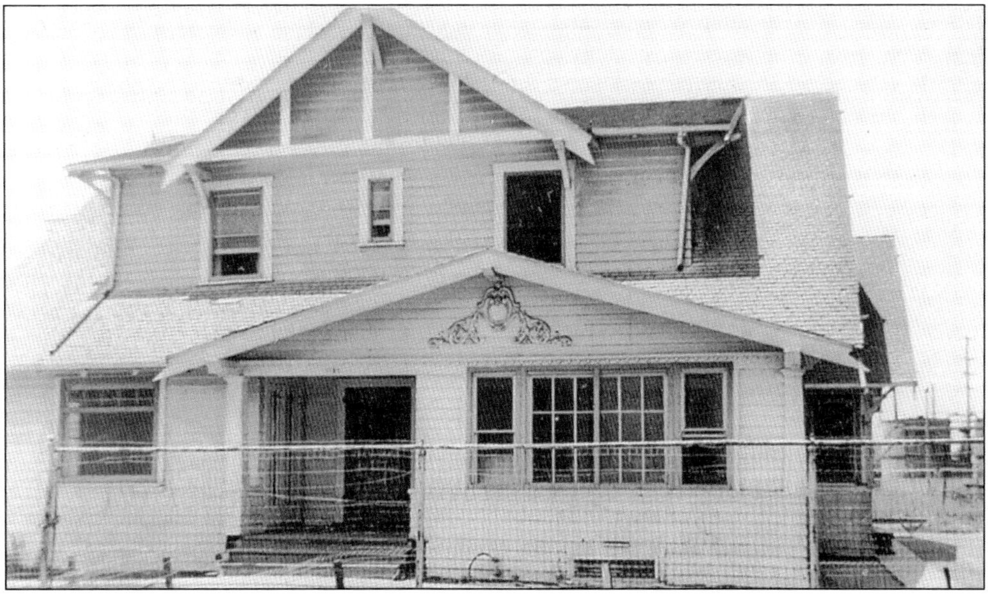

Before the Mahar House was bequeathed to the Roman Catholic Archdiocese of Los Angeles for use as a community center, it was the Mahar family home, well maintained and landscaped. The Mahars came to Wilmington in 1865, and Margaret, the daughter, died in 1937. This photograph was taken shortly before it was demolished and replaced by a new building. For many years after the home was donated, it served the neighborhood through its Catholic Youth Organization (CYO) programs and services. It was the focus point of youth activities. (Alex Areyan.)

Mahar House director Ramon "Baker" Quesada is credited with having been an outstanding mentor and role model for the many youngsters who passed through the agency's doors. Quesada was involved in and promoted many team sports and was a summer 1941 graduate of Banning High. He married Toni Torici, who endlessly supported his activities and accomplishments. He is proud to also have been an interpreter for the 1984 Olympics. (Ramon Quesada.)

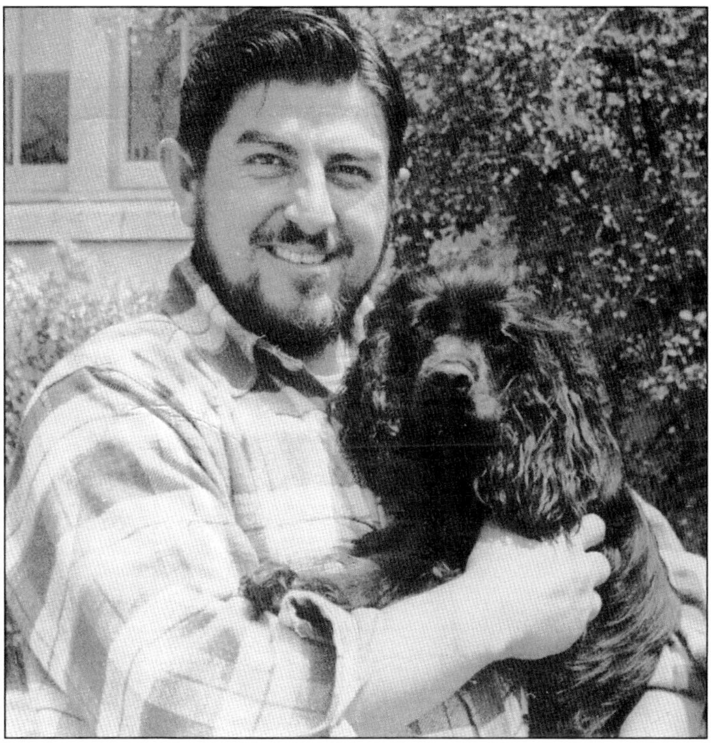

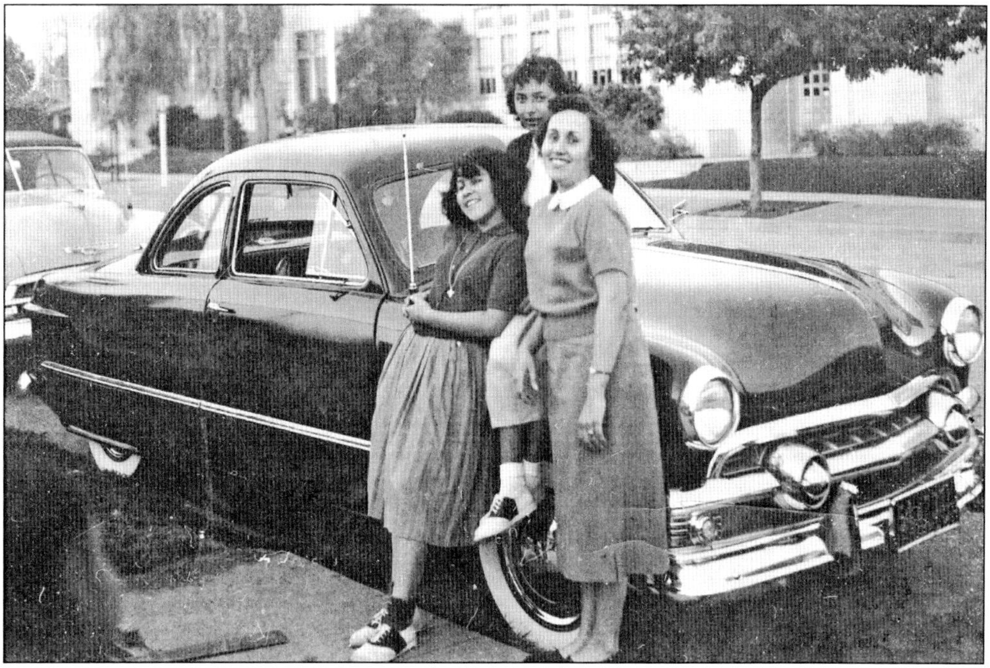

Mahar House stood across the street from Wilmington Park School, which is seen in the background. Leaning against Ramon Quesada's car is Barbara Garcia, and sitting on the customized Chevrolet is Lupe Munoz. Both are wearing the popular saddle shoes of the 1950s. In 1953, counselor Toni Torici joined the girls while her light blue convertible with canvas top was parked further down the street. She, too, was dressed in a fashion fad, the attachable collar. (Barbara Flores.)

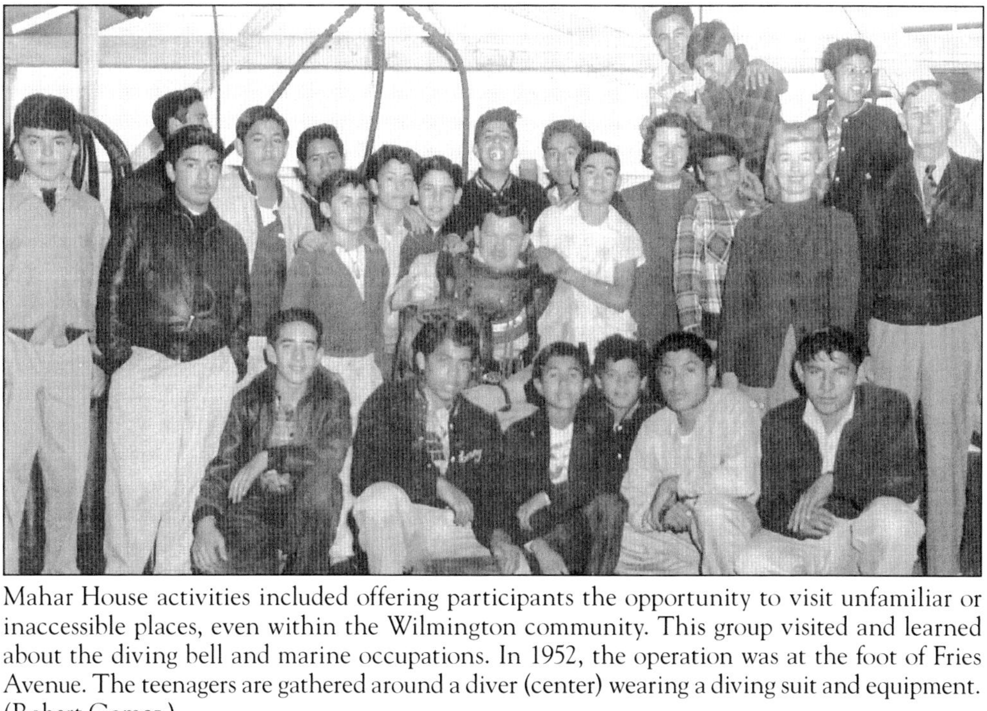

Mahar House activities included offering participants the opportunity to visit unfamiliar or inaccessible places, even within the Wilmington community. This group visited and learned about the diving bell and marine occupations. In 1952, the operation was at the foot of Fries Avenue. The teenagers are gathered around a diver (center) wearing a diving suit and equipment. (Robert Gomez.)

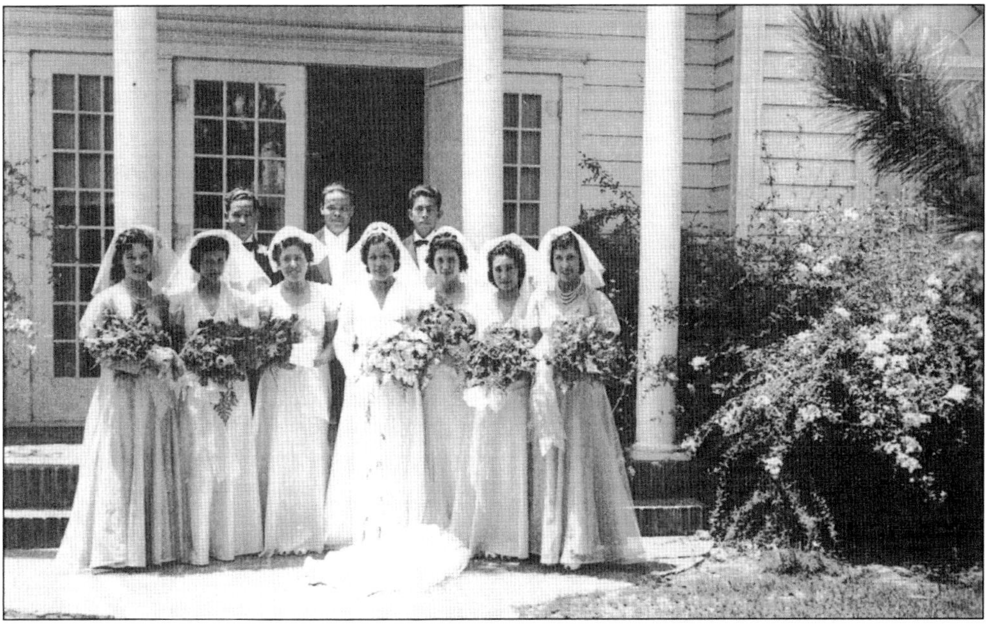

Wilmington Women's Club on Lakme Avenue was the scene of many wedding receptions. It provided an ample, comfortable, and classic setting. Friends of the newlyweds and their families cooperated to make and serve the food. The meal usually consisted of *mole*, rice, beans, salads, cake, and refreshments. A mariachi or *conjunto* (small group of musicians) provided the music for dancing. In this c. 1940 photograph, it is the wedding day of Aurora and Antonio Heredia. (Maria Enriquez.)

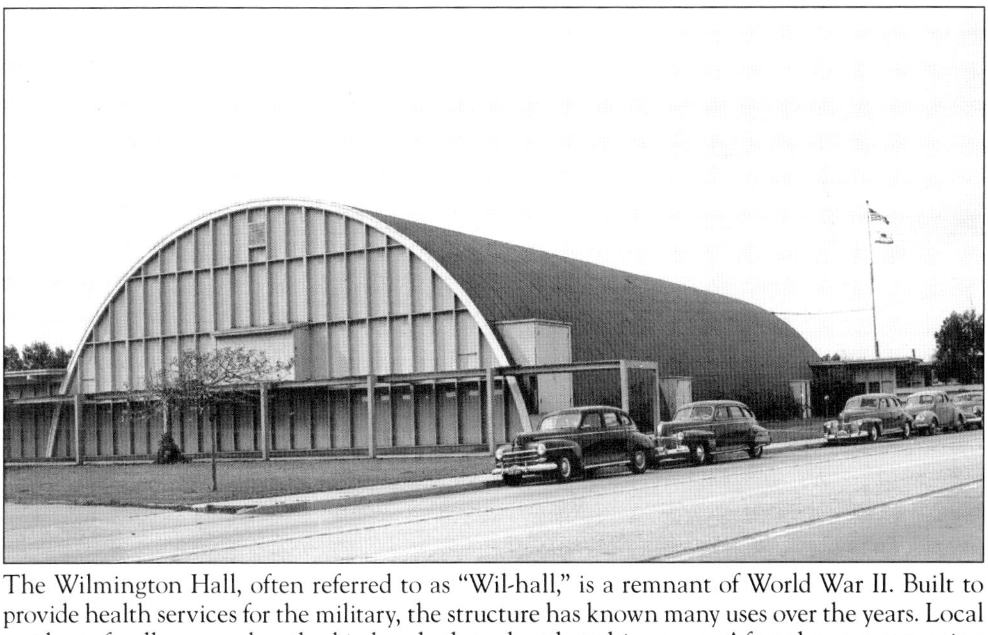

The Wilmington Hall, often referred to as "Wil-hall," is a remnant of World War II. Built to provide health services for the military, the structure has known many uses over the years. Local residents fondly remember the big bands that played at this venue. After the war, returning servicemen were able to buy new "tract" homes built nearby. Housing covenants were lifted, and the generation that had been raised in the community began to move into new homes. (Wilmington Historical Society.)

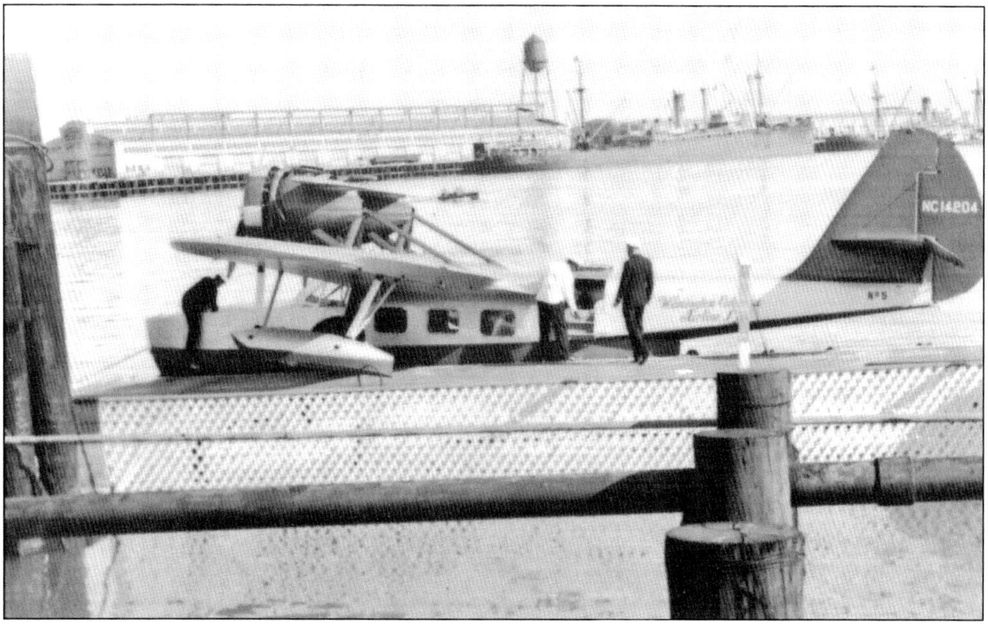

On land and sea, Wilmington had it airports. There was an airplane-landing area at what is now Los Angeles Harbor College, and seaplanes used a location at the foot of Fries Avenue near the Catalina Terminal. In 1919, Charlie Chaplin's half brother began the first seaplane service to Catalina, and in 1931, Philip K. Wrigley, of chewing gum fame, started the Wilmington-Catalina Air Line. On Catalina Island, the company used a turntable to turn the planes around. Donald Douglas designed the main seaplane, and the fee for a one-way trip was $5. (Ramon Quesada.)

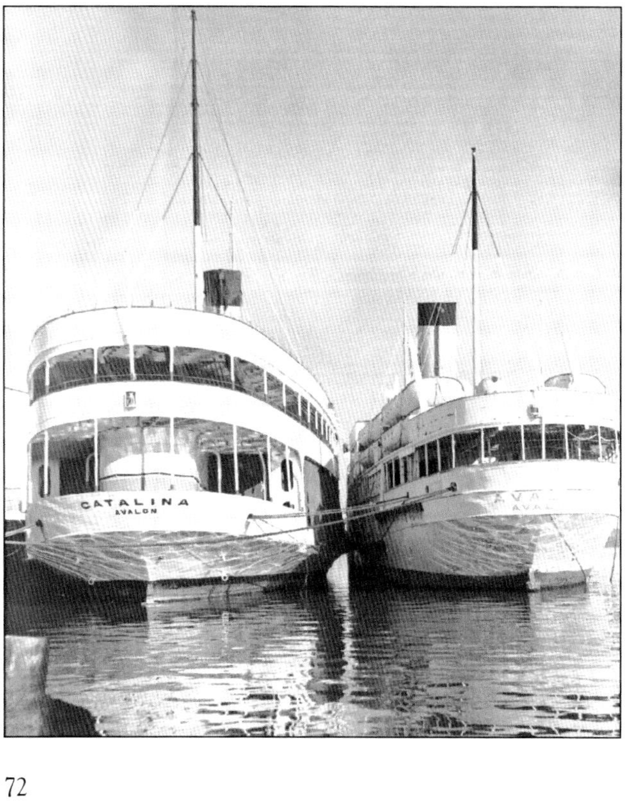

The palm trees lining Avalon Boulevard were designed to direct people to the Catalina Terminal. The S.S. *Catalina*, known as the "Great White Steamer," was built in 1924 and retired in 1975. It carried passengers to and from Catalina Island, and Pacific Electric streetcars had service to the passenger terminal. The Catalina's smaller sister ship, *Avalon*, was moored beside her at the announcement that their passenger-carrying days were over. (Leonard Estrada.)

Brighton Beach, once ranked as a summer playground for the wealthy, was the beach for locals, too. It had a hotel, bathhouse, and boardwalk. The Long Beach Naval Shipyard replaced it. Wearing swimwear fashions of the day, the Gilbert Vaca (far left) family posed for the photographer around 1938. Vaca came from Michoacan and worked in the canneries. His wife, Matilda Acosta (standing next to him), was a forelady at the Pan Pacific Cannery. (Phil Vaca.)

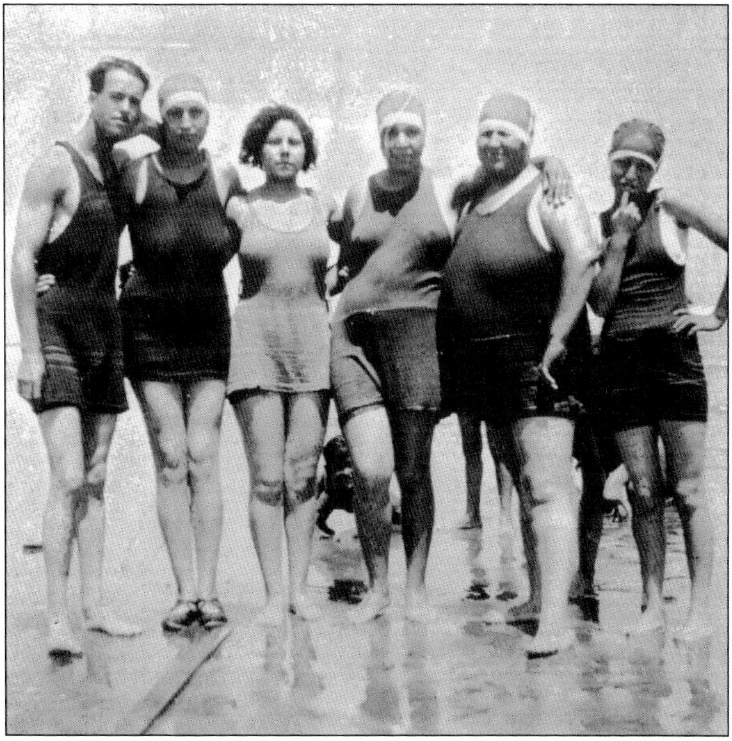

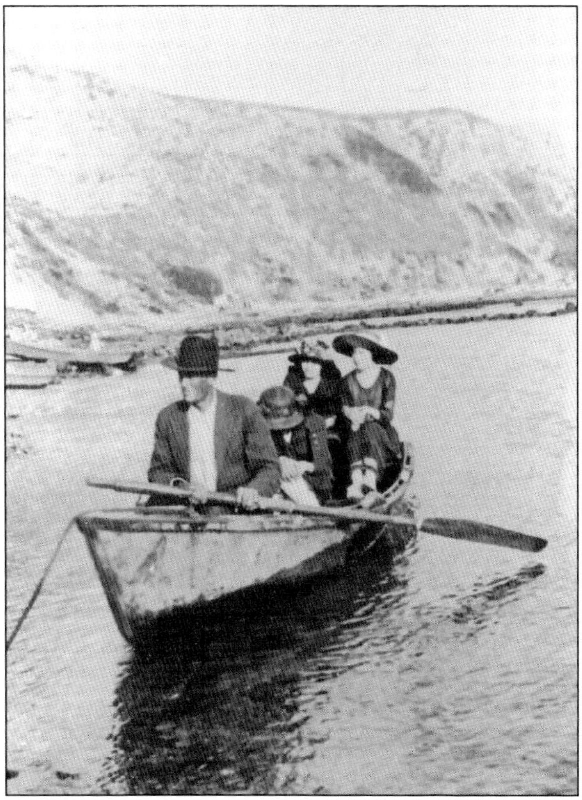

Chon Garcia rowed his family out to Dead Man's Island around 1920. This was a popular outing. Here Rico and Garcia family members are dressed in their Sunday finery for the day's adventure. Dead Man's Island was named *Isla del Muerto* when a sailor was buried there, and later on, those buried on the island were an English sea captain, five crewmen from a frigate, two passengers from a ship in 1851, and in 1855, the wife of a sea captain who never returned from a voyage. The island was leveled in 1927 and became Reservation Point on Terminal Island. (Carlos Rico.)

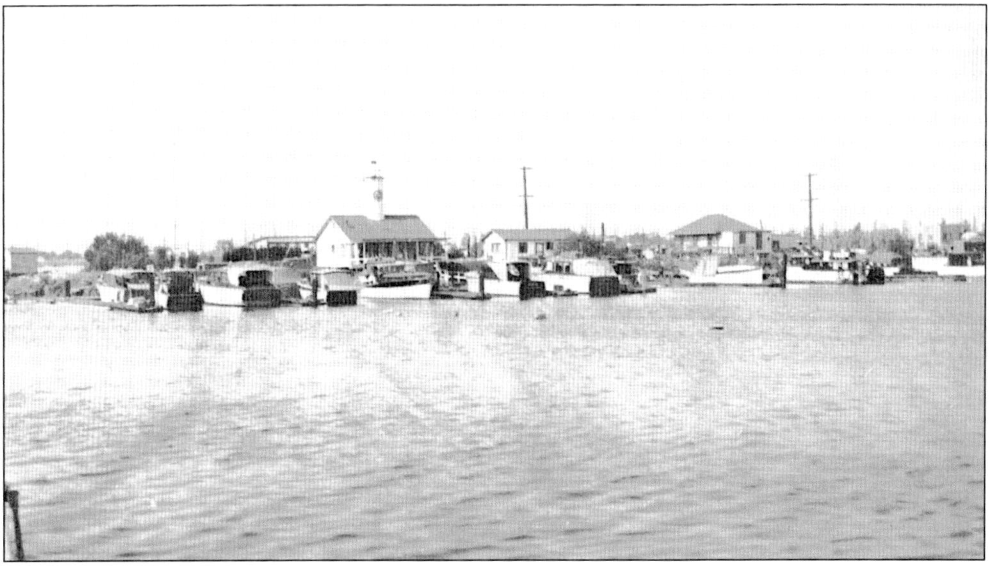

Prior to World War II, many yacht clubs and boat landings were located on Wilmington's waterfront. Most disappeared during the wartime years, giving way to shipyards and port development. As was popular, houses were often moved to other locations in the community rather than being demolished. Visible is Lighthouse Landing, with an office and houses. The author's family home was moved from there to Hyatt Avenue to make way for a shipyard. (Ralph Violante.)

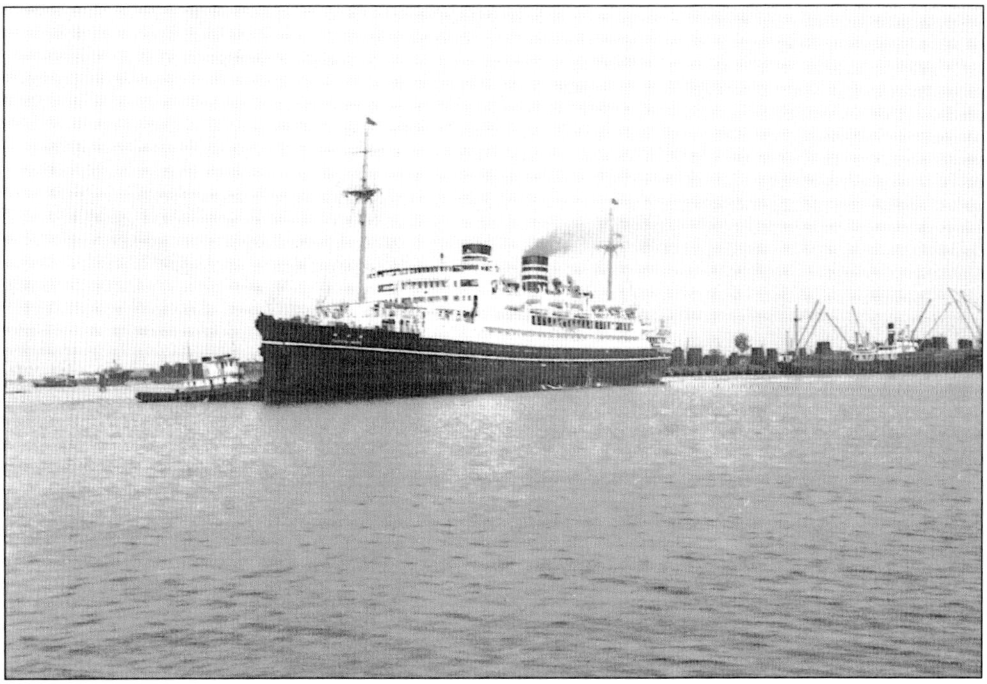

The *Tatsuta Maru* was a Japanese ocean liner owned by Nippon Yusen Kaisha (NYK) and built by Mitsubishi in 1927. An attraction for local residents and photographed in 1939, one of the ship's ports of call was Los Angeles (Wilmington). A few years later, the vessel was used as a troopship for the Imperial Japanese Navy. On February 8, 1943, it was torpedoed and sunk. (Ralph Violante.)

In 2002, a memorial was dedicated to the Japanese Americans who lived in the fishing community on Terminal Island. Mexican Americans and Japanese Americans were friends. They worked and lived with each other. Stories are told about the effects of Executive Order 9066, which sent Japanese Americans to internment camps, leaving everything behind. After the war, some Japanese Americans returned to live in the Wilmington area. (Frank Aguirre.)

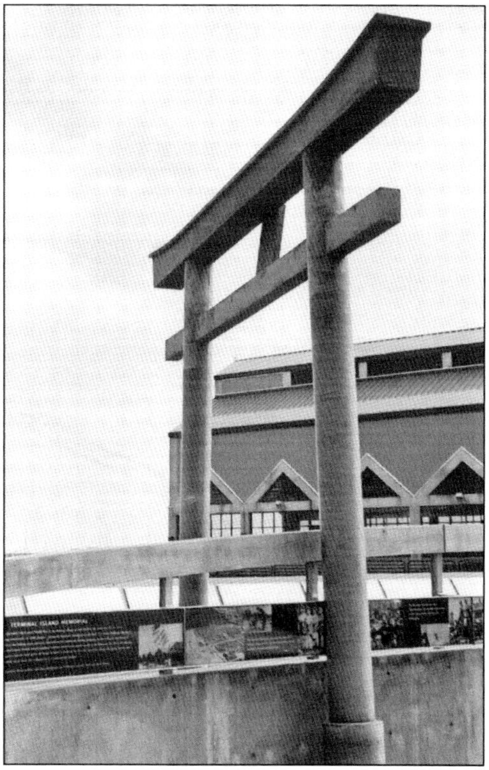

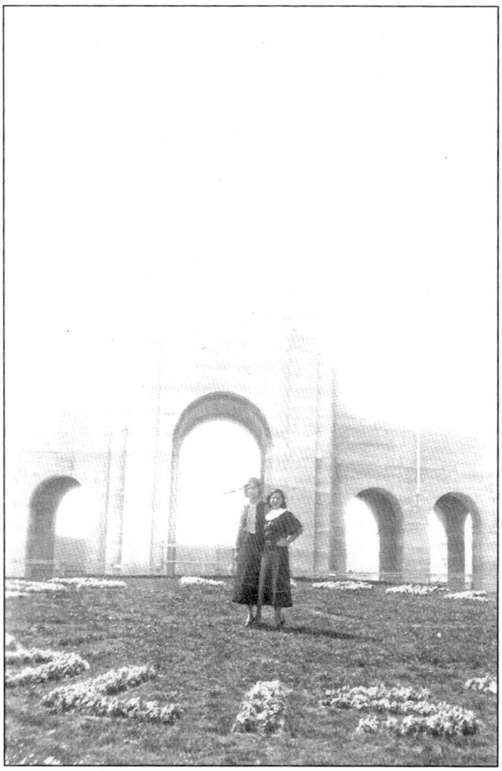

Concha Castro and a friend are enjoying the front garden of the newly built Los Angeles Coliseum in 1932. Concha and Jose McKenna married and lived most of their life in Wilmington. Notice that the letters O, L, I, and S are flower beds that form the partial spelling of "coliseum." It is the only stadium to host the Olympic Games twice, in 1932 and 1984. (Amelia McKenna.)

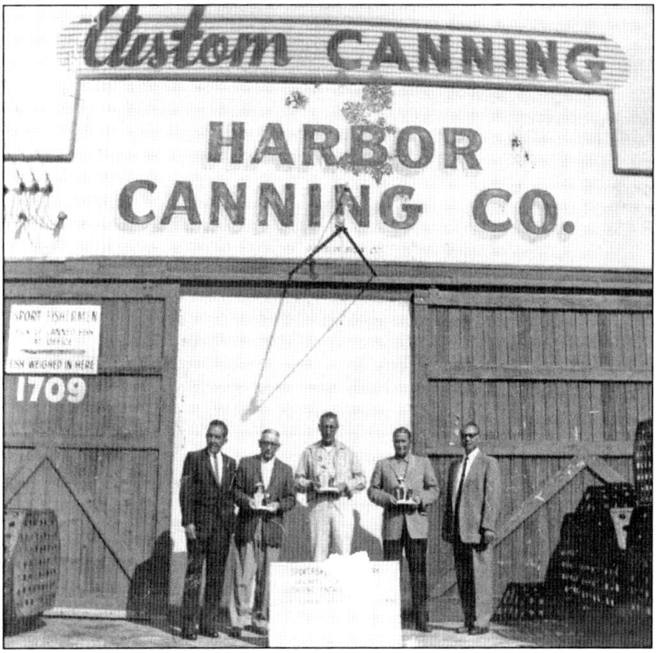

Harbor Canning Company, specializing in fish, was started in 1946 by cousins Albert Guerrero and George De La Torre at 1709 Colon Street. Under the 30-year leadership of George De La Torre Jr. and the label of Juanita's Foods, the company grew into the world's leading producer of *menudo* (tripe soup). The family-owned business shared its success and generosity with the community, both by donations and by employing family and local residents. The founders, Guerrero (left) and De La Torre (right) are pictured with business customers. (Juanita's Foods.)

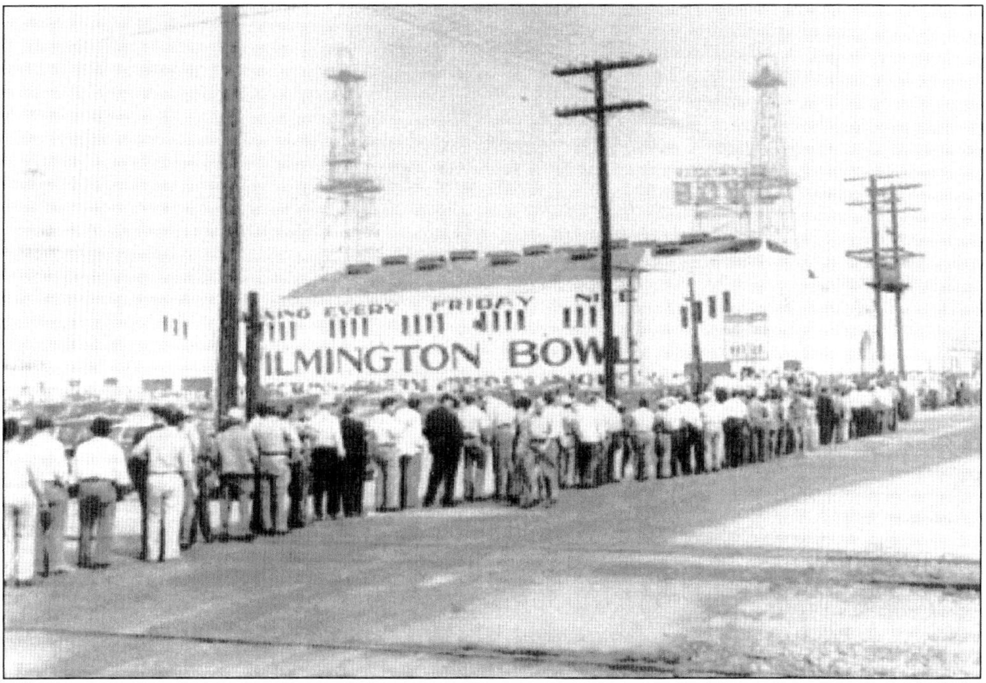

Memories of the Wilmington Bowl linger in the minds of Wilmington's old-timers. It was the place to see big-time wrestling, boxing, roller derby, and to have large meetings or assemblies. Throngs of spectators got off the streetcars at Alameda Street to enjoy the events. Neighborhood boys earned money by collecting tin foil from cigarette wrappers, shining shoes, and selling newspapers, including the *Knock Out* publication for 3¢. In this September 2, 1948, photograph, longshoremen walked off the job for a Union meeting and report on negotiations. (Wilmington Historical Society.)

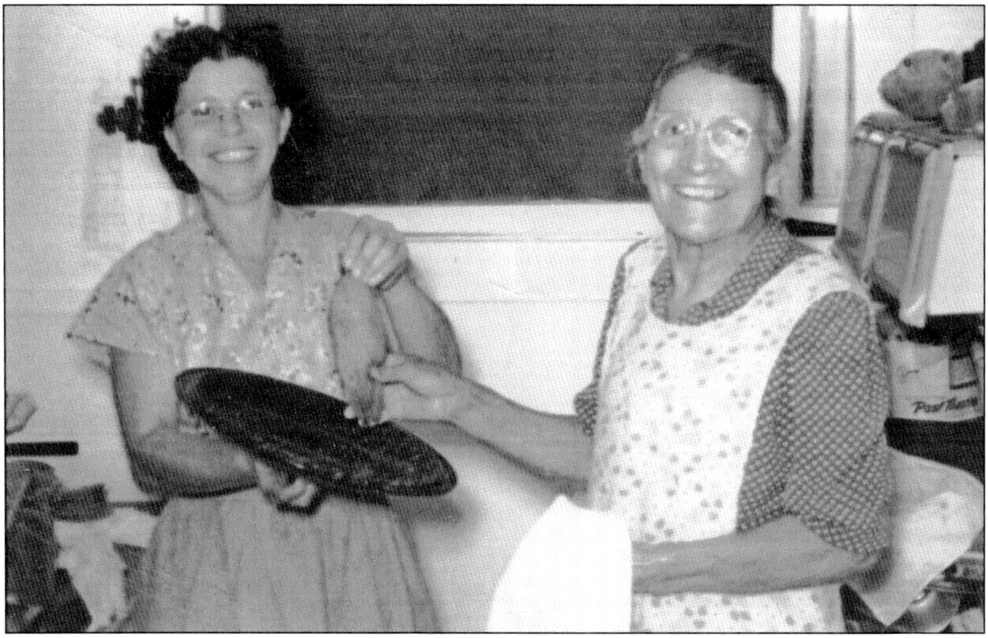

Tamales were the meal of choice on special occasions, especially for Christmas. Making them involved teamwork and mass production for the types and quantities that each family consumed. Wrapping was the fun time when chatter and laughter filled the air. Felicita Ruiz Machado (right) smiled as she and her daughter tested the tamales to determine if fully cooked and ready to be eaten. She used both gas and wood stoves to cook many dozens of tamales. (Anna Mendez.)

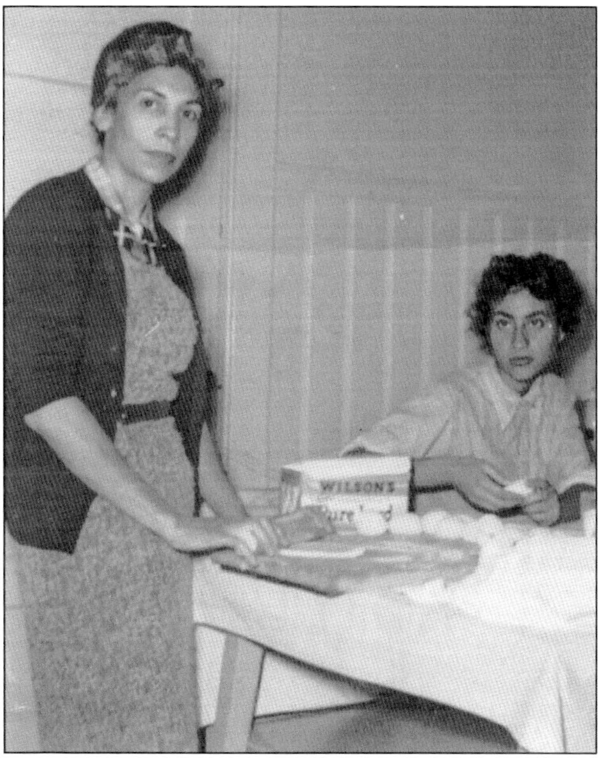

Nowadays, making homemade flour tortillas is almost a lost tradition. Ramona Benavides Hernandez is shown in 1955 at her home on "B" Street rolling a tortilla as her 14-year-old daughter, Leonore, made each ball of dough. The *masa* (dough) was made by kneading together flour, lard or drippings, baking powder, salt, and water. Flour tortillas were not available at markets, and eating a warm tortilla off the *comal* (griddle) spread with butter or filled with refried beans or other homemade fillings was a special treat. (Esther Rendon.)

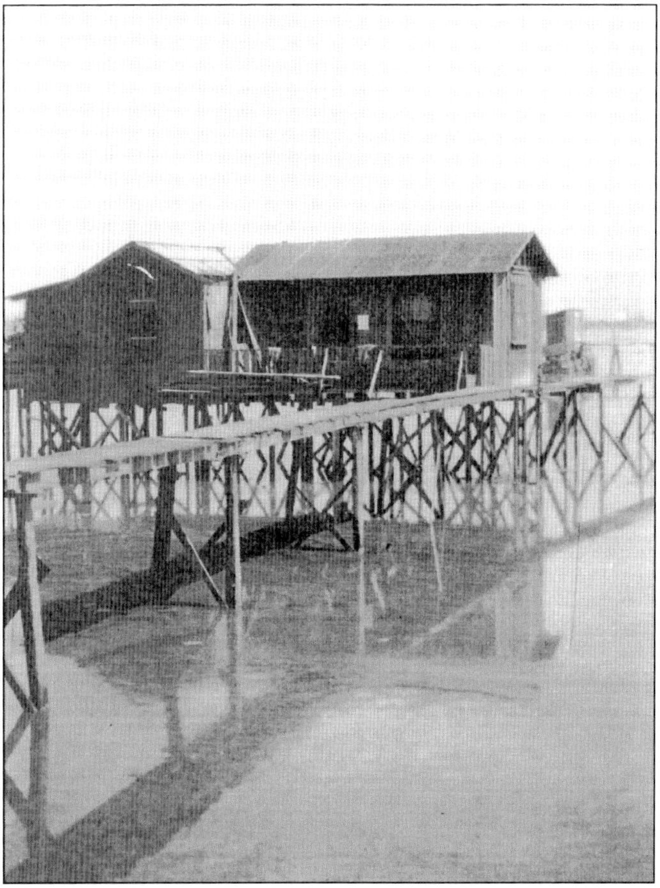

In 1926, the Salcido home sat on stilts at 526 Banning Boulevard. There was no electricity or water in the house. It was located in a swampy area that was affected by high tides and heavy rains. Other homes in Wilmington had the same problem, but it was only an inconvenience. In time, the city used dredged soil to landfill the area. In the picture below, the same house sits on solid ground. This dwelling sat on what became known as the Wilmington Oil Field, and by 1958, was the second most productive field in the United States. (Both, Anthony Salcido.)

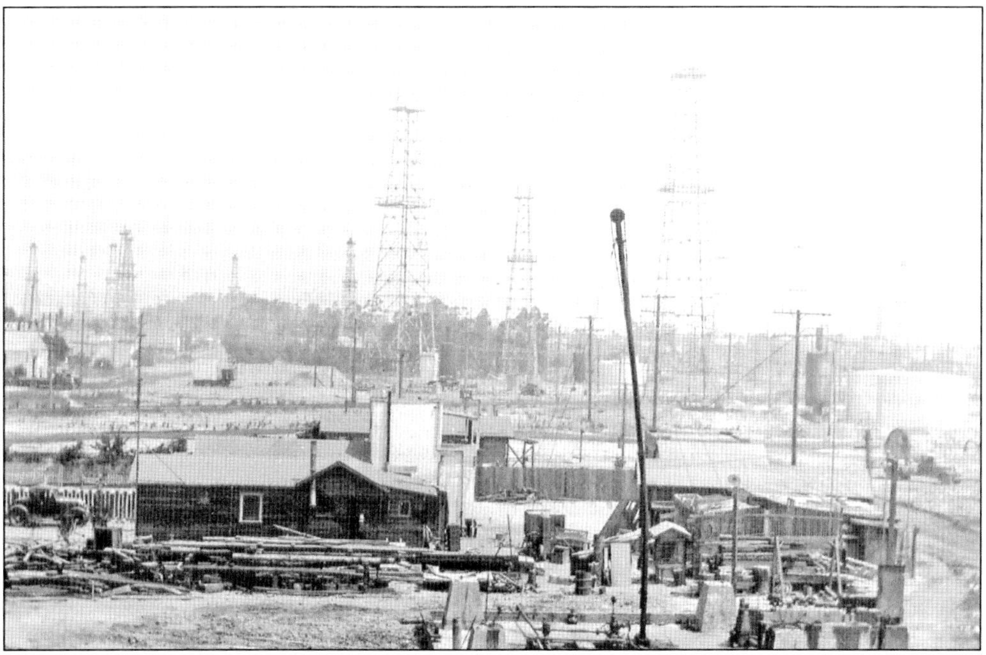

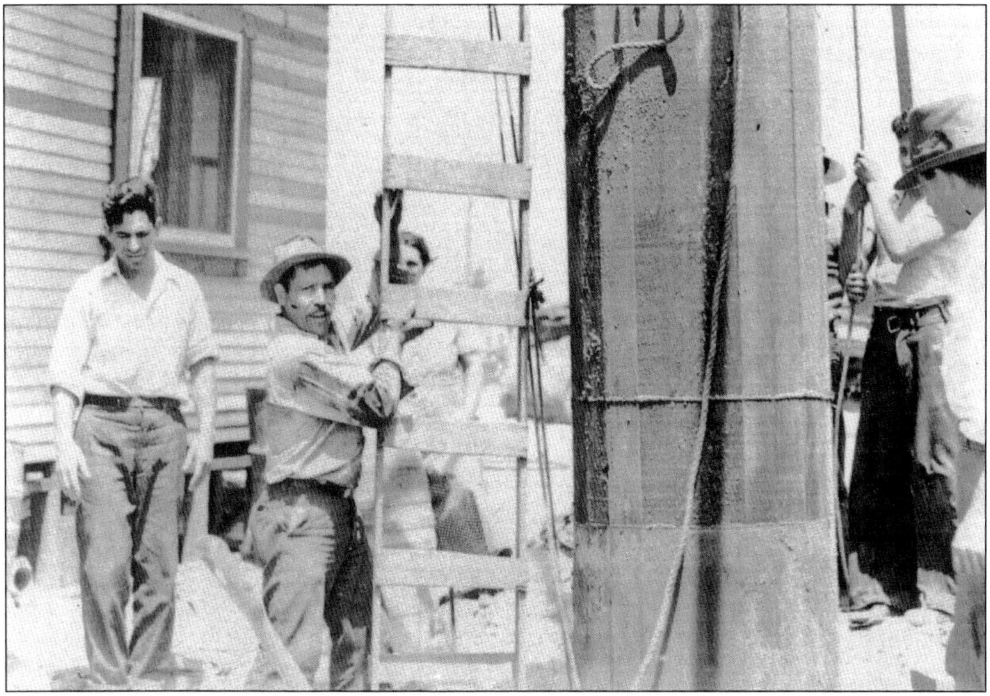

In the photograph above, Cristobal Salcido is working to dig a cesspool, which was to be hooked up to the plumbing system. Instead, what he found in 1935 was a deposit of casinghead gasoline. This unrefined gasoline could be used in cars. He extracted about 13 barrels a day and sold it to prospective buyers. Within a few months, city officials declared the backyard operation a fire risk, and the drilling permit fee was raised from $5 to $100 dollars and $500 dollars for a performance bond for each well hole. He worked as a longshoreman, and his new oil source of income to support the family had faded. The photograph below is reprinted from a newspaper. (Both, Anthony Salcido.)

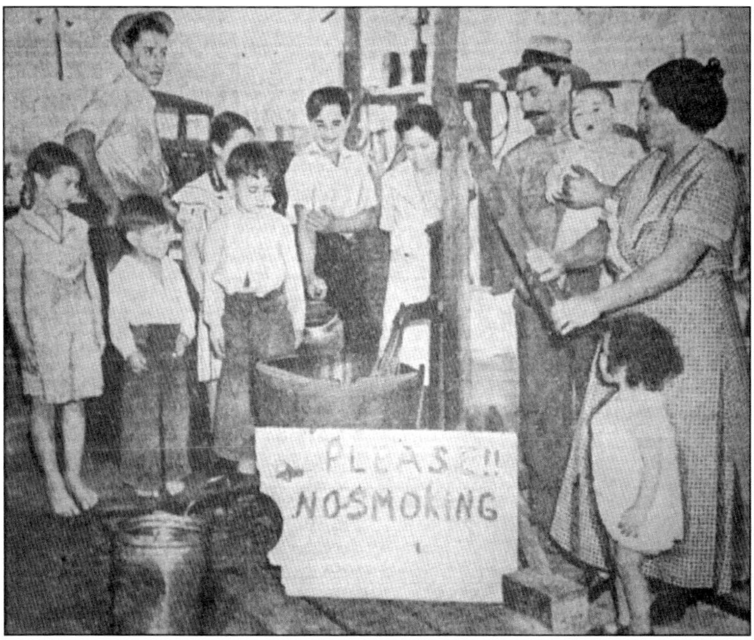

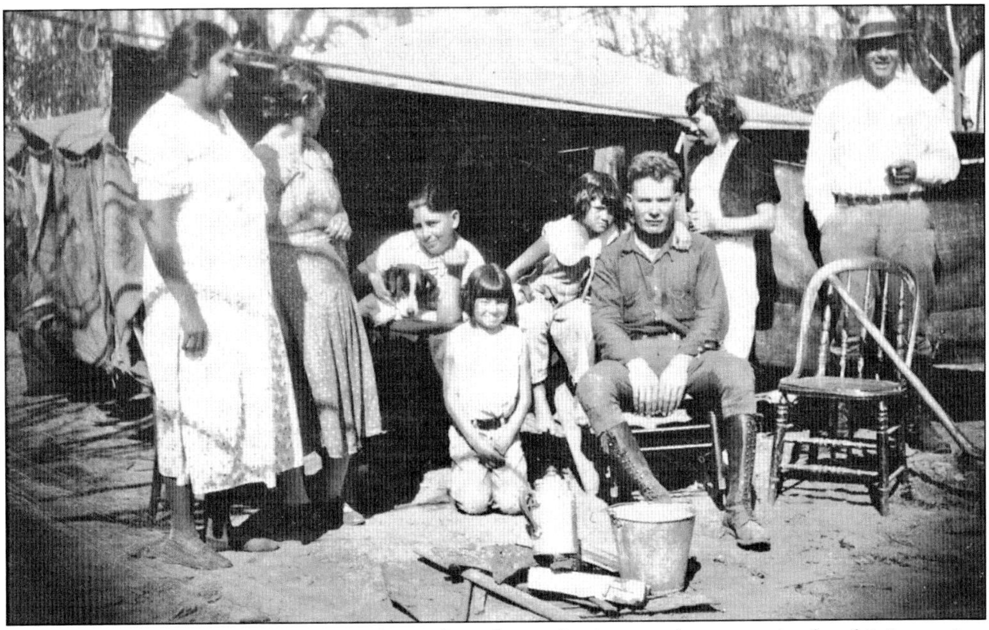

On March 10, 1933, the Long Beach earthquake took place with a magnitude of 6.4, causing widespread damage. Wilmington residents were well aware of the shaking at 5:55 p.m. that afternoon. It rattled their nerves, broke dishes, and caused minor damage to their homes. Some families throughout the community decided it was best to sleep outdoors with the reoccurring aftershocks. (Anna Mendez.)

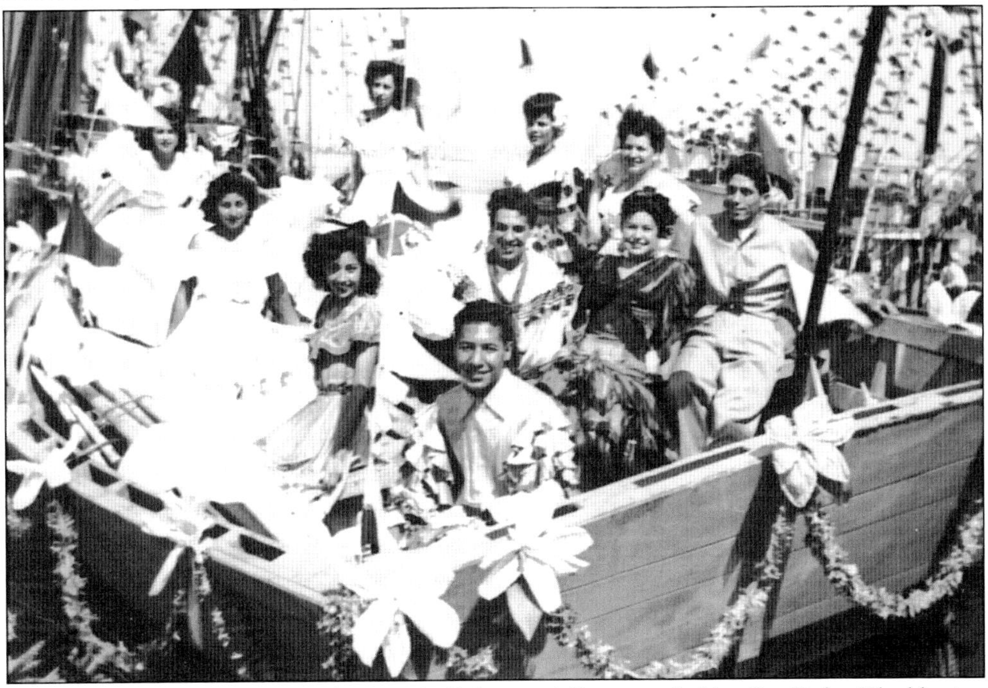

Once a year, during the 1950s and 1960s, the Fisherman's Fiesta was held in San Pedro. The blessing of the fishing fleet attracted hundreds of spectators. Wilmington's Club Lucerna participated in the event and joined the purse seiner parade. (Author's collection.)

An ice cream store was situated on the corner of Eubank and "N" Street, across from Banning Park. It was not a fancy place, but the ice cream was delicious and sold for 5¢ per scoop. It was an after-school hangout. Around 1938, these young women were next door to the establishment and probably bought a malt or ice cream soda with money saved. They are, from left to right, (first row) Stella Miranda, Maggie Espinoza, and Vera Ponce; (second row) unidentified and Ortie Carreon. (Anna Mendez.)

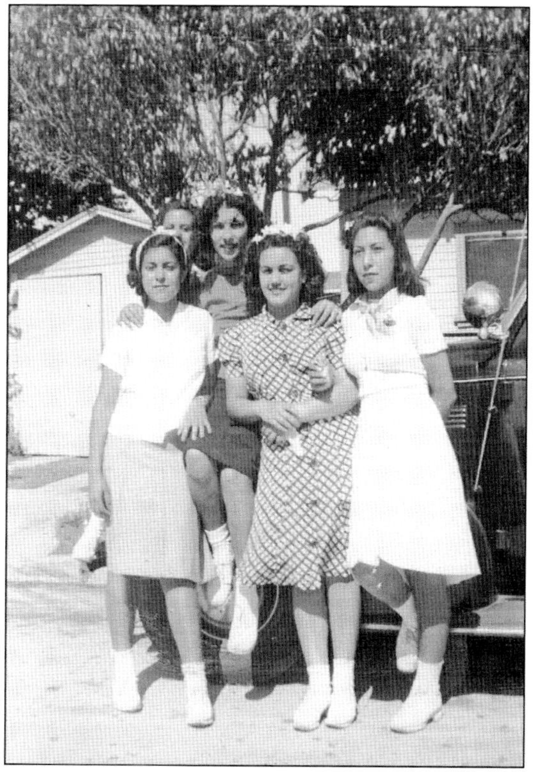

For many years, the Sociedad Cívica held a contest to select a queen and hosted a coronation in her honor. The festivity included speeches, music by local bands, singers, dancing in the closed-off street, food, and game booths. Everyone, young and old, looked forward to the yearly event. Guadalupe Gonzalez was crowned queen in 1939. (Rita Rosales.)

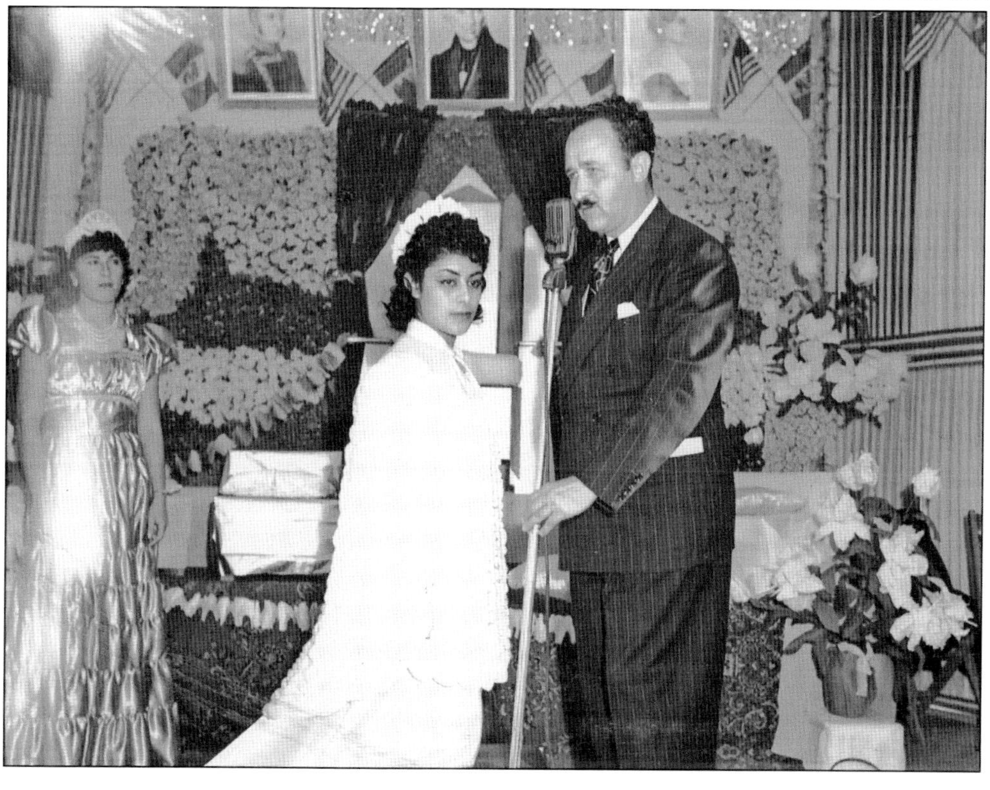

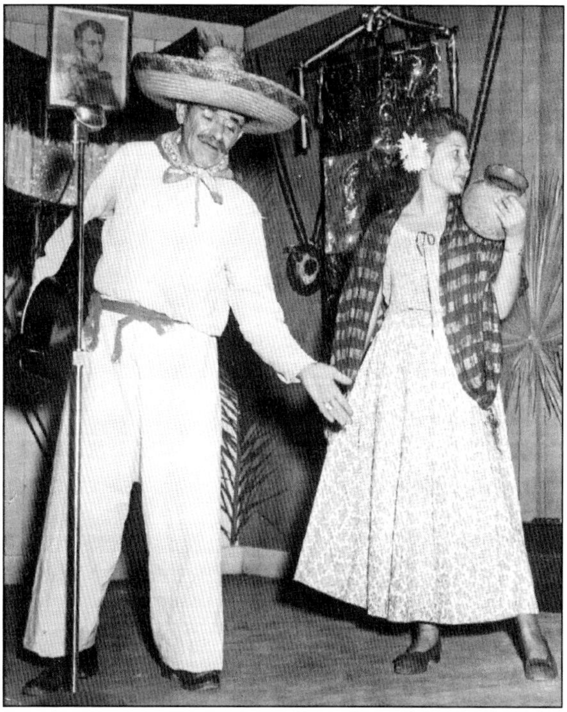

The celebrations at the Honorífica included entertainment provided by local residents. In 1940, at age 53, Marcelino Mota displayed his love of music and dance from his native state of Jalisco. His dance partner was Grace Aguirre. Various bands played on stage, but many remember the bass playing of Francisco Ponce de Leon as he plucked, strummed, and twirled his shiny, stringed, wooden instrument. His musical family played in school bands and orchestras, and his son, Frank, played in the Marine Corps Marching Band. (Ralph Mota.)

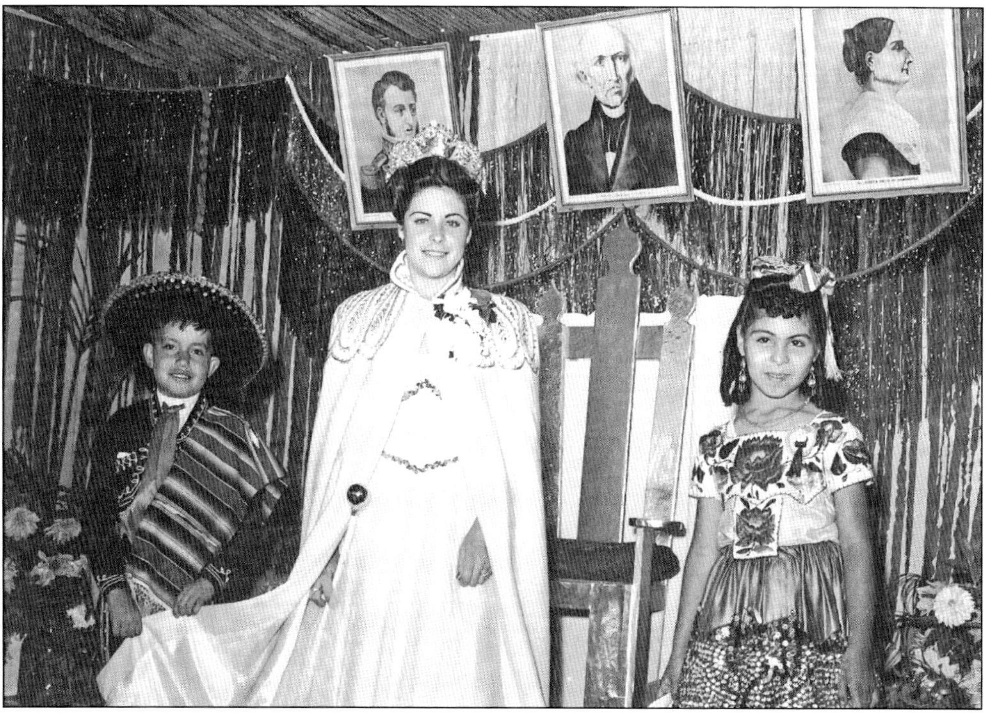

On the anniversary of the 131st year of independence from Spain, the Mexican Independence Day program was witnessed by over 1,500 persons in 1941. Queen Rosalie Perez is shown with two young attendants Rogelio Cruz (left) and Margarita Cabrera (right). The princesses were Catalina Salcido, Nena Hernandez, and Margarite Corrales. (Rosalie Medina.)

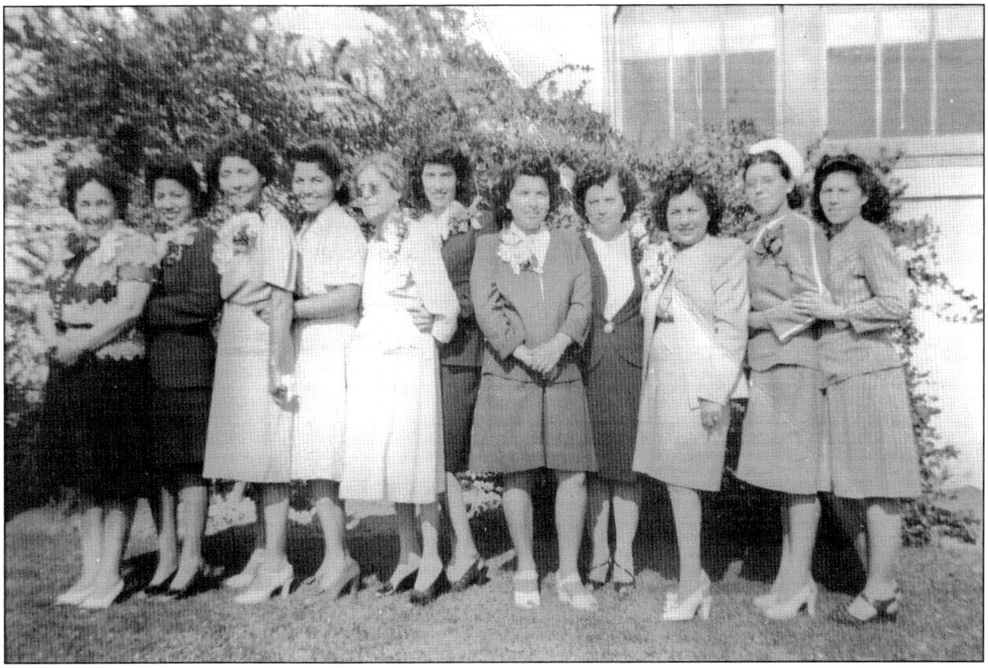

Participants of the Mother's Day celebration at Mahar House on May 12, 1946, are shown in the two photographs. Mothers (above) wore the corsages presented to them by their daughters, and their daughters (below) showed their joy in honoring their mothers. The guest of honor was Andrea Uribe Gomez (above, far right), a Van Camp cannery worker and mother of six children. In 1935, she spearheaded the effort in organizing the Cannery Workers Union. (Anna Mendez.)

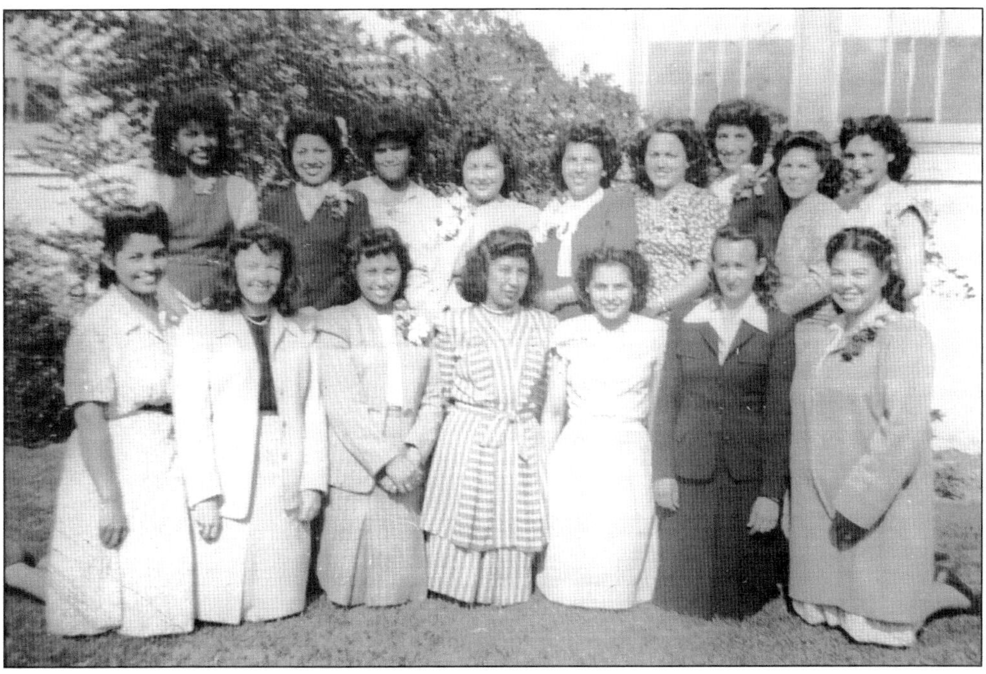

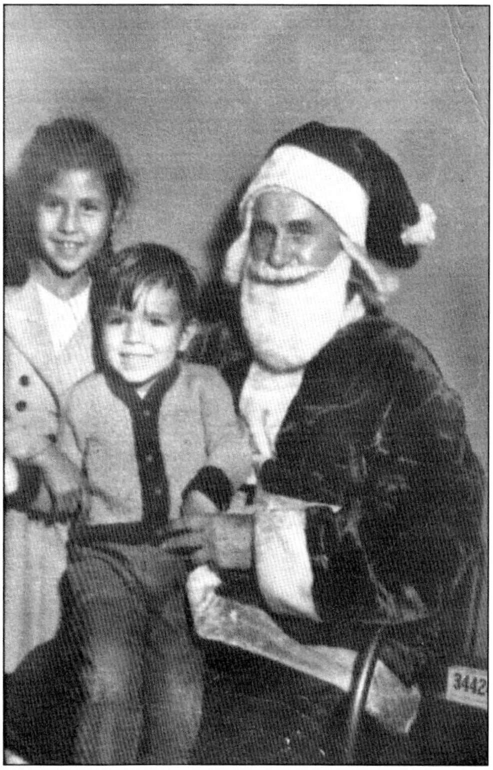

The Christmas season was welcomed by children. They bought or made gifts for their brothers and sisters, and in some homes they helped set up the *nacimiento* (nativity scene). Midnight Mass and church were important to the season. Yet, the opportunity to meet Santa Claus either at a store, park, or workplace was exciting. Otila Gallegos and her brother Jose Manuel are smiling with Santa around 1947. (Otila Sorensteene.)

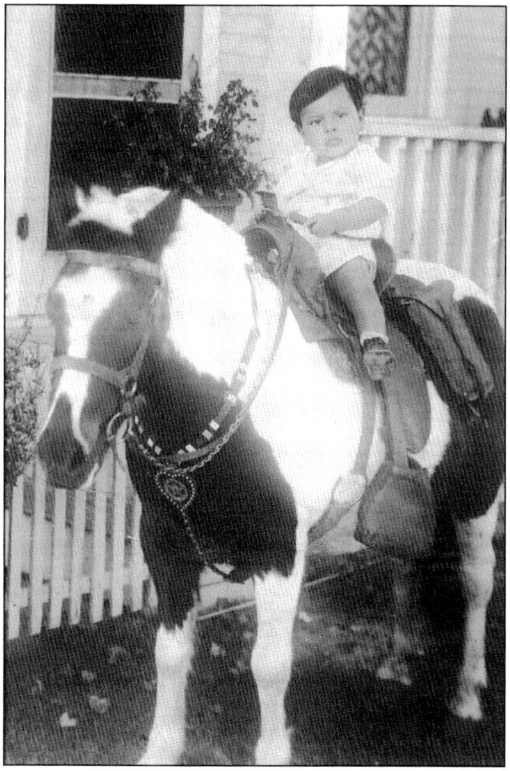

Roger Gonzales sat upon a pony for a memorable photograph in 1938. Whenever the traveling photographer walked through the neighborhood, children followed him. They were hopeful to have the opportunity to pet the animal. Gonzales and his sister Aurora were raised on Rubidoux Street, and he became a longshoreman. Their parents, Juan and Jesus Gonzales, had come from Tequila, Jalisco. (Roger Gonzales.)

WILMINGTON CENTENNIAL PAGEANT

1858 - 1958

This Is The Story

THIS IS THE STORY OF A HARBOR

This is the story of a harbor—the vision of one man, then the dream of a few, a challenge of a nation's Congress, the benefit of countless thousands around the world.

One of the festivities for Wilmington's centennial was a hometown play held in the Phineas Banning High School auditorium on June 6, 1958. These images show sections of the 100th birthday pageant program, which lists the fiesta folk, townspeople, and orchestra. The supporting cast of actors were also local residents. (Both, author's collection.)

FIESTA FOLK—Hortensia Delgadillo, Paul Gutierrez, June Munoz, Benny Sierra, Virginia Salcido, Sylvia Romero, Carol Romero, Teresa Romero, Elva Cueva, Patricia Hoover, Judy Wilson, Donna Carpenter, Marilyn Eltraham, Shirlee Kimbrell, Sonoma Jenne, Sandra Enright, Pat Hiller; Los Matachines of Mexican Civic Association, George Fimbres, Joe Alfred Fimbres, Pancho Gonzales, Raymond Hernadez, Francisco Islas, Tony Lara, Lind Murry, Carlos Macias, Antonia Paredes, Sergio Rodriguez, Lorenzo Sigala, Jose Sigala, Carlos Soliz, George Soliz, Bobby Trani, Eilisa Gutierrez, Jesus Caldera, Gerardo Nolaso, Eutimio Saucedo, Director.

TOWNSPEOPLE—Roberta Ryan, Dorene Lees, Joanne Eshelman, Janet Partin, Rosa Kidder, Gloria Rice, Beulah Holstein, Genevieve Partin, Esther Scott, Ellen Eitel, Arlene Thompson, Rawson Gorsh, Roger Landesman, Jim Poindexter, Jim Davis, Barney Spencer, Carole Dennis, Claudette Garnichaud, Emilie Janish, Barbara Queen, Patricia Murphy, Marion Spencer, Genevieve Bruno, Molly Markham, M. Hoxworth, Marie Yadao, Cecil Ricks, Larry Wilson, Ruth M. Adams, Lois Black, Marge Bowling, Ethel DeVore, Florence Foat, Juanita Harvey, Winifred Hill, Charmagne Hobbs, June Kelso, Virginia King, Margaret League, Joan Lorenzen, Blanche Sebesta, Florine Stevenson, Marge White, Lucille Wilson, Mildred Trujillo, Mae Nishimoto, Mary Crandall, Mary Carter, Lucy Brockway.

ORCHESTRA—Don Rowland, Allen Dennen, Ned Dennen, Betty Dale, Janet Coffelt, Kay Westall, Myrna Hill, Edwin James, Sharon Stowell, Gloria Moyer, Linda Morphew, Suzanne Lee, Stephen Whelchel, Julian Garcia, Pat Ngoho, Gary Gabriel, Helen Christian, Tom Anderson, Bill Lees, Dale Martin, Joe Ratliff, Don Hall, Michael Ryan, Francisco Ponce deLeon, Kenneth Haar, Bob Ryan, James Lees, Guy Barnett, Alan Ryan, Ed Sandison, Bob Eitel, Larry Nelson, LeRoy Transler, Glenn Moore, Guilford Clopton, Ronnie Blanchard.

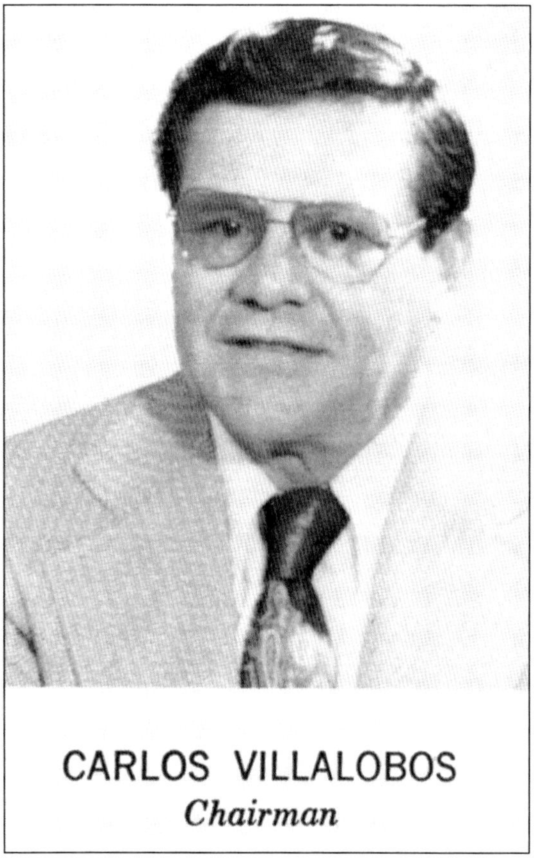

For 84 years, Carlos Villalobos lived in and loved his hometown. As chairman of the Harbor Hispanic Bicentennial Committee, Carlos and his committee enriched and brought recognition to Wilmington for its celebration of the 200th birthday of the United States. Community organizations and businesses joined and enjoyed the program, parade, and dance. Villalobos had been a disc jockey and boxing trainer at the Wilmington Bowl, a merchant marine, active in the community, and also ran a tax and insurance business. (Carol Maldonado.)

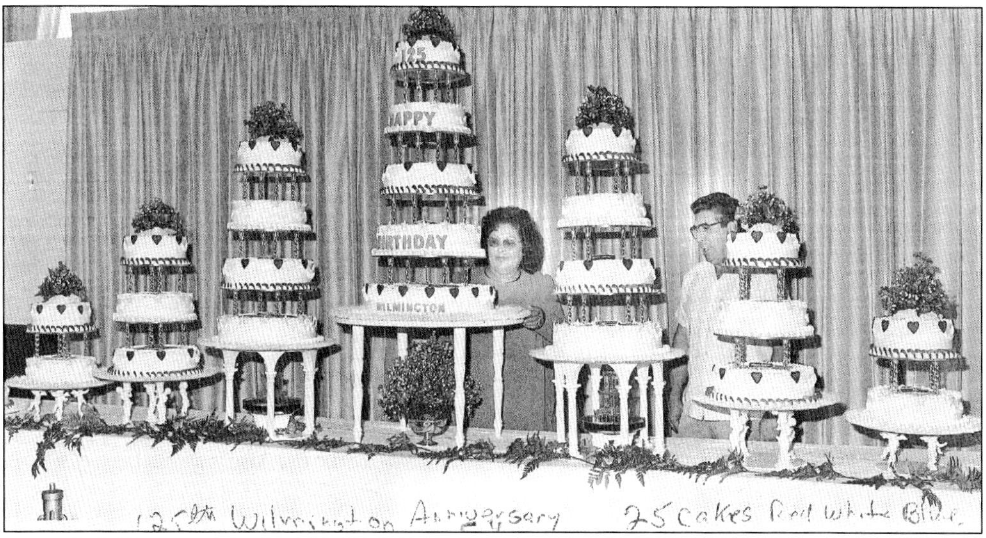

In 1983, Wilmington reached its 125th anniversary in a display of sweetness. Eleanor Robles Montano provided 25 red-white-and-blue cakes. She is standing behind the center tier. Montano lived on East Cruces Street and recalls the army radio station in the family's garage during World War II. She has been a volunteer for 36 years, working to make the community a safer place for residents and police officers. (Eleanor Montano.)

Five

Work and Play

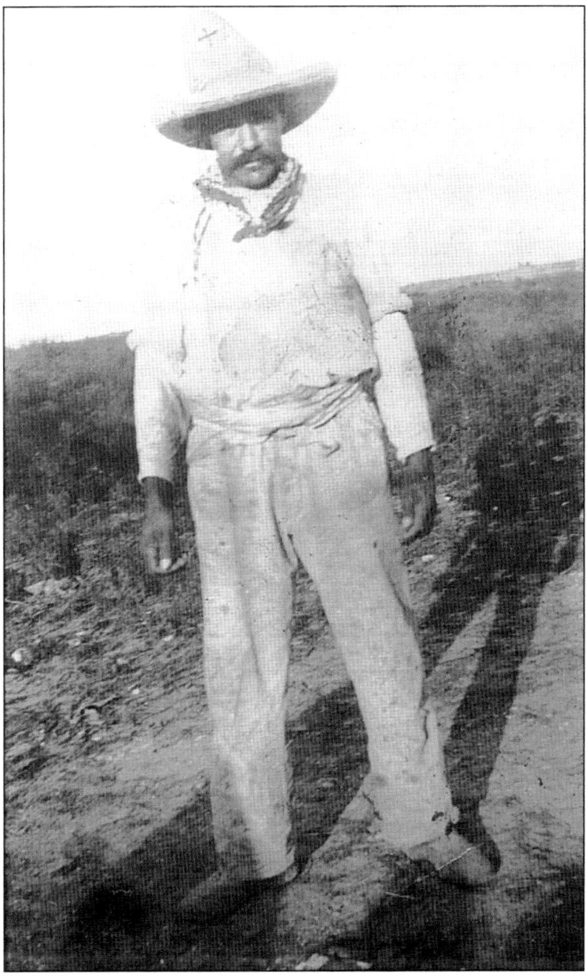

Ignacio Manzo was born in Michoacan in 1880 and came to this country in 1900. He worked cattle and traveled back and forth across the border to sell them. Concerned about safety and long periods of separation, his wife, Juanita, stayed in Wilmington near relatives. In retirement, he enjoyed the company of his grandchildren who lived near him on Cruces Street. He and Juanita are buried in the historic Wilmington Cemetery. (Joe Manzo.)

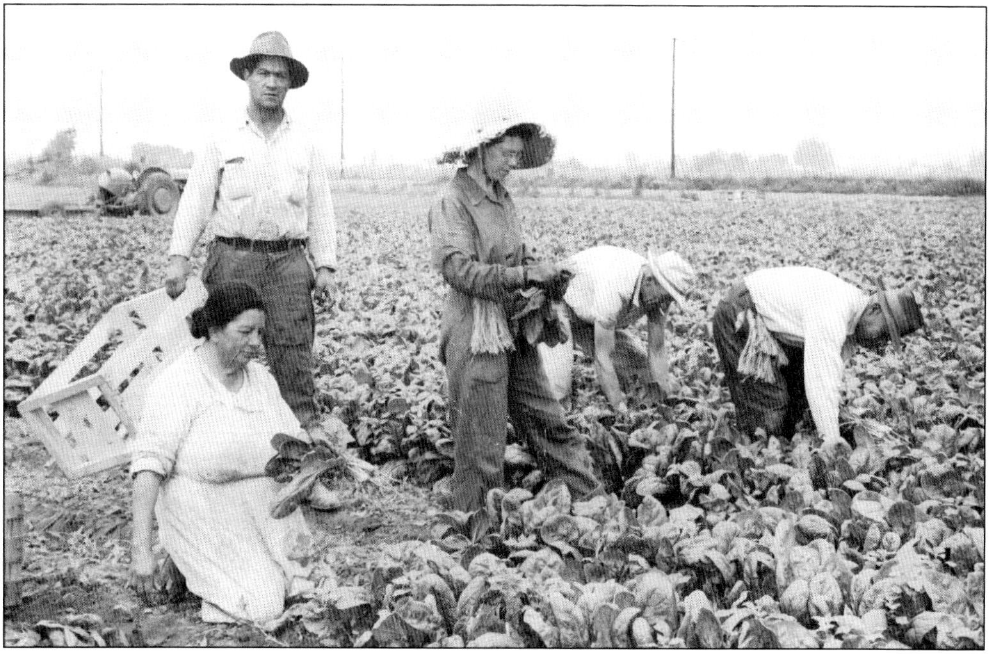

Early families worked farms, orchards, dairies, or their own land. Some had farmed in Mexico, but others did it to provide for family. From the Midwest to California, from children to older adults, with machines, horses, and hands, they toiled. Picking spinach on the Machado farm are Doña Remedios (kneeling) and standing from left to right, James Machado, Catalina ?, Carl Boatwright, and Don Luti. Strings at their waist were used to tie each bunch of spinach. (Anna Mendez.)

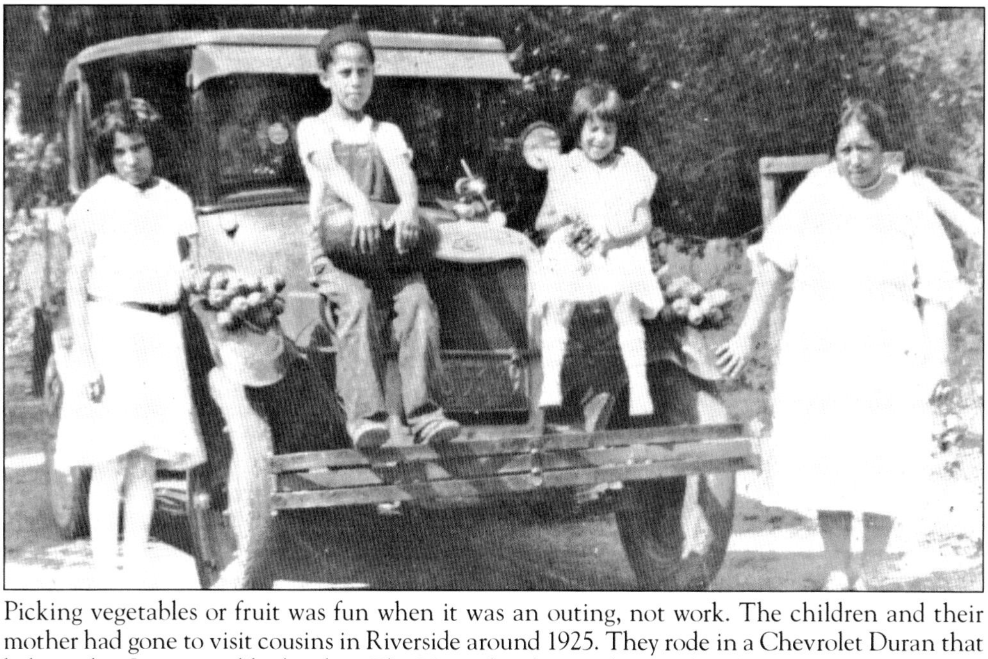

Picking vegetables or fruit was fun when it was an outing, not work. The children and their mother had gone to visit cousins in Riverside around 1925. They rode in a Chevrolet Duran that belonged to Jesus, an older brother. The Urrea family was about to head home with some prized fruit, a watermelon, and *tunas* (prickly pears). Pictured are, from left to right, Esperanza, Lino, Helen, and Luisa Urrea. (Eleanor Urrea.)

Longshoremen who worked the Long Beach and Los Angeles ports were of many ethnic backgrounds. They formed friendships and working relationships that were strong, and they depended on each other for their safety. Generations of Mexican Americans have worked as longshoremen and as union officers and representatives. The membership book and working card for Santos Calderon is displayed, showing his initiation day as May 1938. (Connie Calderon.)

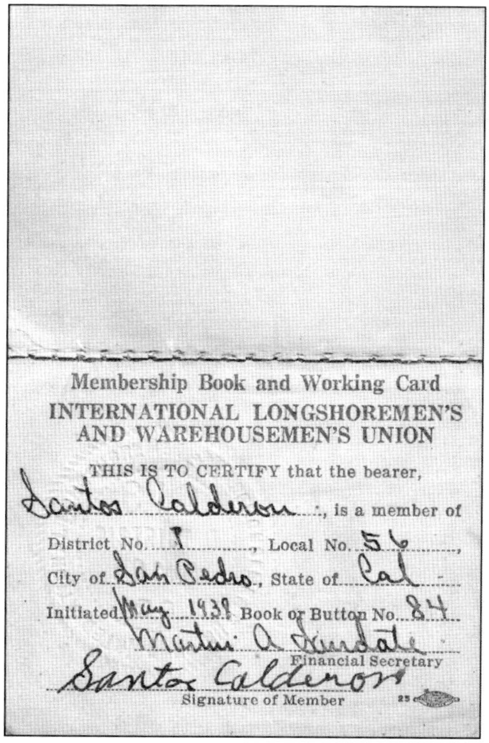

Membership Book and Working Card
INTERNATIONAL LONGSHOREMEN'S AND WAREHOUSEMEN'S UNION

THIS IS TO CERTIFY that the bearer, Santos Calderon, is a member of District No. 1, Local No. 56, City of San Pedro, State of Cal. Initiated May 1938 Book or Button No. 84

Martin A. Lindale
Financial Secretary

Santos Calderon
Signature of Member

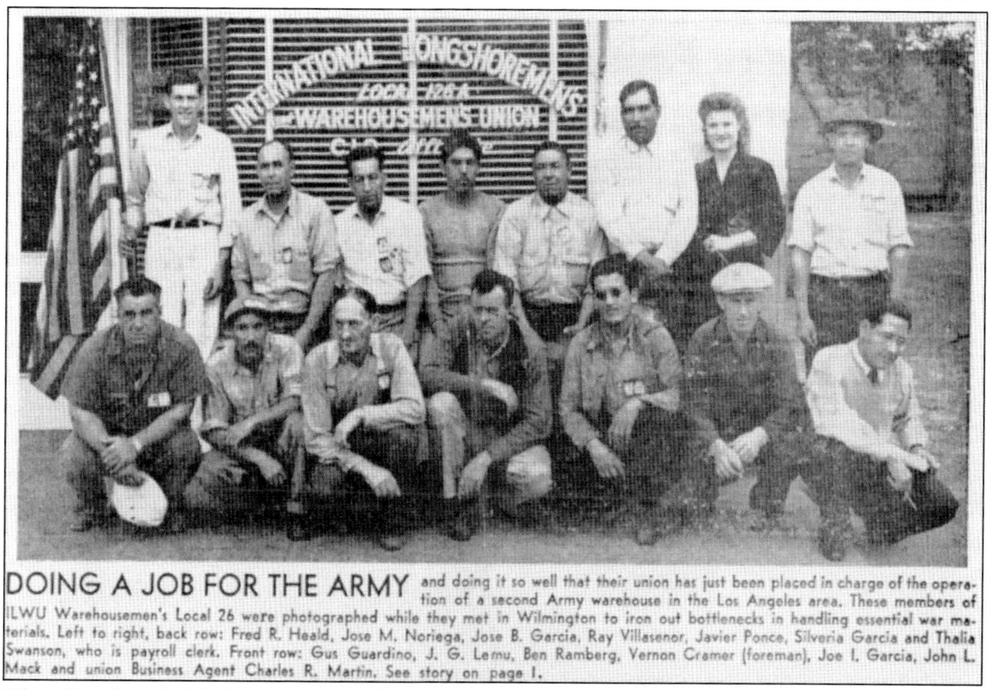

DOING A JOB FOR THE ARMY and doing it so well that their union has just been placed in charge of the operation of a second Army warehouse in the Los Angeles area. These members of ILWU Warehousemen's Local 26 were photographed while they met in Wilmington to iron out bottlenecks in handling essential war materials. Left to right, back row: Fred R. Heald, Jose M. Noriega, Jose B. Garcia, Ray Villasenor, Javier Ponce, Silveria Garcia and Thalia Swanson, who is payroll clerk. Front row: Gus Guardino, J. G. Lemu, Ben Ramberg, Vernon Cramer (foreman), Joe I. Garcia, John L. Mack and union Business Agent Charles R. Martin. See story on page 1.

This October 1, 1943, newspaper clipping from the *Labor Herald*, a Congress of Industrial Organizations (CIO) publication, demonstrated the commitment to the war effort by a ILWU local. Several of the members shown and Thalia Swanson were residents of Wilmington. (Glenn French.)

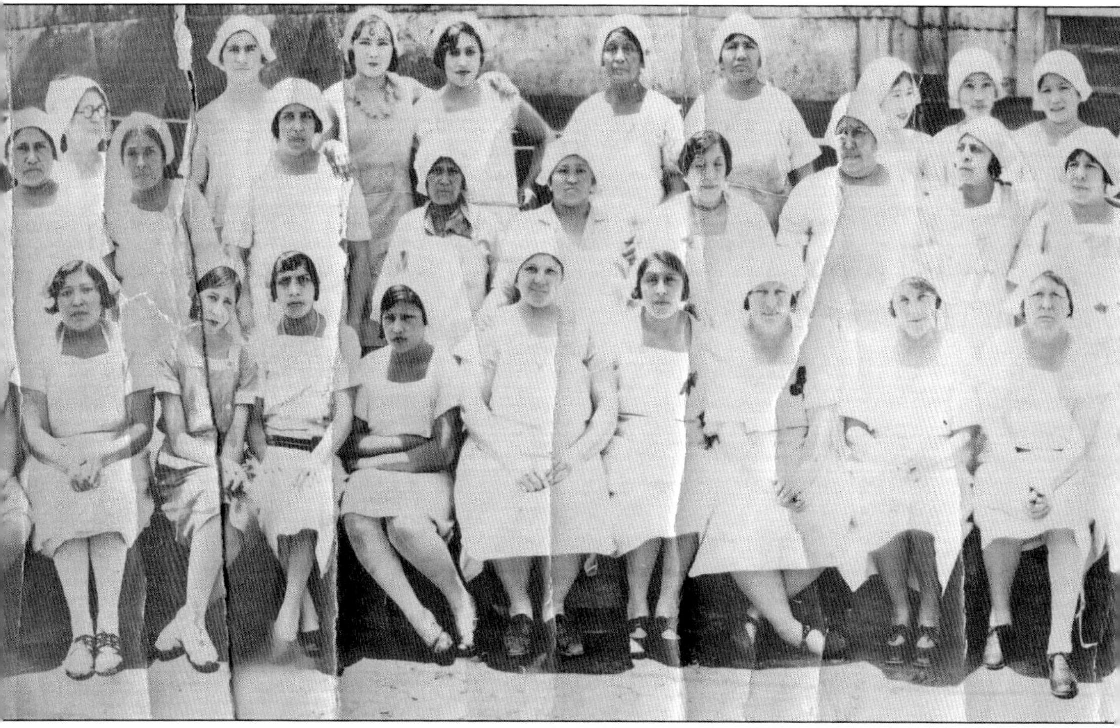

Pictured are women workers who, in 1929, cleaned and packed fish at Coast Fishing Company in Wilmington. The men worked in the warehouse, on the machines, or distributed the bins of fish. Working in a fish cannery was hard work, but it was available to everyone. When work was not available at this cannery, the workers sought work at the Terminal Island canneries. It meant

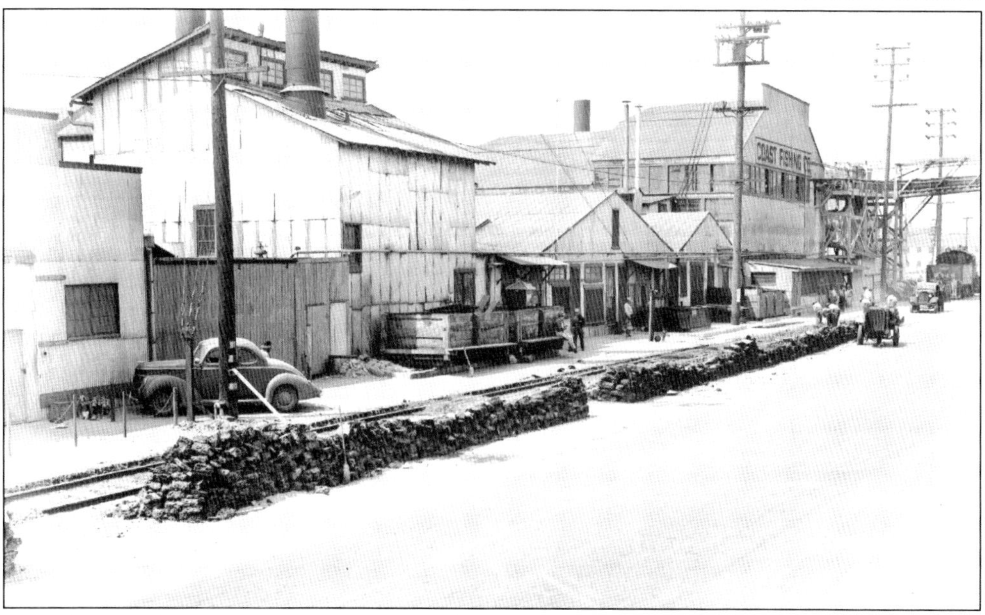

Coast Fishing Company provided work for the men and women of the harbor area. It processed tuna, mackerel, and sardines. Later it became a division of Quaker Oaks and canned Skippy dog food and Puss 'n Boots cat food. (Wilmington Historical Society.)

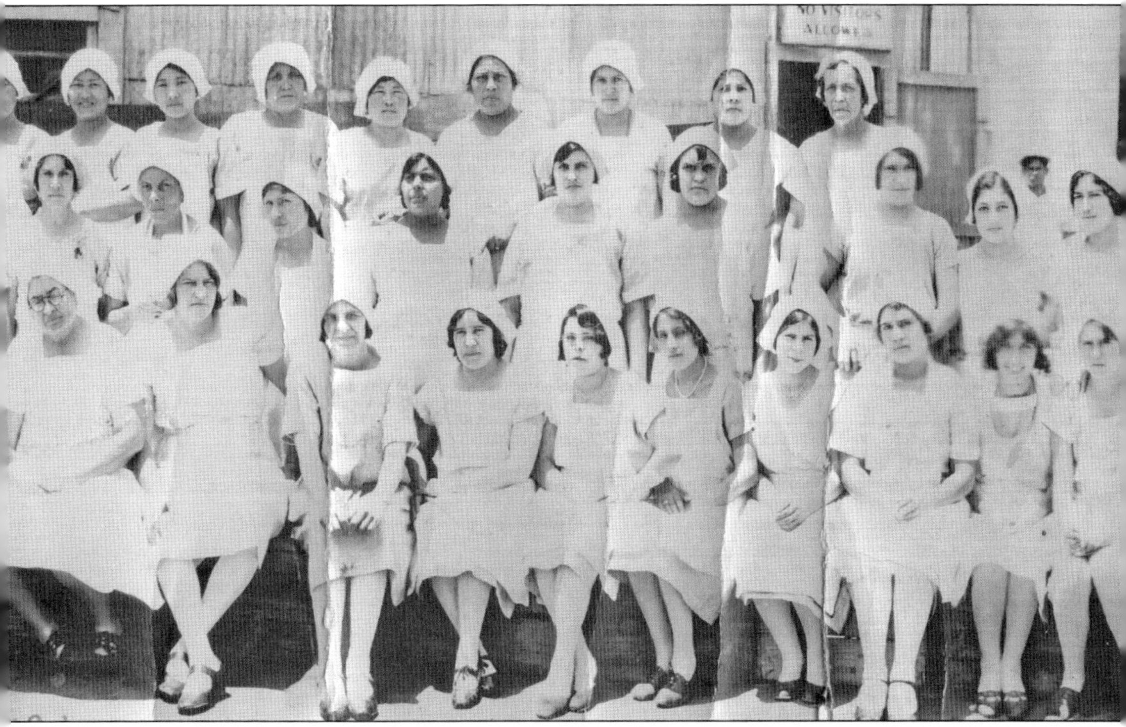

standing outside when there was work and waiting to be chosen to replace vacant spots at the work stations. Transportation involved carpooling, and since refrigeration was limited, the hours were irregular. The family of Trinidad Caracoza Cruz (first row, sixth from right) provided this photograph, and at the present time Cruz is 102 years old. (Eloise Cruz.)

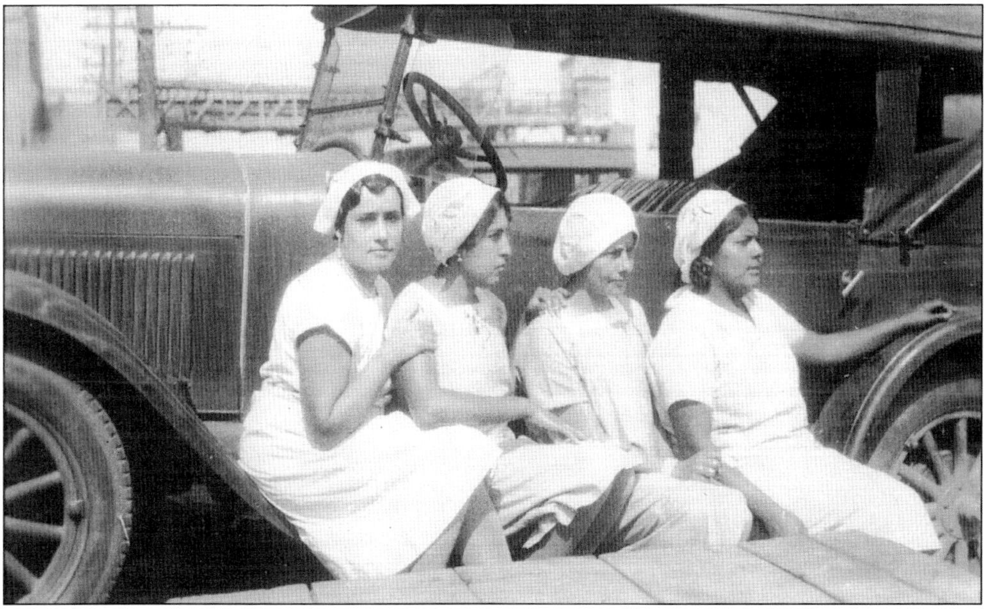

Four cannery workers relax during their lunch break around 1935. Visible in the background is the conveyor bridge that crossed over Fries Avenue. The fish were unloaded from the boat and transported via the conveyor to the cannery. (Maria Enriquez.)

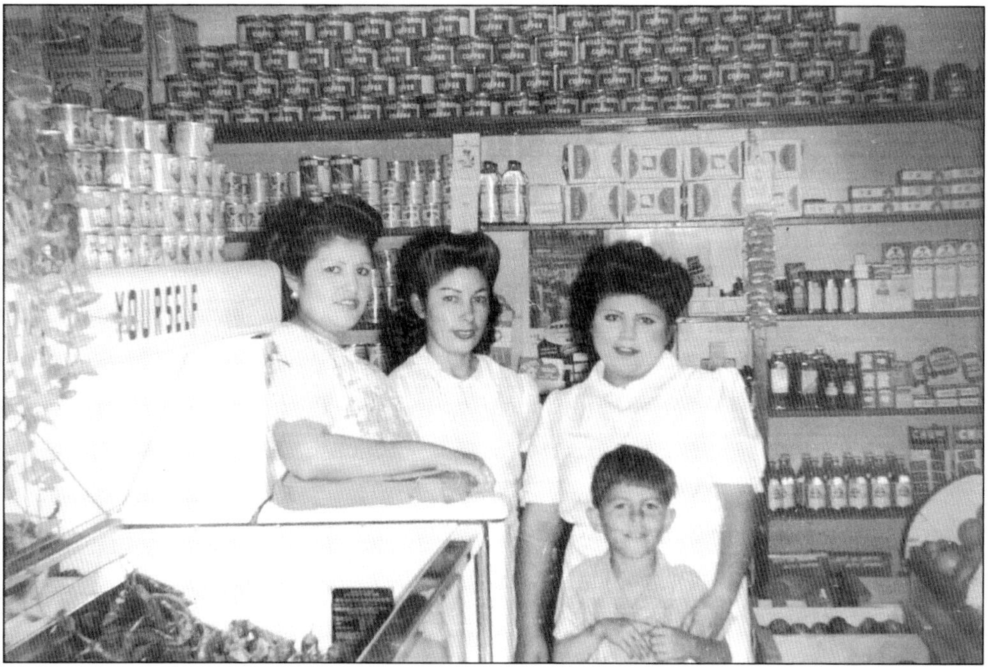

La Jaliscience, a store owned by Fermin Quesada, was located at 1115 East "L" Street. The store was a bakery and corn tortilla factory and sold Mexican staples and spices. On Sundays, during the 1940s, about 600 dozen tortillas and as many as 100 copies of *La Opinion*, a Spanish-language newspaper, were sold. The store was managed by daughters Dolores, Gertrude, and Belen, pictured from left to right with younger brother Ramon. During World War II, packages of tamales and tortillas were sent to Wilmington's servicemen fighting in every theater of operation. (Ramon Quesada.)

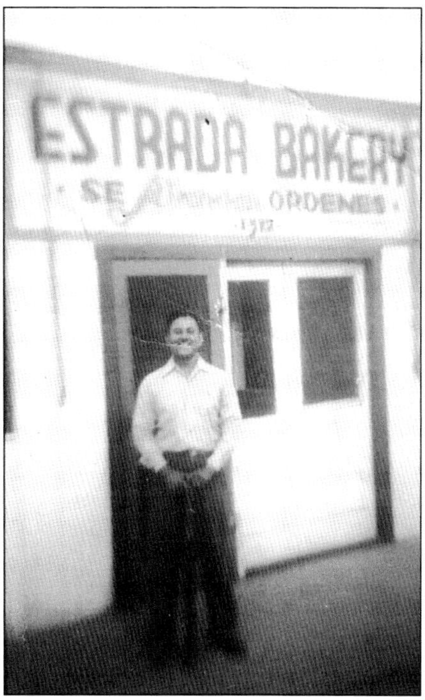

Estrada Bakery was located at 1312 Eubank Avenue. The Estrada family immigrated in 1920 to the United States when threatened by the politics of the revolution. They had owned two bakeries in Sonora. After working as a baker in Douglas, Arizona, and in Corona, California, Manuel Estrada opened this bakery, baking bread in an old brick oven located behind the Fermin Quesada residence. Estrada's son Herman (in front of bakery) worked in the paint department at Shell Chemical. (Cynthia Pratt.)

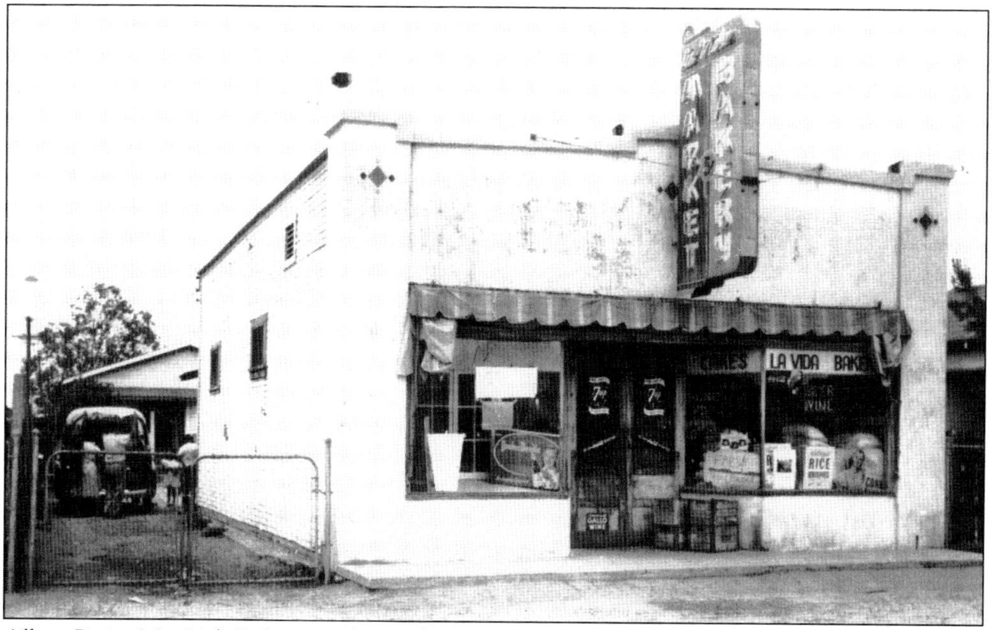

Albert Patino's La Vida Bakery was located at 1126 Sanford Avenue. This site has served as a bakery and grocery store for many years. It is now named La Perla Bakery. Family-owned grocery stores were popular and common in the neighborhood. There was the market on Blinn Avenue that Andres Rutoskey opened in 1918 and operated for 42 years. Other markets included Watson Avenue Grocery (Jose and Eleuteria Mares), La Mexicana (Ernesto Vega), Fries Avenue Market (Salvador and Lucy Aguirre), Duran's Liquor Store (Jose Duran), Arroyo's (Luz and Jesus Arroyo), La Jaliscience (Fermin Quesada), Villagomez Market (Cayetano Villagomez), and others. (Eugenia Porras.)

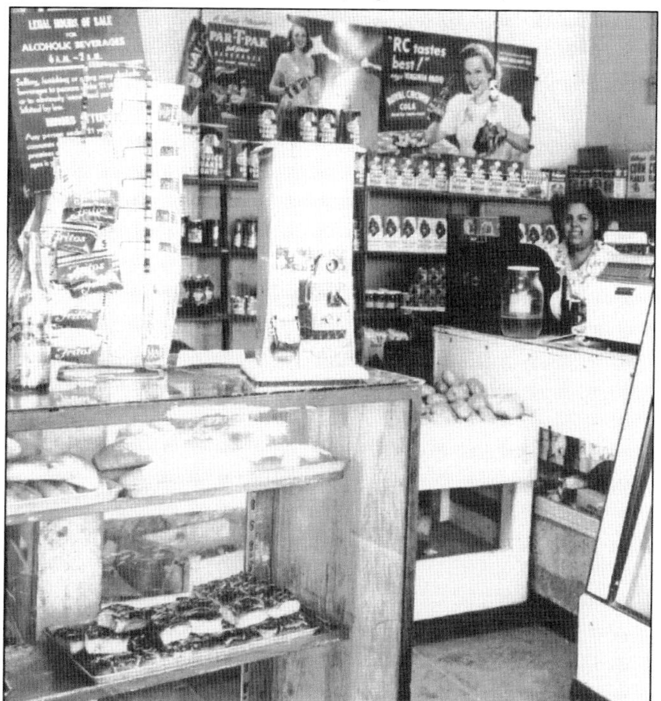

The owner's daughter stood at the cash register in La Vida Bakery. Food products are neatly displayed with the poster behind the Fritos display announcing the legal hours of sale for alcoholic beverages. The bakery sat in an ideal location, one block from Holy Family Church. After Sunday Mass, churchgoers found it convenient to buy *pan dulce* (Mexican bread). They bought *elotitos* (little corn), *conchas* (shells), *semitas* (wheat buns), *cuernos* (horns), *empanadas* (turnovers), *polvorones* (powdered cookies), *bolillos* (French rolls), and cakes. (Eugenia Porras.)

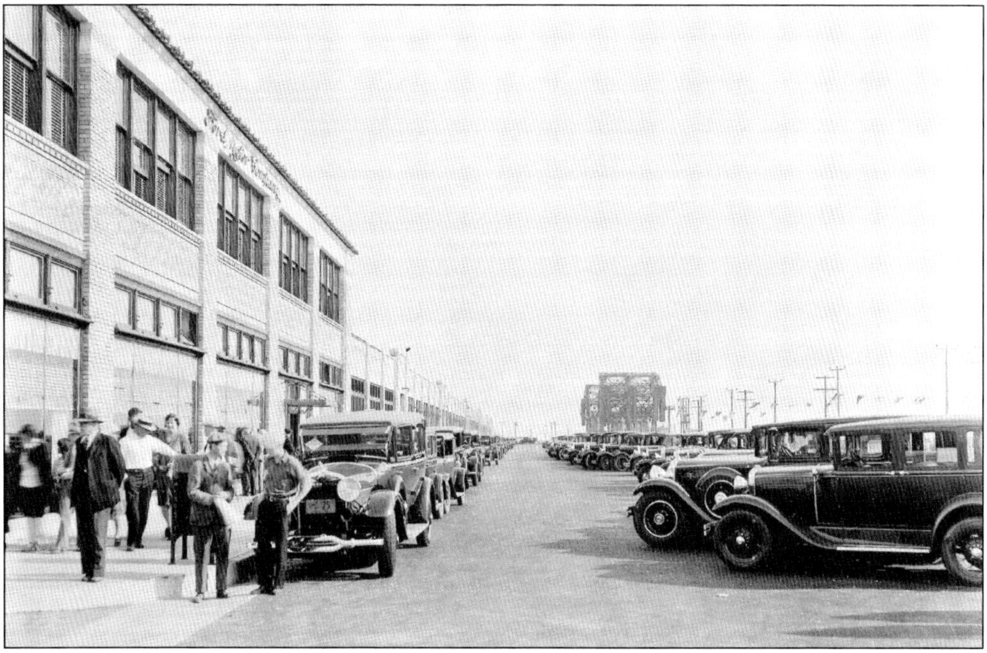

In January 1936, production at the Ford Motor Company plant on Henry Ford Avenue in Wilmington rolled 205 automobiles off its assembly line per day. In those days, over 1,200 men were employed. Around 1959, the plant closed at this location and moved operations to Pico Rivera. The Badger drawbridge, often referred to as the Henry Ford drawbridge, is visible in the background. (Wilmington Historical Society.)

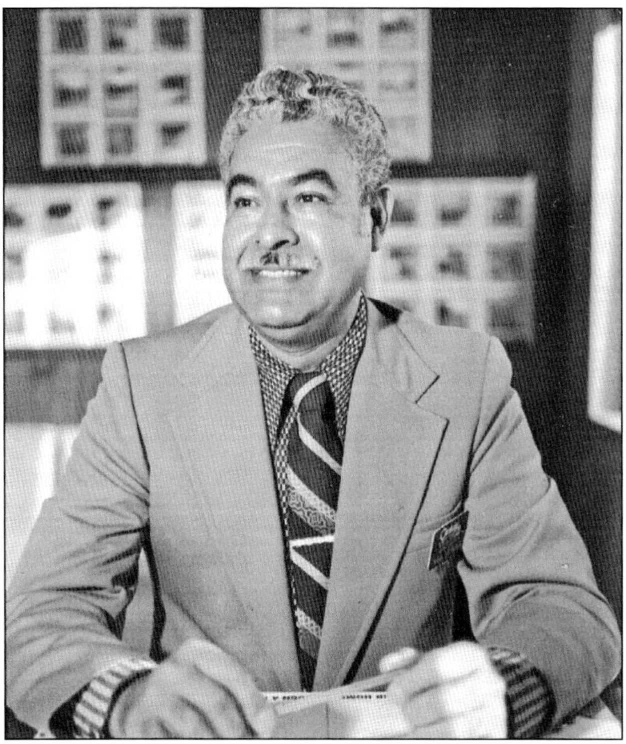

While Frank Herrera served in the U.S. Army, his parents moved to Wilmington from Arizona and his father found work at Todd Shipyard. In 1946, Herrera joined them when he was discharged from Fort Mac Arthur in San Pedro. Herrera worked many jobs through the years, and like other returning servicemen, the G.I. Bill provided him the opportunity to go to college. Advancement promotions at Ford Motor were not granted, so he moved to General Motors in South Gate and became the first Mexican American superintendent of a department. (Frank Herrera.)

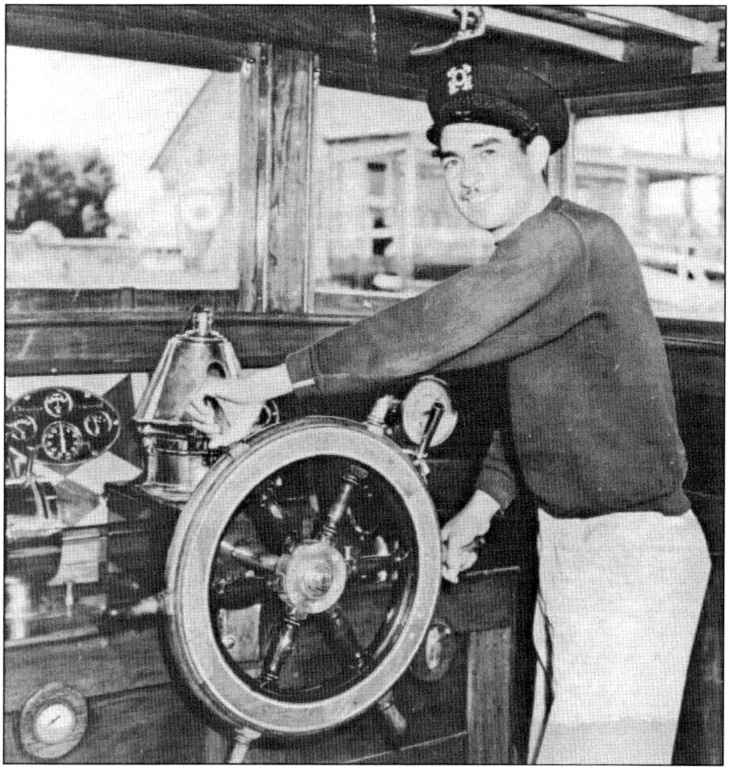

The pleasure boat scene with its many yacht clubs in Wilmington allowed young men to work beyond their sphere of reality. They came from humble homes to work in luxury as deckhands, pilots, and in marina occupations. David Gonzales was one of many who found work in this challenging and enjoyable aquatic environment around 1940. As the marinas disappeared, Gonzales opened a successful furniture business, Harbor Furniture, on Avalon Boulevard. (Raul Gonzales.)

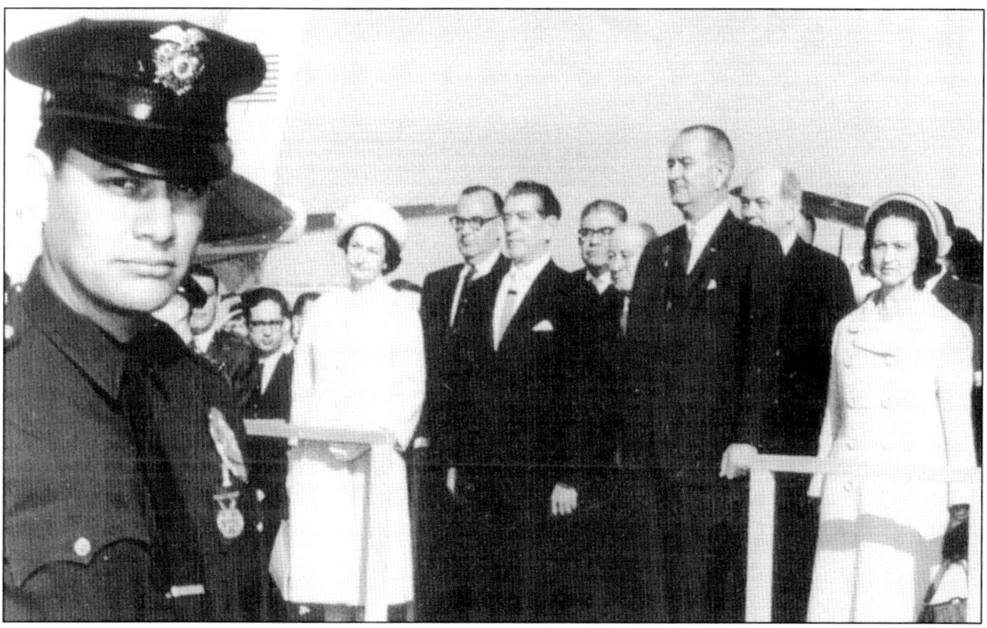

In 1964, the Metropolitan Division of the Los Angeles Police Department provided security on a tour of Los Angeles for Pres. Lyndon Johnson, First Lady Claudia "Lady Bird" Johnson, Mexico's president Adolfo López Mateos, and his wife, Eva Sámano. Shown on duty is officer Alfredo Pacheco. He served for three years as president of Los Angeles Law Enforcement Association (LA LEY). (Margaret Pacheco.)

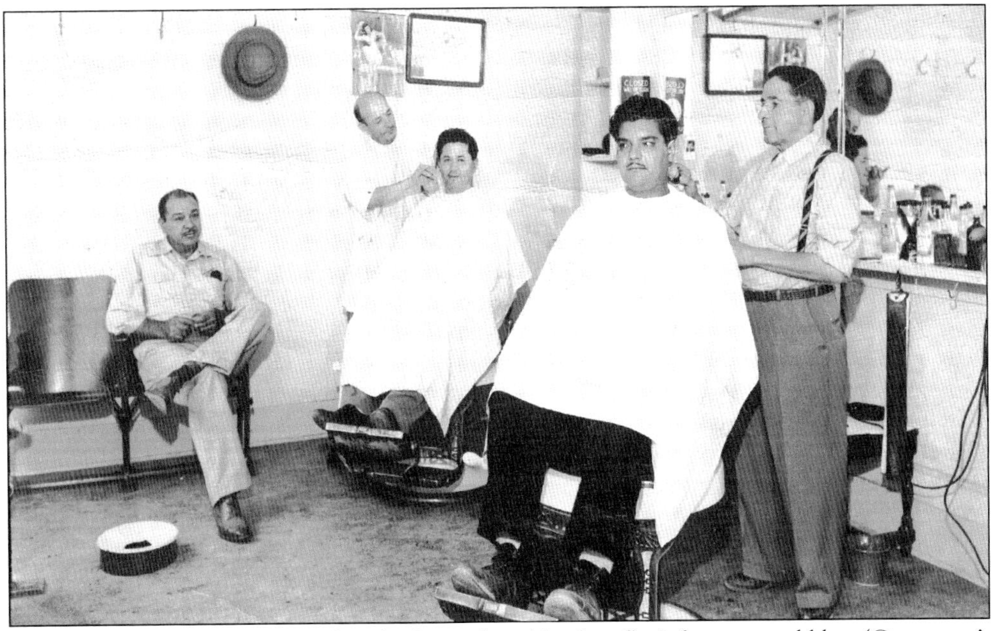

Everyday services were provided in the *barrio* (neighborhood). A few were cobblers (Camarena's Shoe Repair), beauticians (Inez Beauty Salon), produce vendors (Don Daniel Cabrera), meat providers (Medrano's), filling stations (Knotty Pine Station), flower shops (Massey's Flowers), and barbershops. This barbershop was on Young Street and its owner, Ignacio Ramirez (far right), is giving Manuel Yanez a haircut. Joe Rico is waiting and is seated near a spittoon. Jose Mares is the customer in the center. (Carlos Rico.)

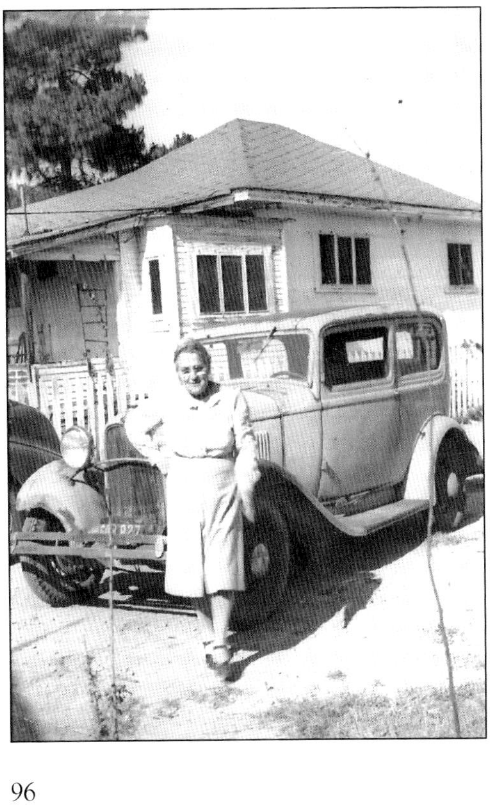

Standing in front of her Model T is Inez Amezcua. She came from Sinaloa in 1916 and resided at 1040 Watson Avenue. Amezcua was an independent businesswoman, having had several different businesses, including working in the canneries and being a "Watkins lady." The Watkins Company, in business since 1868, sold natural ingredient products using door-to-door salespersons. (Amelia McKenna.)

Quirino De La Torre was the patriarch of a family that established itself into the roots of the community. He had come from Durango and worked on the railroad, fish canneries, and lumberyards and farmed on lots north of the Pacific Coast Highway. He grew corn, beans, zucchini, pumpkins, and more, plowing with his horse or mule. He had a roadside stand where his children sold the produce, but he would share his bounty with the soldiers based on nearby East Cruces Street during World War II. The army guarded the barrage balloons set up to protect against low-flying aircraft. (Eleanor Urrea.)

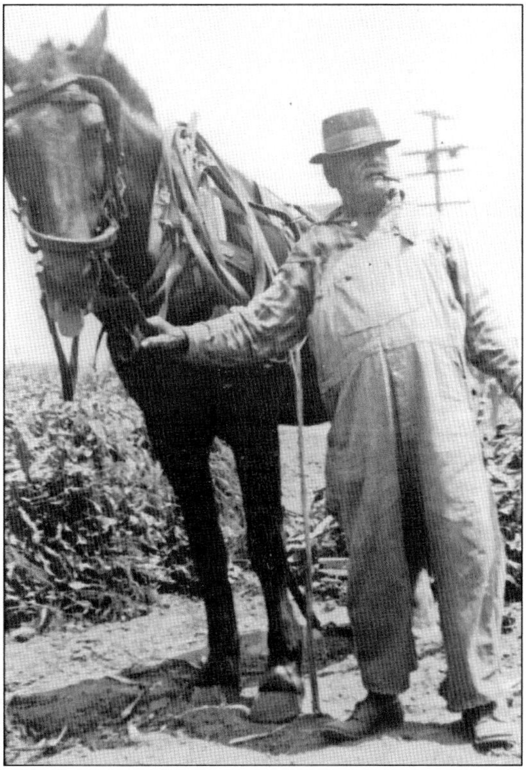

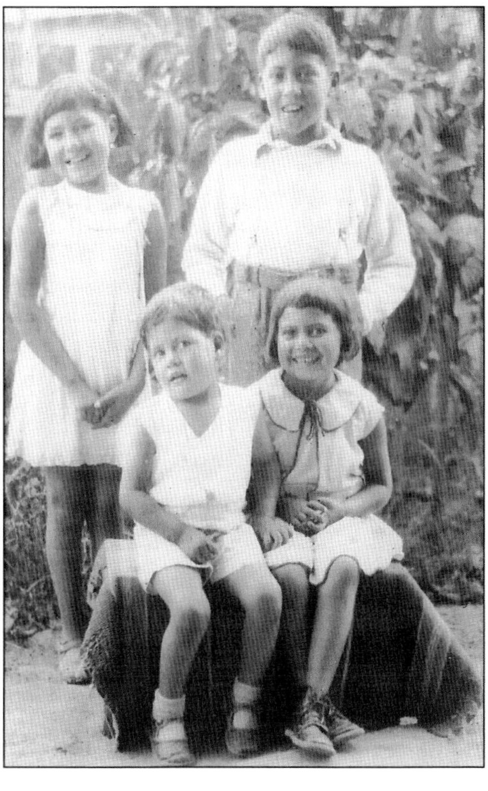

Four of the Juan Gonzales children are shown in 1929. They are pictured next to the family's cornfield. From left to right are (first row) Raul and Emma; (second row) Lilly and Arthur. Gonzales raised his seven children on Sanford Avenue behind a bakery, and they learned commitment and strong work ethics. As young men, the two boys served in the South Pacific. Raul Gonzales became both a merchant seaman and paratrooper, often taking hazardous assignments to earn extra money to send home. (Raul Gonzales.)

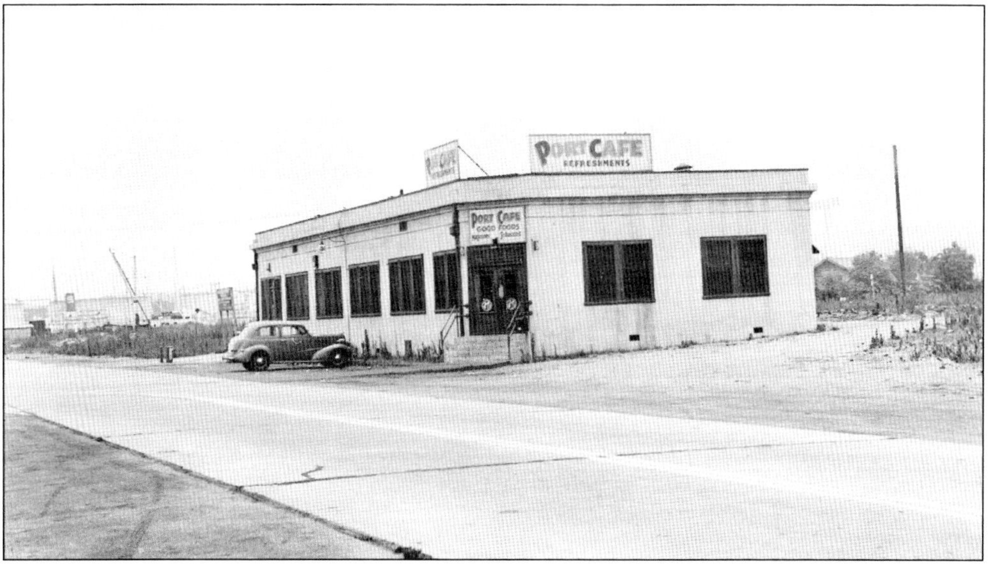

Port Café was built in 1941. It was a diner that served workers employed near its location on Mormon Island. The island area had already been landfilled to connect it to Wilmington. Oil and banana docks, Borax, Union Ice, and the Catalina Terminal were nearby. The "Red Bus" used the location for a turnaround spot since the street wound around the café. Although many workers had homemade lunches, they stopped for soft drinks and tobacco as seen advertised. (Wilmington Historical Society.)

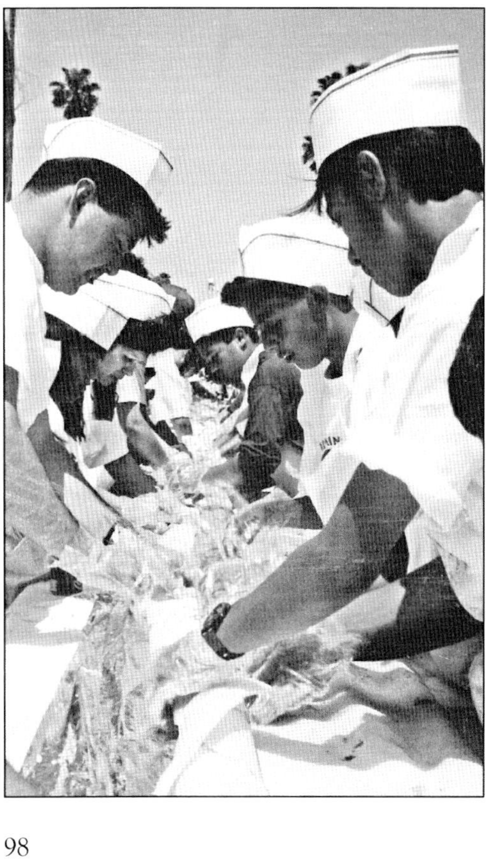

On April 11, 1992, a 2,000-foot burrito was made by about 750 residents. It put Wilmington in the Guinness Book of World Records by breaking the previous record of 1,597 feet. Abelardo De La Peña, president of the Wilmington Coordinating Council, wanted to show a positive side of the community. The donated ingredients consisted of 3,300 tortillas, 800 pounds of refried beans, and 150 pounds of cheese. The burrito was made atop 250 tables along Avalon Boulevard and cut into pieces, which sold for 25¢ to raise money for the council's scholarship fund. (Dolores Marquez.)

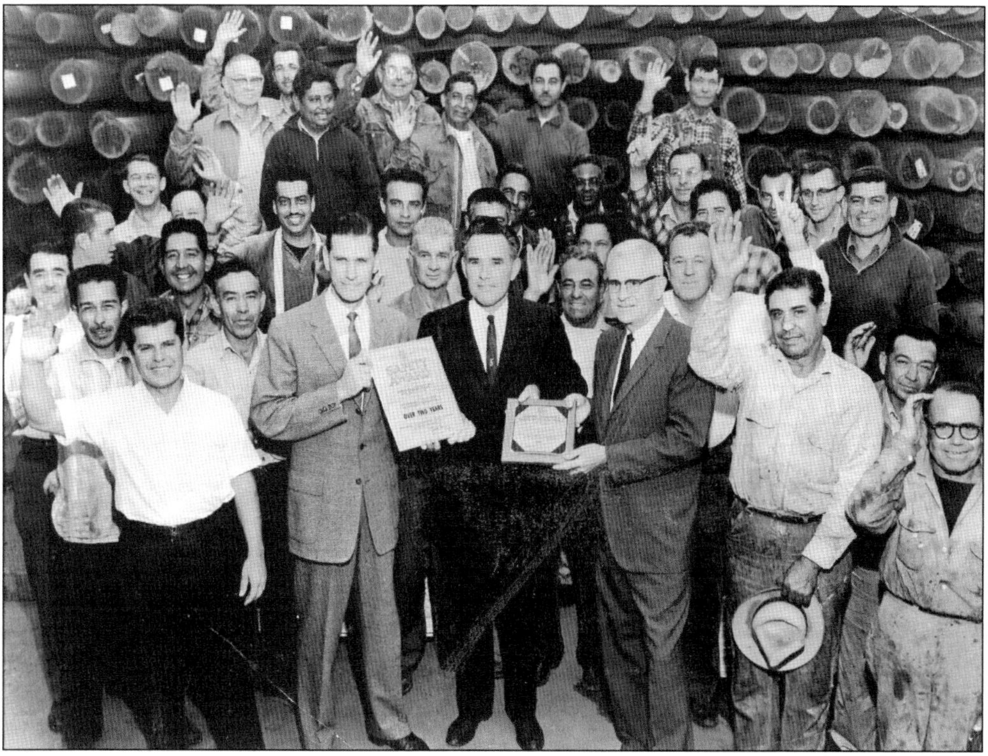

Trustworthy and dependable workers often did the unwanted hard and dirty jobs. They toiled, grateful to have employment, to feed, clothe, and provide for their families. This 1945 photograph shows management and workers of Koppers Company accepting a safety award for more than two years of compliance. The plant was a creosote wood treatment facility that handled railroad ties, utility poles, and pilings. Workers identified are Louie Lopez, Manuel Madrigal, Leno Galvan, Julio Serrano, Trino Romero, and Eulogio Gomez (first row, far right). (Robert Gomez; Carmen Galvan)

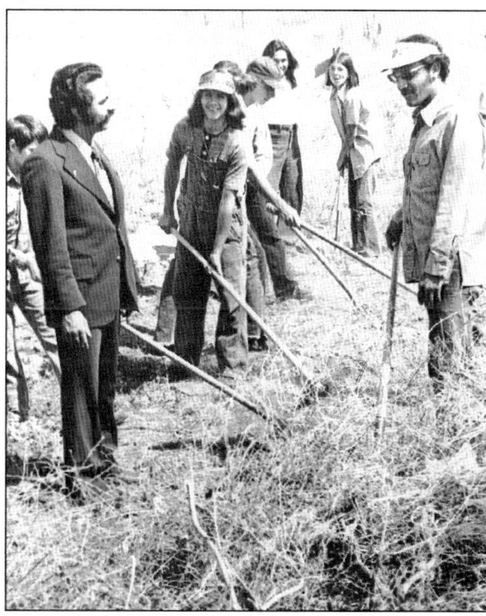

Jay Cees played two important roles in Wilmington. The organization promoted and built leadership opportunities for its members, and it was a vital contributor to the community's well-being through its many programs and endeavors. In this 1973 photograph, Joe Infante (left) observed youngsters enrolled in a summer job program as they participated in Community Clean-Up Day. Jay Cees forged the group to receive national recognition for its ballpark development (Jay Cees field at Figueroa Street, John Gibson Field at Opp Street, and the Green Belt Park at "L" Street). The club held centennial celebrations in 1948, 1958, 1968, and sponsored health fairs, Blackbeard Olympics, and track meets. Proceeds were donated to many charitable organizations. (Joe Infante.)

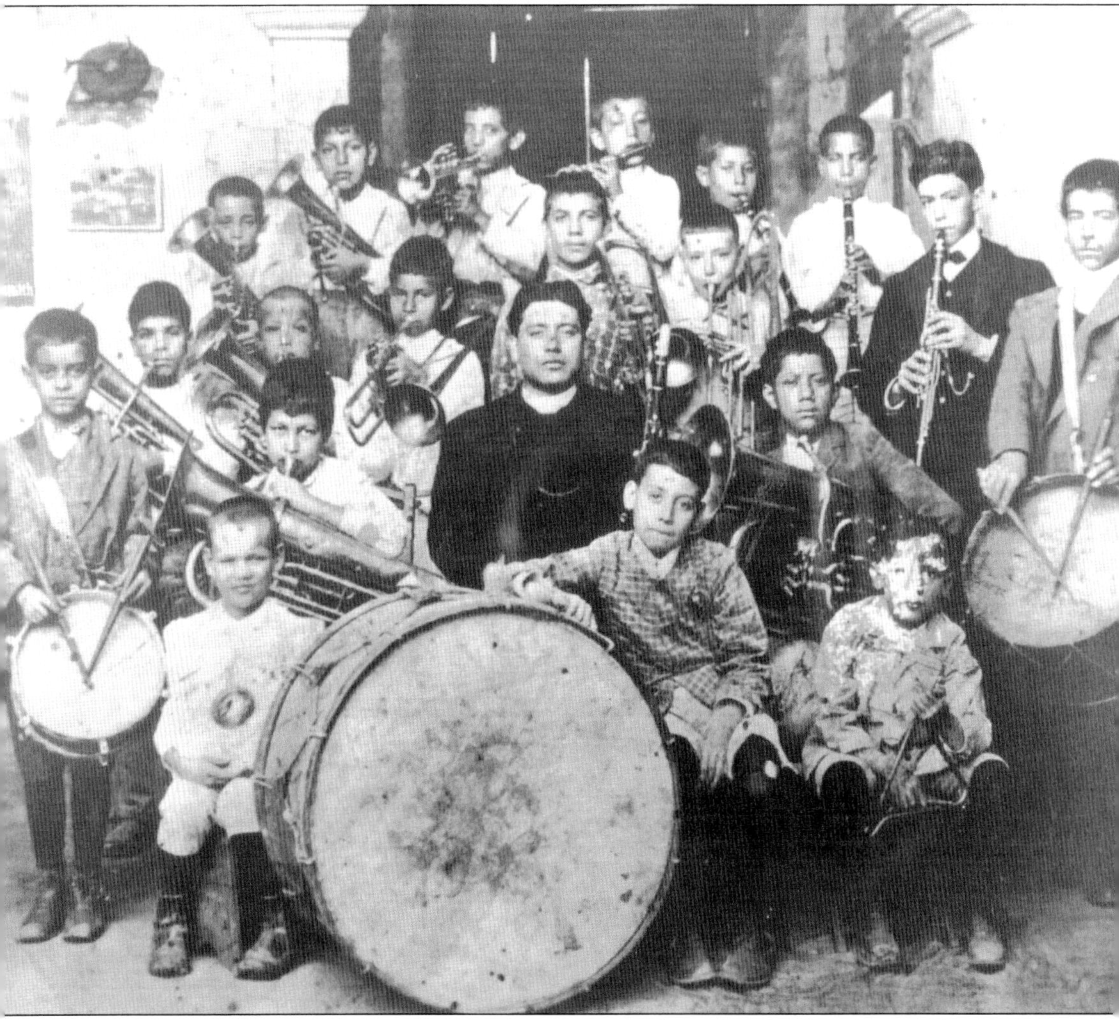

The priest in Tequila, Mexico, gathered the young band members for this photograph. It was 1906, and soon after, Mexico found itself facing religious persecution. People and priests fled for safety and religious freedom. Many early Mexican families came to Wilmington during this turbulent period. They joined family and found work. Juan Gonzales (top row, farthest left) came to Wilmington after suffering severe wounds from fighting armies in his homeland. (Roger Gonzales.)

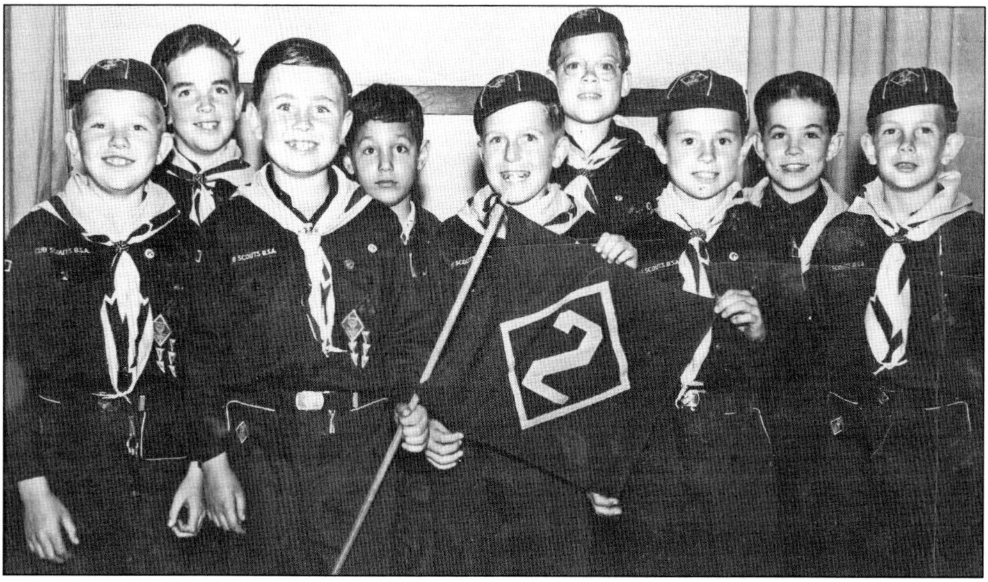

The Boy Scouts of America celebrated its 100th anniversary in 2010. Although one of the largest youth organizations, its outreach was limited. In 1954, Gary Estrada (second from left, back row) is surrounded by fellow troop scouts. Estrada graduated from St. Anthony High School in Long Beach and became a Vietnam veteran. In the 1940s, Boy Scout Troop No. 225 met at the Honorífica site for their meetings. (Cynthia Pratt.)

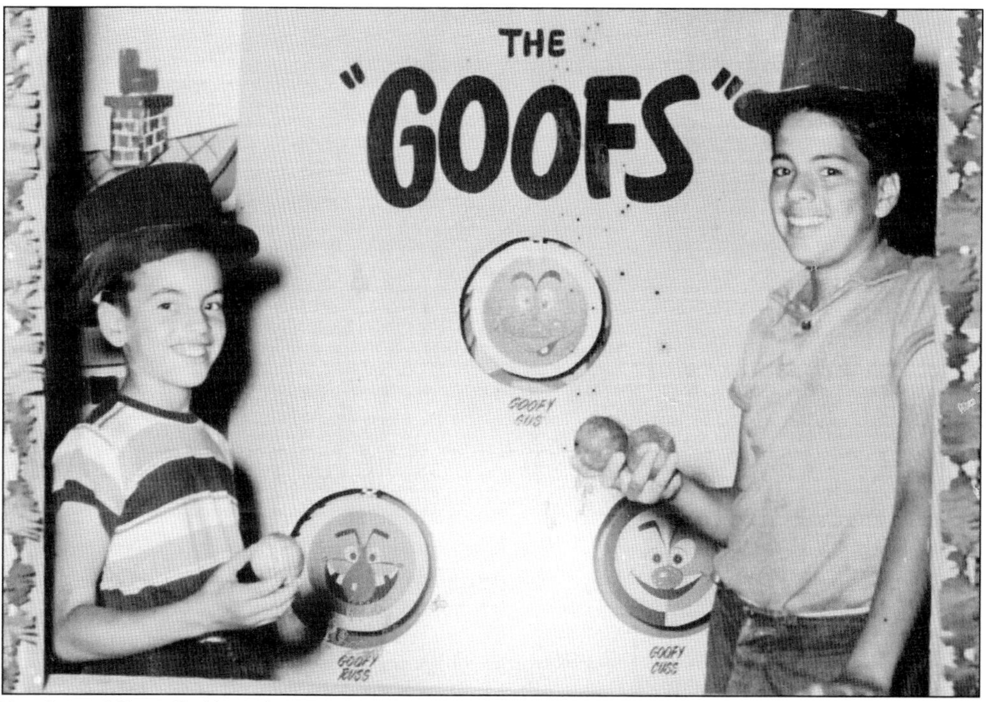

Brothers Albert (left) and Ernest Munoz were in charge of a "Wil-hall" carnival booth around 1951. Big smiles encouraged onlookers to test their throwing skills. The boys' mother, Alberta Munoz, had lived on Terminal Island and worked in the canneries, and their father, Ernest Munoz, worked at the Long Beach Naval Shipyard. (Wilmington Historical Society.)

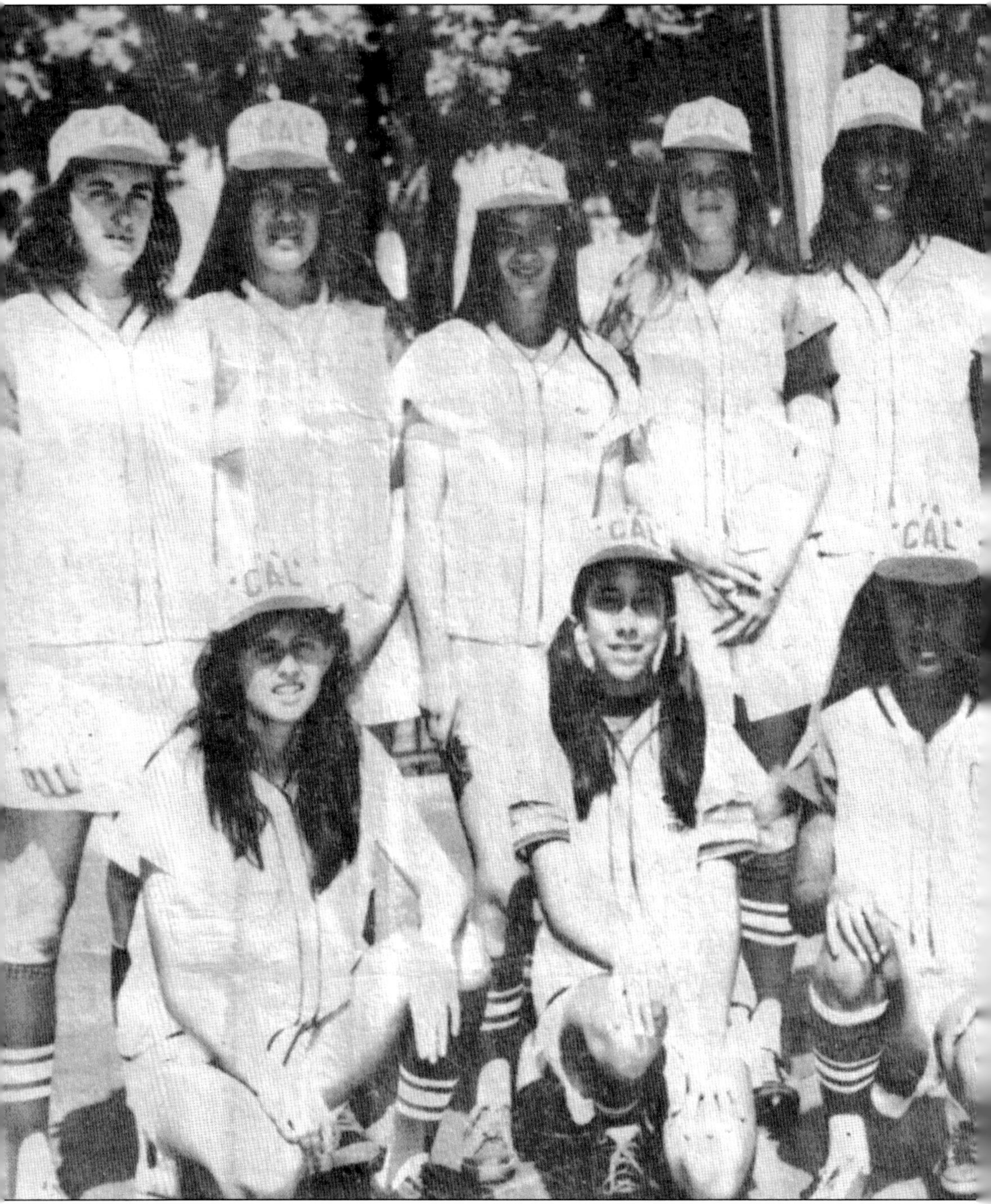

The Wilmington-Carson Softball team is shown as Minnie Mouse's guest of honor. In 1974, this team won the National Miss Softball America Championship in Odessa, Texas, with a final 4-2 win despite overcoming incredible experiences going to the tournament. Half the team was in a near plane crash over Arizona, and the others suffered food poisoning on the bus. The first game was played into early morning hours and, although sick and exhausted, the girls won. Their tournament play was 15 wins, 1 loss. Participation countrywide involved about 50,000 teenage

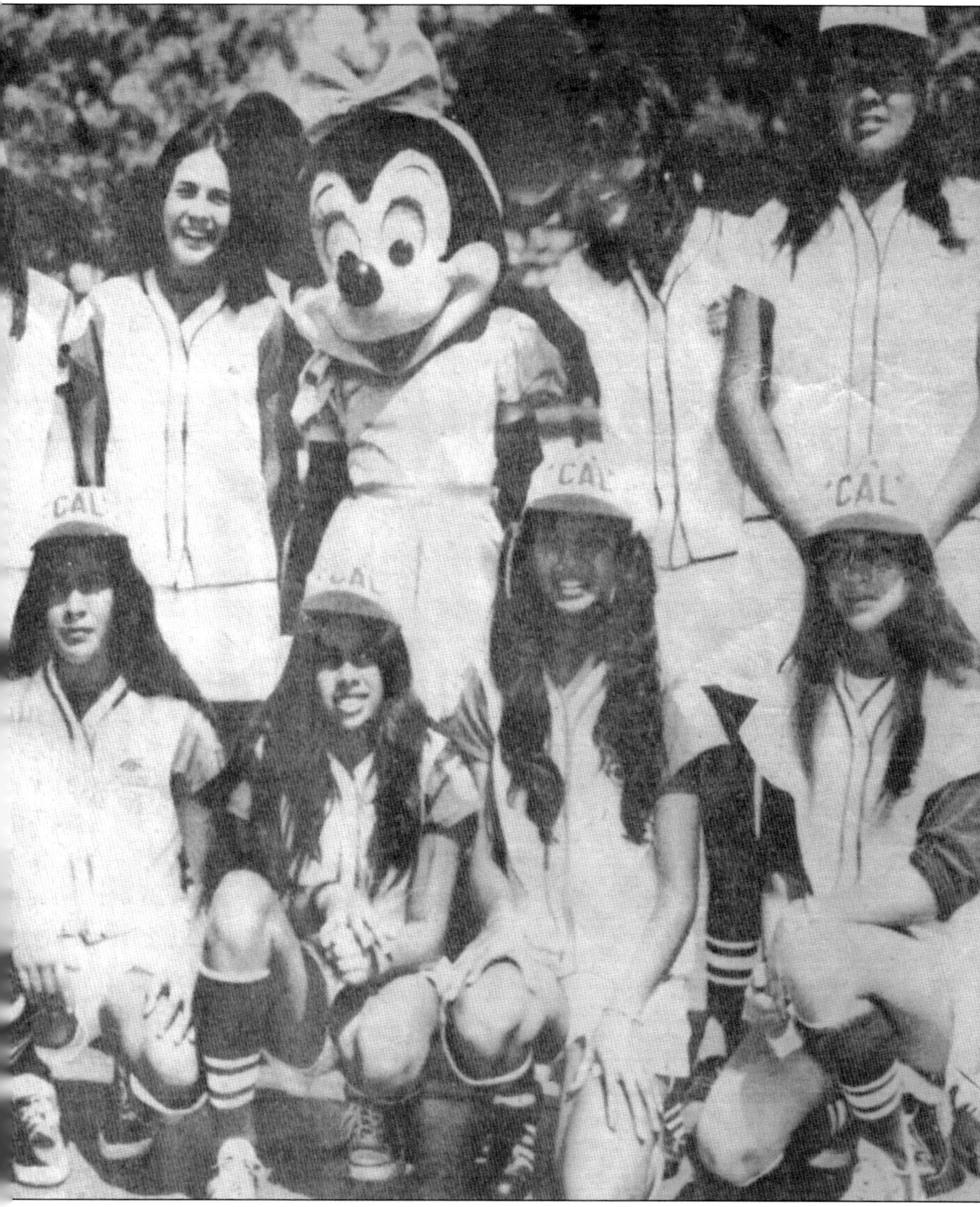

girls. The players were, from left to right, (first row) Donna Nieves, Charlotte Smith, Josephine Tuli, Charlotte Murillo, Rachel Quijada, Julie Hernandez, and Esther Rendon; (second row) Patty Christie, Nancy Gillespie, Terri Cipriano, Susan Pinkham, Renee Gray, Bonnie Mauricio, Moana Garcia, Minnie Mouse, Carrie Villanueva, and Donna Calac. Not pictured are coaches Ron Smith and Crama Gray; manager Marilyn Smith; and chaperone Andrea Gray. (Esther Rendon.)

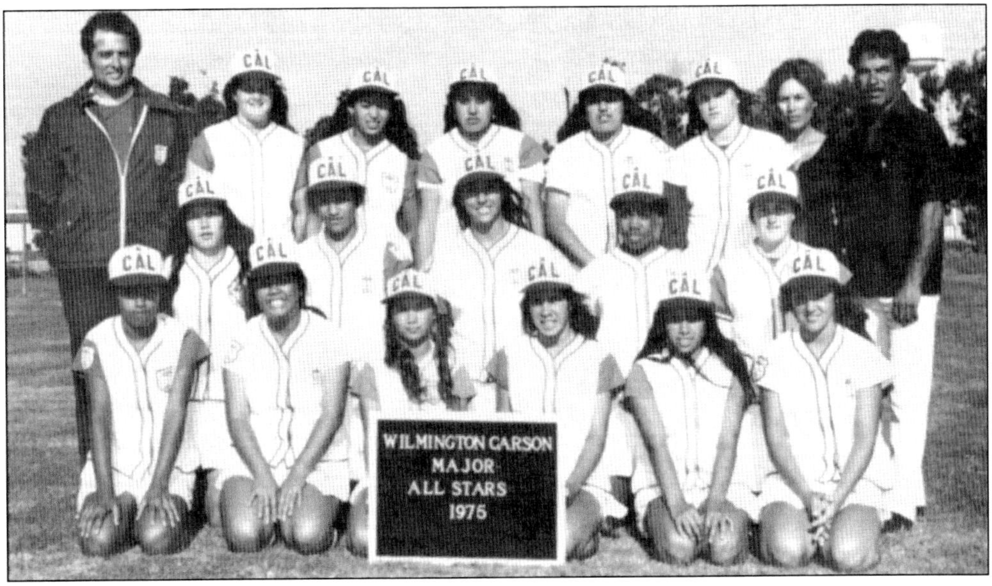

Above, the defending national champions to the Miss Softball America Tournament, Major Division, in 1975, were these all-star players. Each year, participation countrywide involved about 50,000 teenage girls. The Wilmington-Carson All-Star teams returned several years as defending champions. Most girls went on to play for Banning High School teams. Below, these all-star players participated in the Senior Division at the tournament in 1975. (Both, Esther Rendon.)

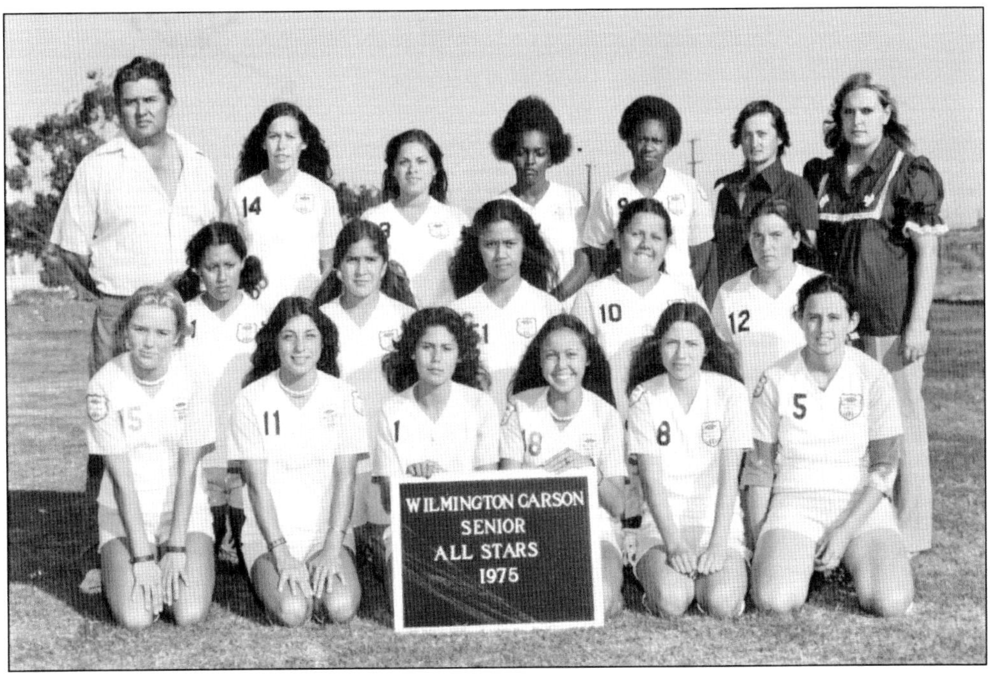

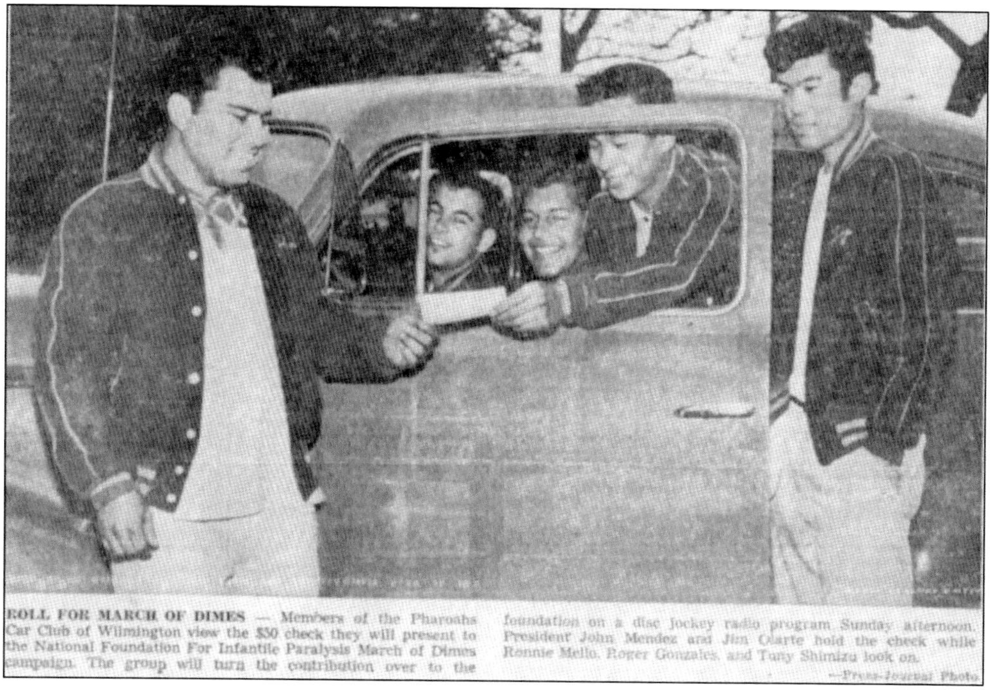

ROLL FOR MARCH OF DIMES — Members of the Pharoahs Car Club of Wilmington view the $50 check they will present to the National Foundation For Infantile Paralysis March of Dimes campaign. The group will turn the contribution over to the foundation on a disc jockey radio program Sunday afternoon. President John Mendez and Jim Olarte hold the check while Ronnie Mello, Roger Gonzales, and Tony Shimizu look on.

—Press-Journal Photo

The Pharaohs Car Club was launched in 1953 at Banning Park; the club's charter officers were Bobby Gonzalez, Edward Mendoza, John Chambers, and Sonny Velasco. Above, in a clipping from the *Wilmington Press-Journal*, the group was making a donation to the March of Dimes. Below, in 1956, a reliability run was being advertised by the membership. A Pharaohs jacket is seen in the center of the picture. (Above, author's collection; below, Roger Gonzales.)

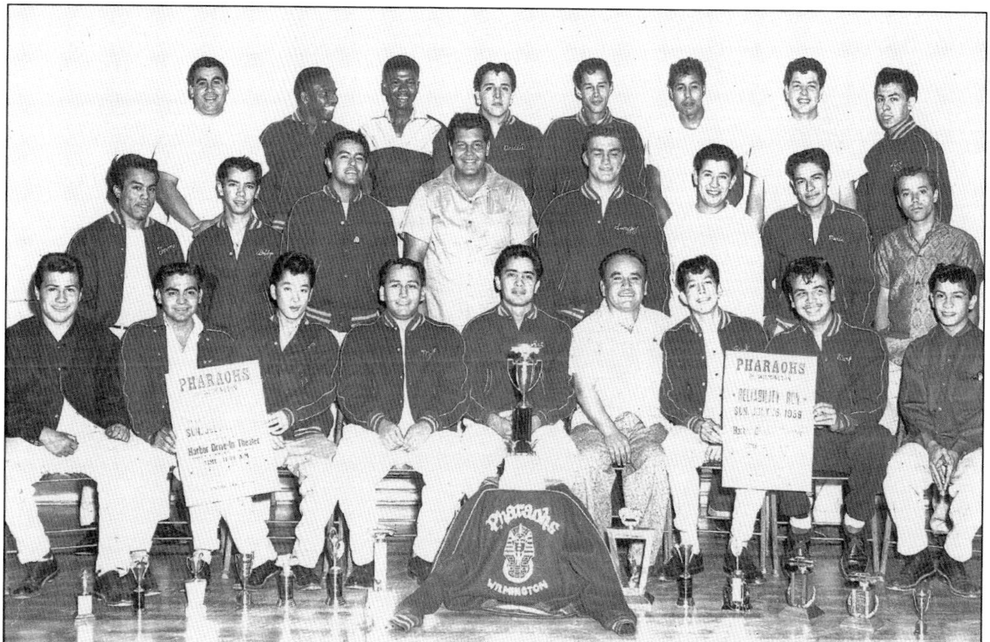

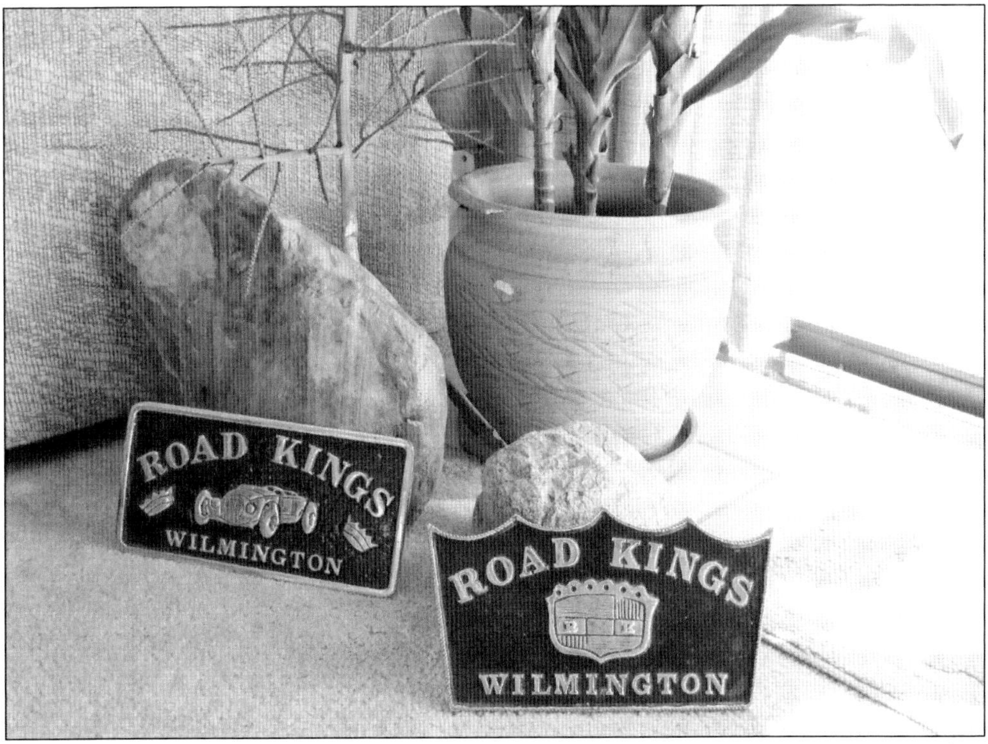

The Road Kings began at the Mahar House around 1952. The club's primary interest centered on cars, and it participated and sponsored car shows and reliability runs. Additionally, if a member provided roadside help, a card was handed out saying "assisted by a member of Road Kings Car Club." The card, plaque, shirts, and jackets made the Road Kings identifiable. Charitable donations were important fund-raising goals, and of special interest was City of Hope, which was treating a member's daughter. Eastside residents gave $1,300 in one weekend's door-to-door effort. The plaques above were made by the Buddy Azpeita foundry in Wilmington. Below, the car club displays trophies won at events. (Above, author's collection; below, Phil Vaca.)

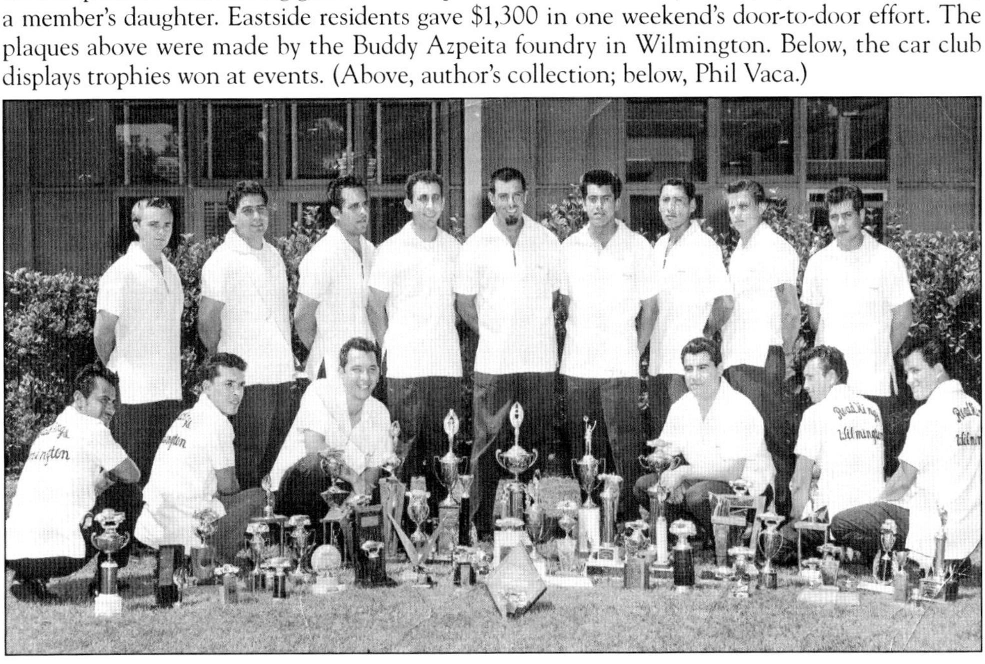

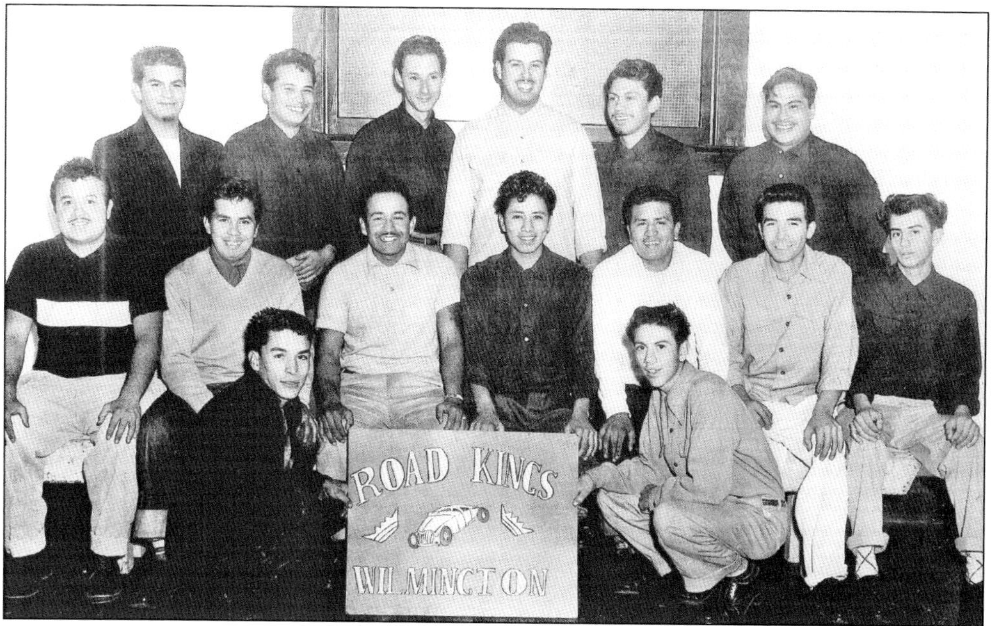

This group picture of the Road Kings was taken at the Mahar House on December 12, 1950. The members were, from left to right, (first row) Eddie Shaw and Bobby Morales; (second row) Edward Morales, Edward Reyes, Danny Lares, Mike Calderon, unidentified, Abel Garcia, and Bobby Slader; (third row) Joe Jalomo, Mariano Alpine, Sandy Sandoval, Phil Vaca, Jack Slader, and John Almojuela. (Phil Vaca.)

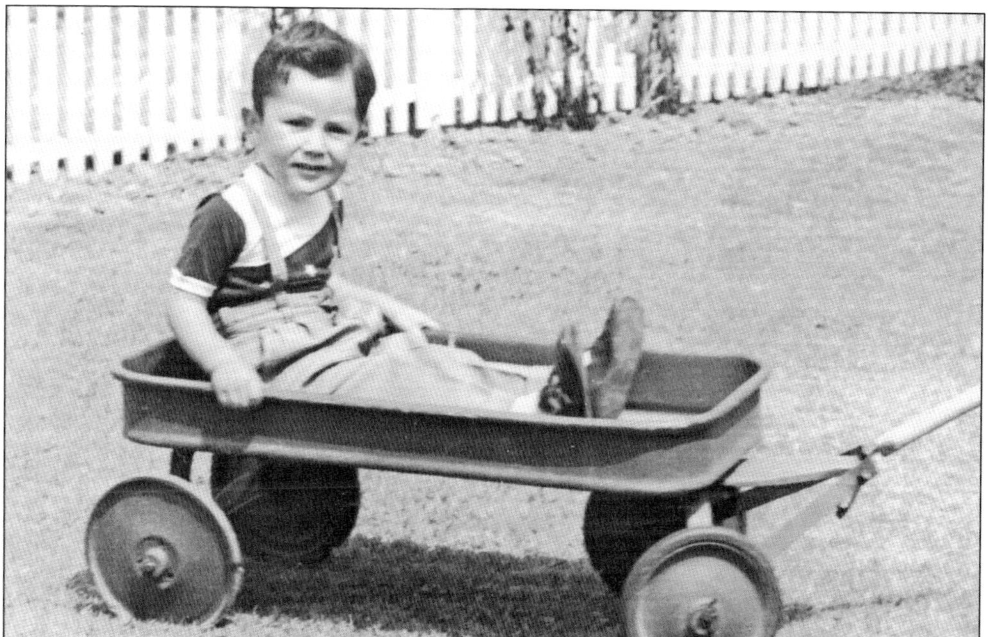

Too young for a car in 1952, Michael Caro enjoyed the ride and comfort of his wagon. Families had many uses for wagons, including to take home groceries. Caro, like young men in an earlier decade, participated in the California Conservation Corps (CCC), and he retired as a boilermaker from the Long Beach Naval Shipyard. (Maria Enriquez.)

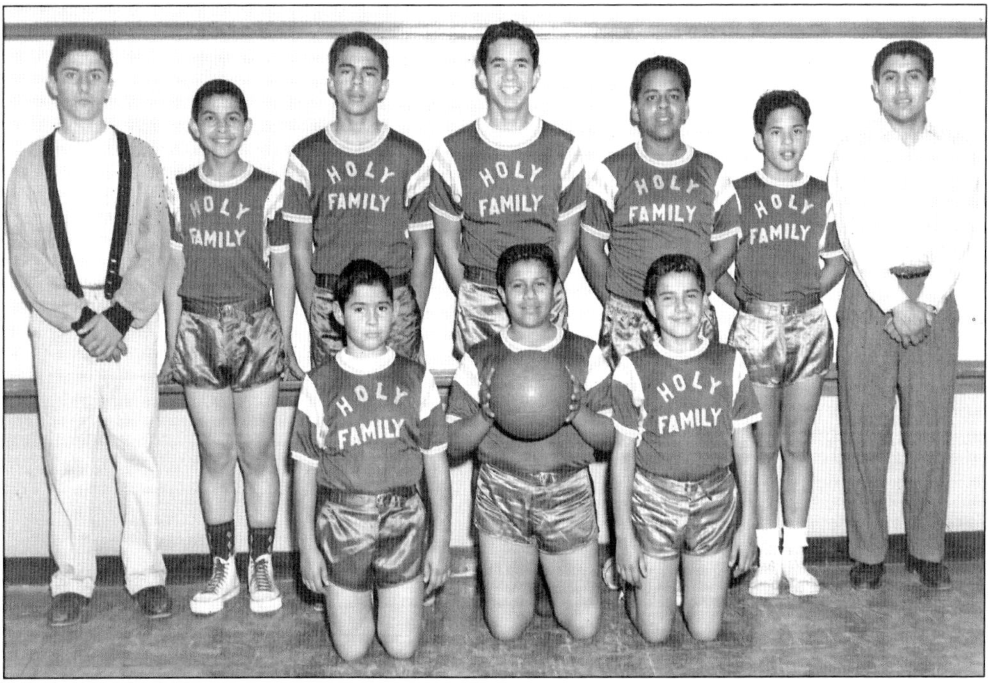

Sports were an integral component of the curriculum at Holy Family School. Teamwork and leadership were important skills developed through sports. Basketball was popular, and this photograph shows a team around 1950. (Amelia McKenna.)

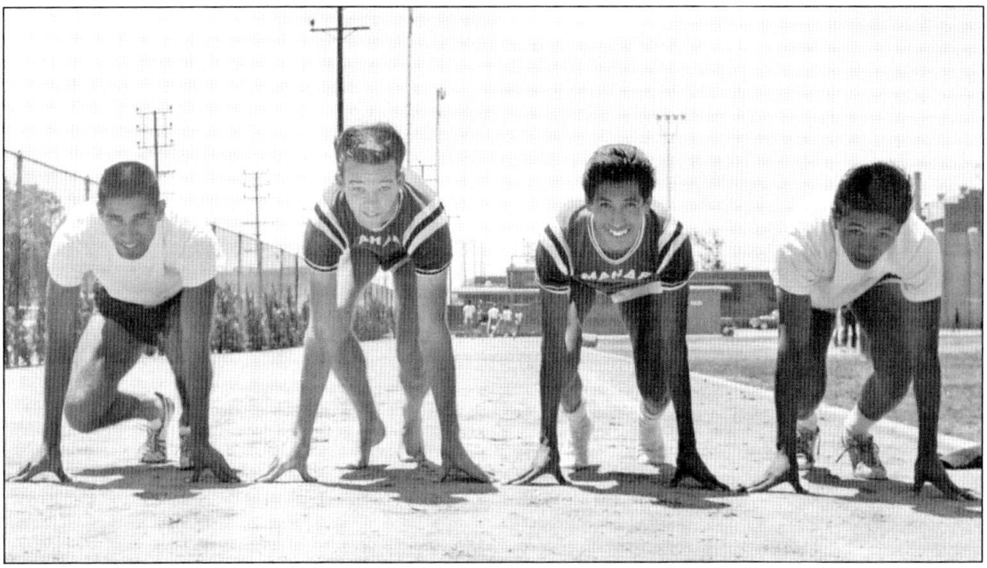

At Banning High School, success in track and field events was guided by coach Pete Zamperini. He coached from 1947 to 1977, and he was a 1935 NCAA 1-mile winner. Ready to run in 1960 are, from left to right, David Esparza, Tommy Williams, Rudy Monarrez, and Curtis Nuez. Esparza was a Los Angeles Catholic Youth Organization 100- and 220-yard dash champion. A 1949 champion at the school was Manuel Ceja. He set a Los Angeles city schools pole vault record of 13 feet, 3 inches with a bamboo pole. Ceja also held records in the high jump and high hurdles. (David Esparza.)

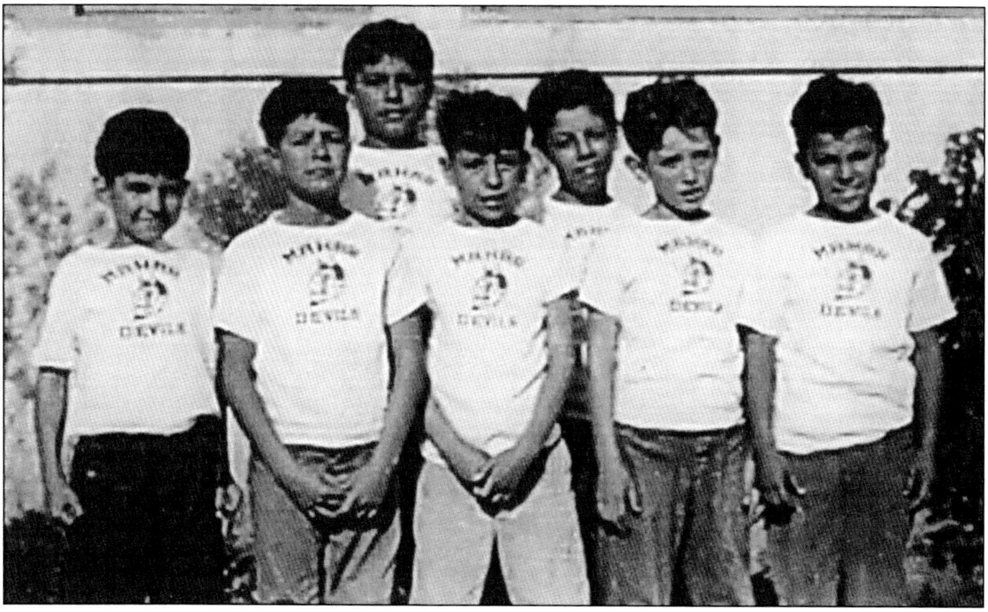

Most of the players in these two Mahar House photographs continued their interest and ability to compete in a variety of sports. Above, the Devils were young ballplayers in 1947. They are, from left to right, (first row) Molo Martinez, Christie Medina, Eugene Montgomery, Edward Mendoza, and Dick Garcia; (second row) John Urrea and Louie Rios. Below, boys on a 1946 team were (first row) "Wedo" Mendoza; (second row) Gabby Mendoza, George De La Torre, Corly Rojas, and Ruben Calderon; (third row) Pete McKenna, Manuel Pacheco, Ed Martin, Vincent Silva, Sonny Flores, and Mike Calderon. (Both, Gabriel Mendoza.)

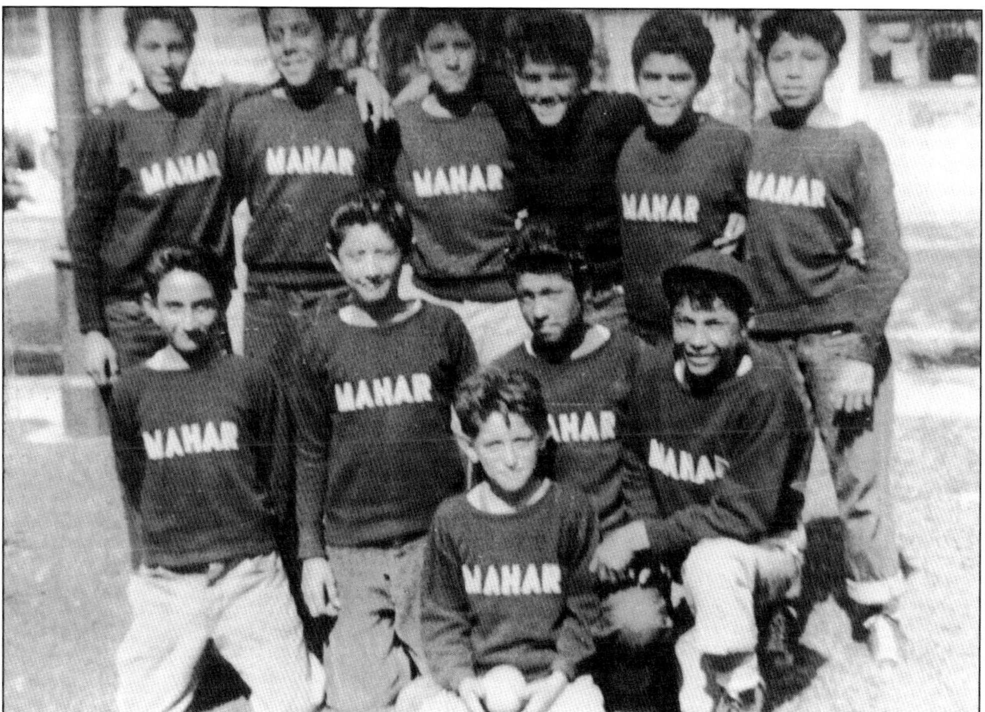

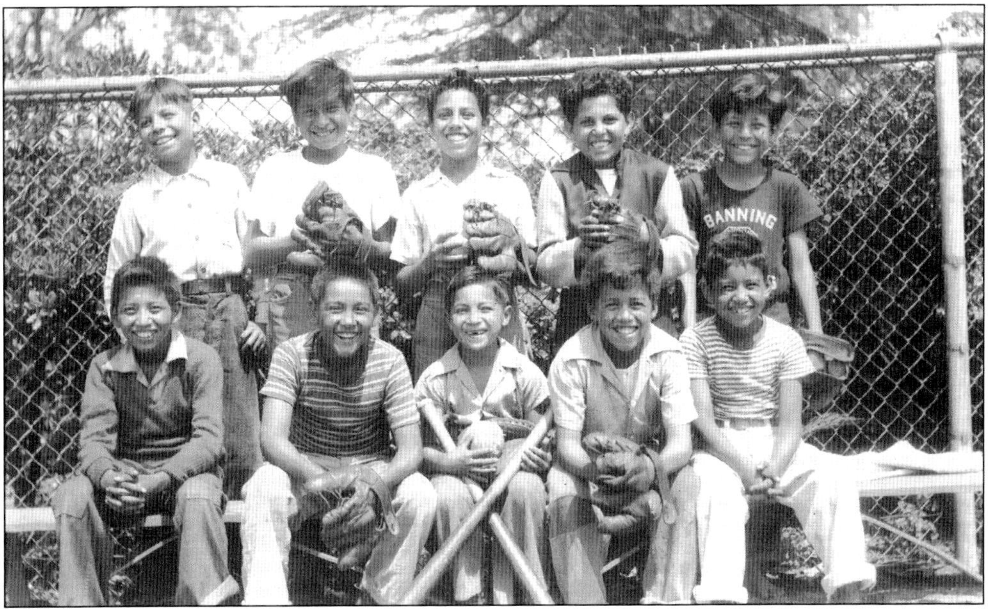

Two Banning Park baseball teams are shown. Above, the News Boys were friends, brothers, and cousins of the Dominguez, Escudero, Gonzales, Pacheco, Ramirez, and Ramos families. Below, a team stood poised on the main field. The park's gymnasium building is in the distance, and a variety of sports areas and playground equipment involved young and old in year-round activities. (Above, author's collection; below, Ramon Quesada.)

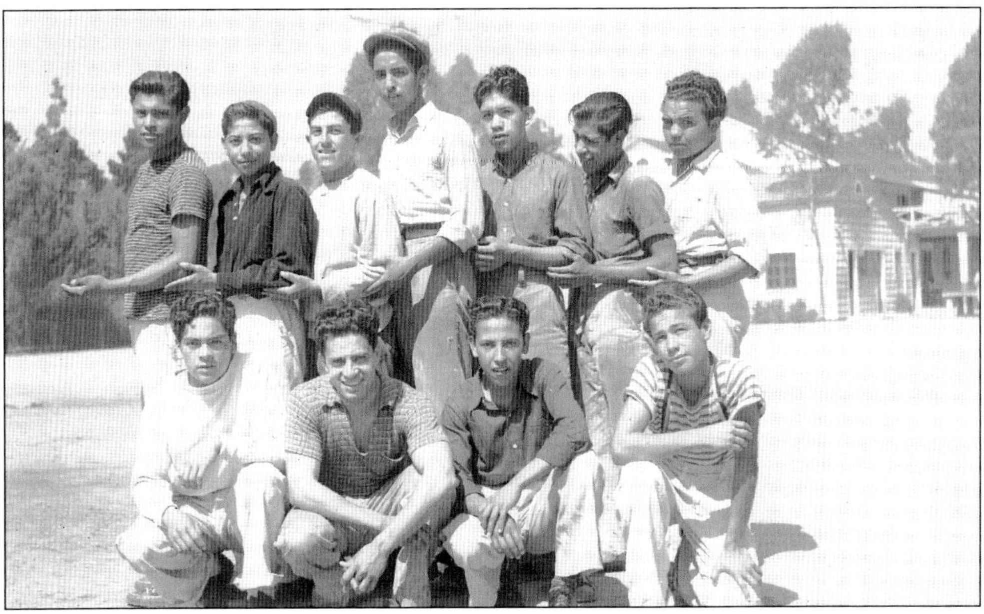

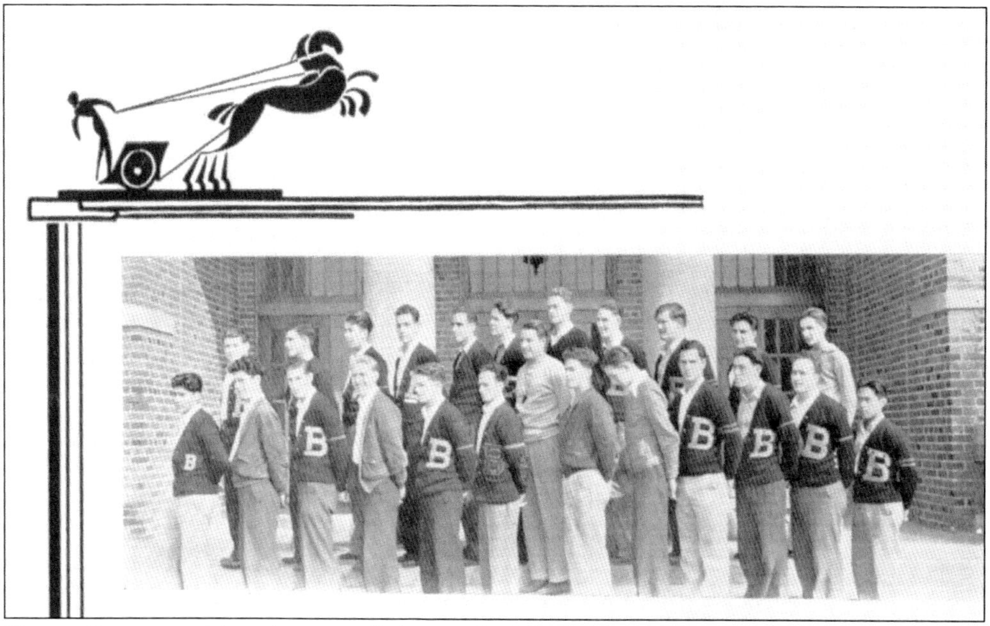

Phineas Banning athletes have excelled on and off the field, track, and gymnasium. Shortly after the school opened, coach Eugene Patz organized the Varsity Club. Among the founding members in 1928 were Charles Gonzales, Joe Duran, and Louis Sapien. Standing at the front entrance of the main building are members of the 1930 Varsity Club, a few wearing letterman sweaters. (Raul Gonzales.)

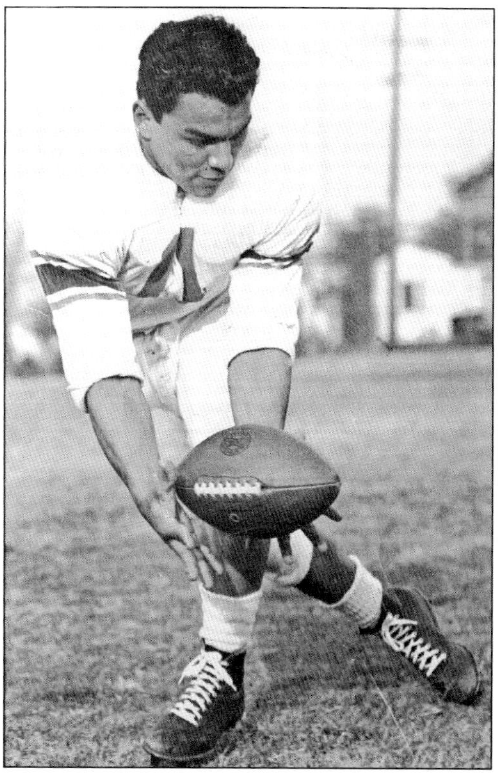

In December 1953, Dick Garcia was named Los Angeles City Player of the Year. He earned the honor as a junior and led the team to the city's championship. Garcia was joined on the first All-City team by Albert Aguilar, and the second team included Mich Yamamoto and Edmund Paculba. In other years, Player of the Year honors went to Banning tailbacks Jack Hernandez, Gabriel Mendoza, and Dan Espalin. (Barbara Flores.)

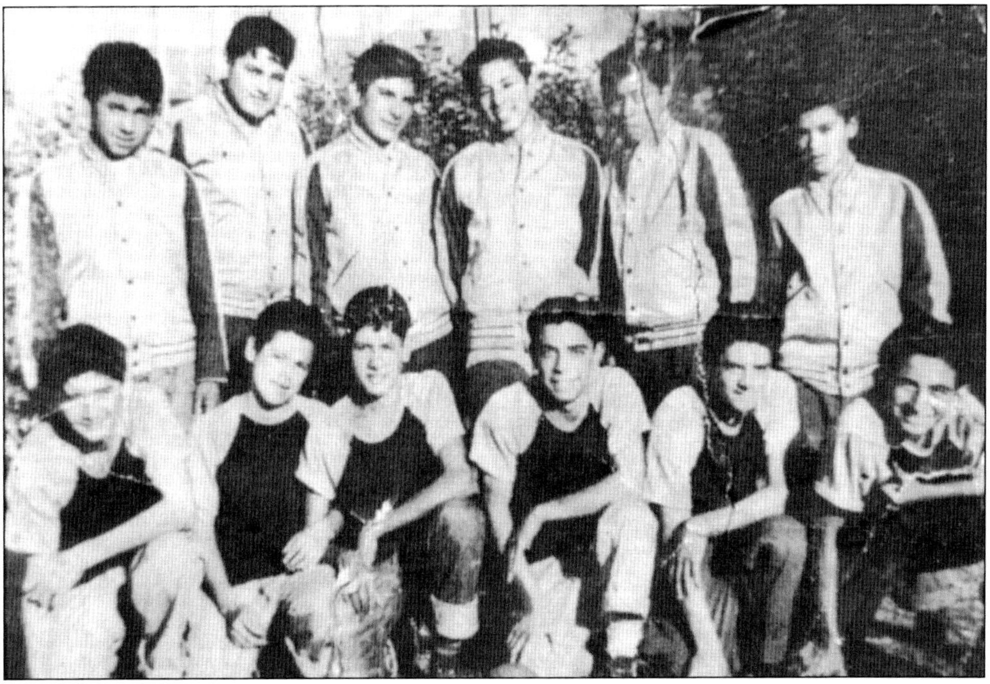

In 1947, the Mahar Vultures earned first place in softball in the division of the City of Los Angeles's Department of Recreation and Parks. (Gabriel Mendoza.)

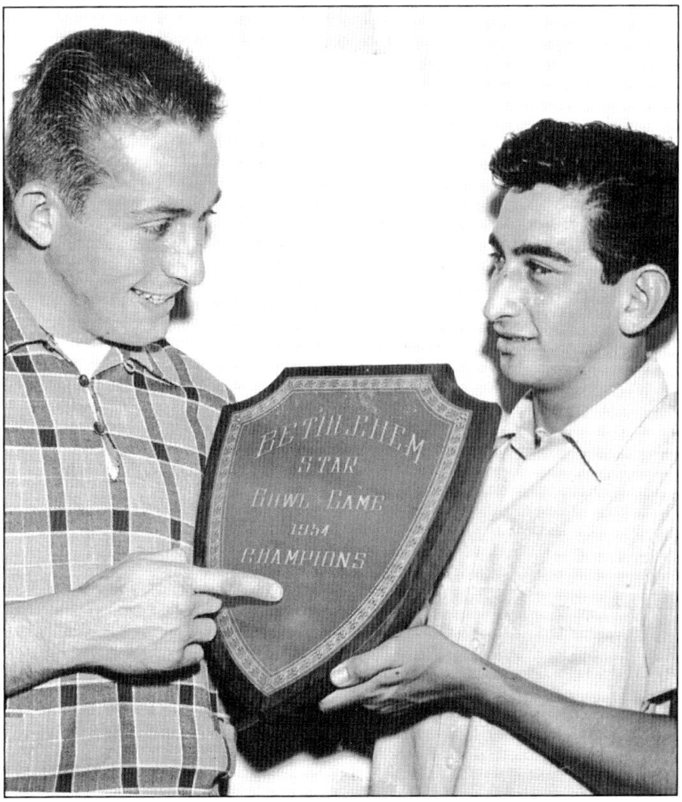

After successful sport experiences at Banning High, Gabriel Mendoza (right) lettered two years at Harbor College. He was an outstanding player and the Seahawks team captain, and he accepted honors in the Bethlehem Star Bowl Game in 1954. Mendoza began working at a warehouse for Smart and Final and retired 37 years later as manager. He played semipro football and liked photography and adventure. As a youngster, Mendoza redeemed 5¢ coupons to get a camera and enjoyed long bicycle rides to Long Beach, Terminal Island, and then crossing on the ferry to San Pedro on the free ride direction. (Gabriel Mendoza.)

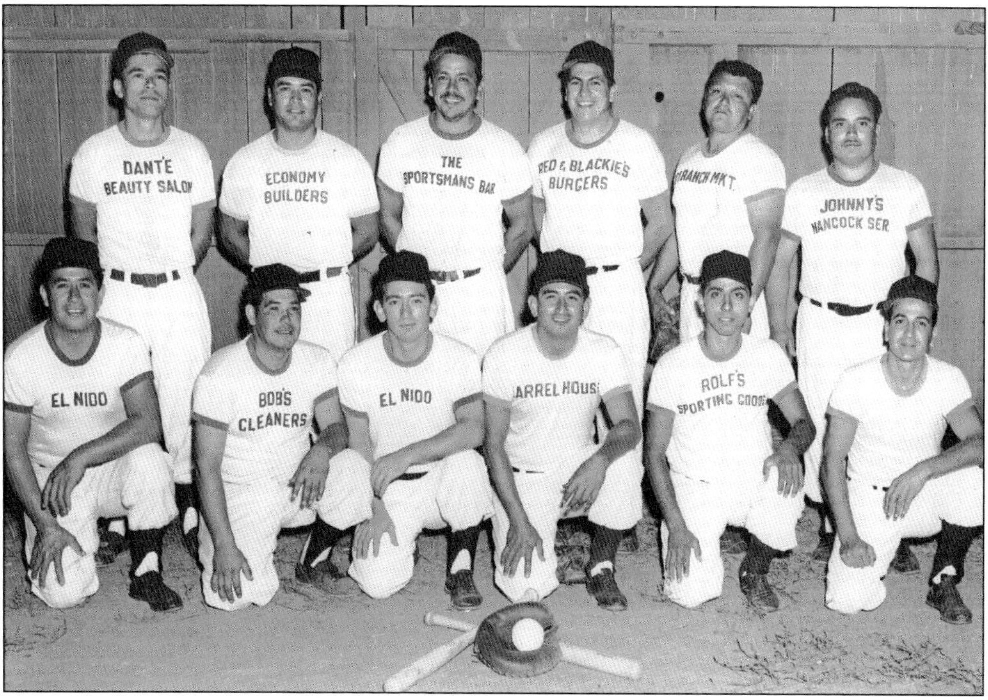

This team of Wilmington baseball players was the 1961 Long Beach "A" League Champs. They are, from left to right, (first row) Art Hernandez, Tony Rivas, Wedo Mendoza, Gabby Mendoza, Elmer Fematt, and Ruben Aguirre; (second row) Dick Rivas, Dick Mendez, Jack Montgomery, Gene Montgomery, Tony Manzo, and John Mendez. (Gabriel Mendoza.)

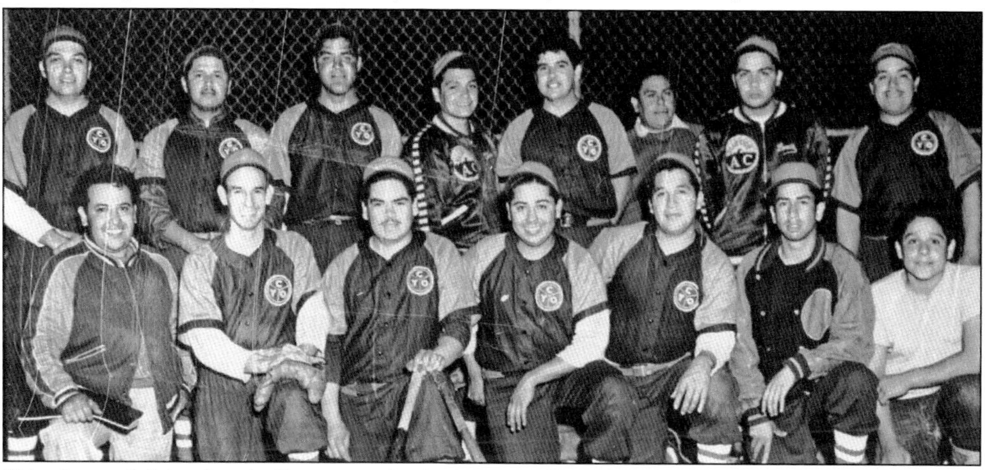

"It's a beautiful day for a ball game . . . Let's play two!" Ernie Banks, a Major League player for the Chicago Cubs, tagged the catchy phrase above, expressing his wish to play a doubleheader. The players on this team did doubleheaders, worked full-time jobs, and played baseball. Players are, from left to right, (first row) Jessie Ramirez, Art Calderon, Leonard Rodriguez, Mike Ramirez, Manual Hernandez, Ralph Violante, and Amado Espino (bat boy); (second row) Charles Rico, David Flores, Trinidad Camarillo, Tony Manzo, Lino Arriaga, Tony Martinez, Louie Manzo, and Ernest Hernandez. Just a few of their nicknames were Tubby, Chapo, Square Deal, Chief, and Popeye. The team coach was Ramon "Baker" Quesada, not shown because he took the team's picture. (Wilmington Historical Society.)

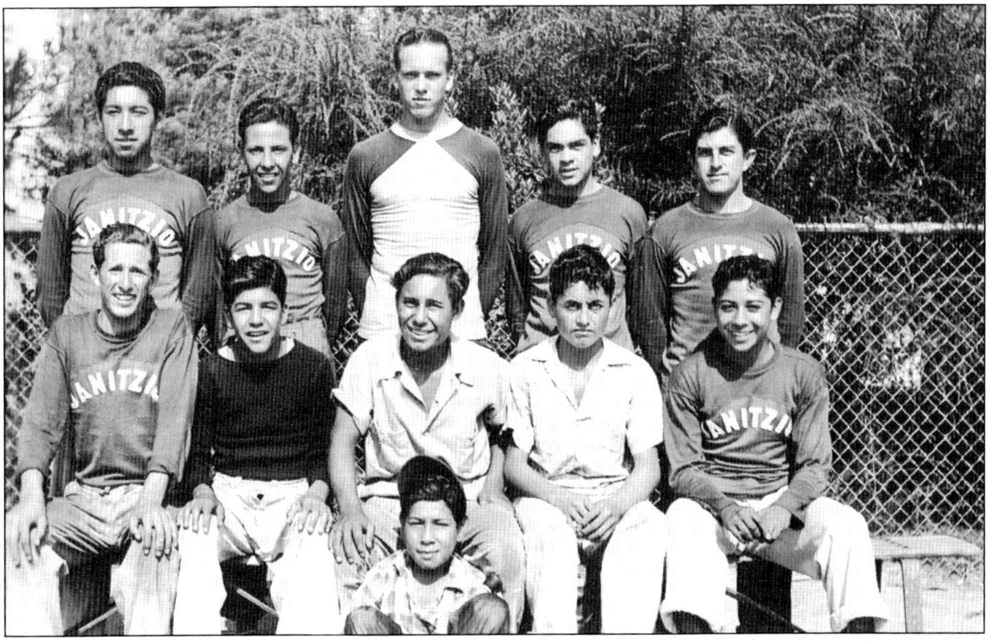

"Take me out to the ball game, Take me out with the crowd," are the beginning chorus lyrics to the Tin Pan Alley tune which became the traditional song of baseball. It symbolized the community's appreciation for the sport. In an empty field, on the street, or in a park playground, games were organized and fans gathered to watch and cheer. The Janitzios and other Wilmington teams played in the neighborhood, in leagues, and in special games at Terminal Island prison and other venues. (Ramon Quesada.)

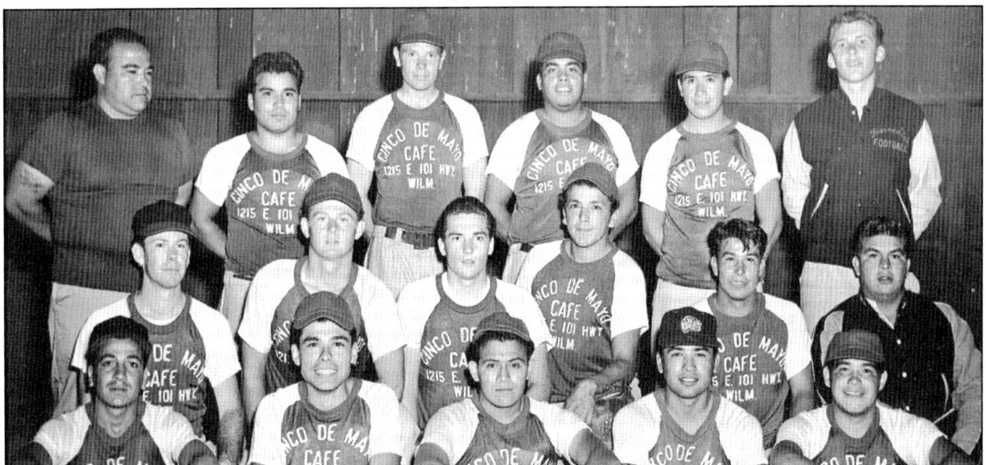

The 1953 season of the Cinco de Mayo softball team showed the diversity and team spirit of 17 and 18 year olds. The business community was very supportive of sponsoring teams. The Cinco de Mayo restaurant was located on the Pacific Coast Highway (formerly 101 Highway) at Watson Avenue and owned by Manuel Gonzales and sons. Team members are, from left to right, (first row) Ruben Aguirre, Dick Rivas, Alfonso Macias, Dick Mendez, and Tony Rivas; (second row) Dick Thompson, Harold Ezell, J. C. Lewis, Jack Montgomery, Fred Ortega, and Joe Jalomo; (third row) Nick Ortega, John Mendez, Bob Miller, Bob Menes, Art Hernandez, and Bob Raines. (Alfonso Macias.)

Six

In War and Peace

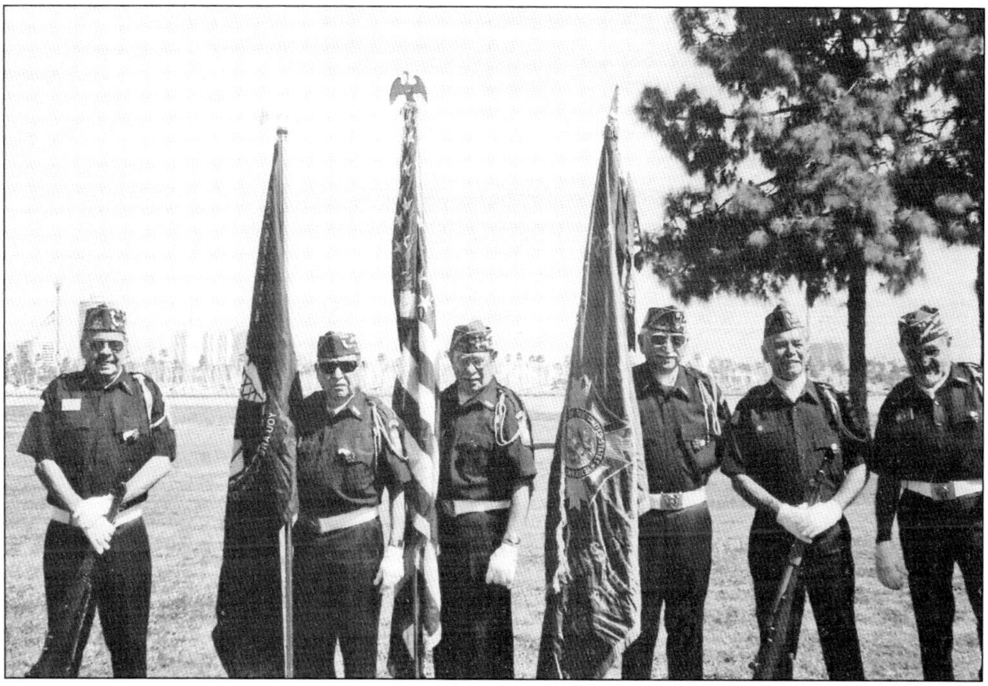

Veterans of Foreign Wars (VFW) Post 2967 is a group of veterans whose mission is to "honor the dead by helping the living" through its actions. In the photograph, Wilmington's VFW Honor Guard participated at the Harry Bridges Park dedication in Long Beach in 2010. The honor guard members are known for their dedicated service and are called upon to officiate at many different functions and venues, from funerals to civic ceremonies. (Gabriel Mendoza.)

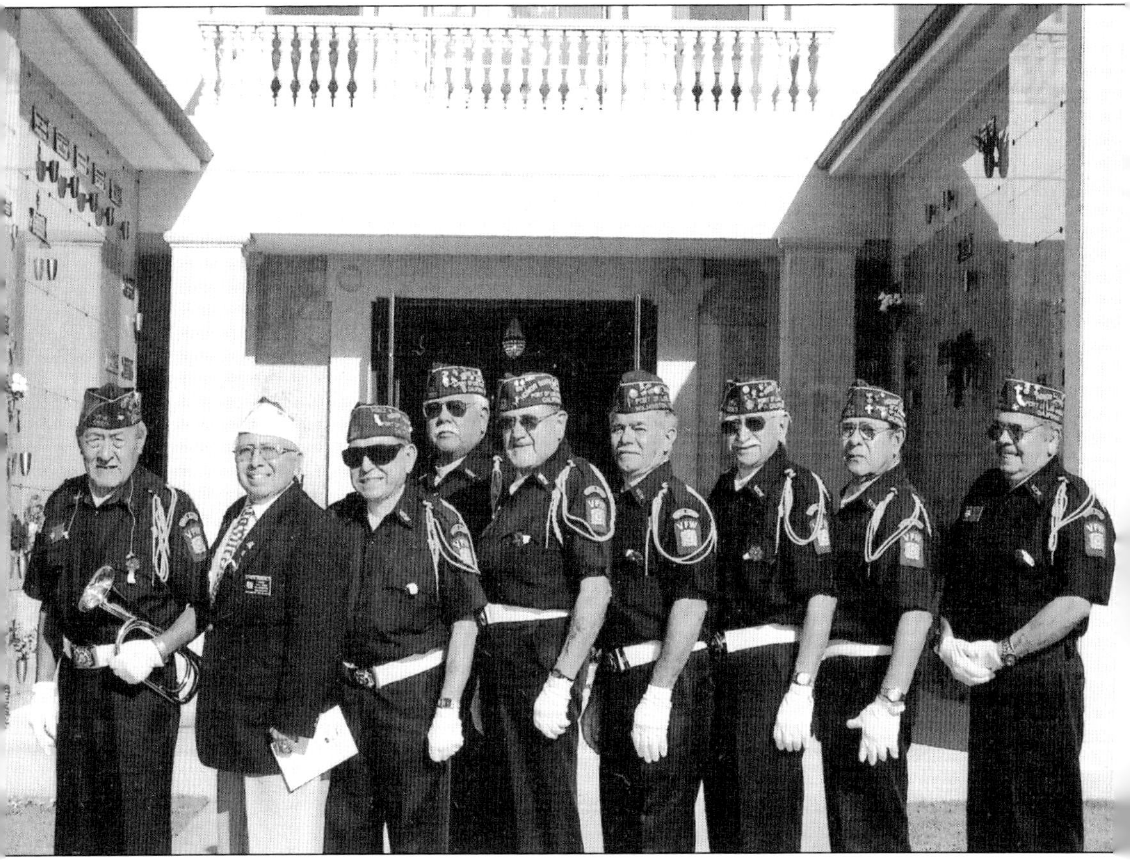

The national VFW traces its roots back to 1899 when veterans of the Spanish-American War (1898) and the Philippine Insurrection (1899–1902) founded groups to secure rights and benefits for their service. They were also instrumental in establishing the Veterans Administration, creating the G.I. Bill, developing the national cemetery system, fighting for issues that are affecting Vietnam and Gulf War veterans, and helping fund the military memorials in Washington, D.C. The local post supports and sponsors many activities and programs. Comdr. Martin Chacon, Honor Guard captain Art Rodriguez, and Ladies Auxiliary president Irene Gonzalez guide the volunteer activities of Post 2967. (Gabriel Mendoza.)

The U.S. Maritime Commission presented Jose McKenna a certificate of merit for his invention. The award was presented on July 27, 1945, and recognized his initiative and service rendered for the war effort in originating a meritorious suggestion for increasing production of ships for victory. His action resulted in the invention of an upside jig that allowed shipbuilders to get into tight places. Jose worked at Todd Shipyard where he is shown with his created device. He arrived in Wilmington from Guanajuato in 1920 and never ceased to apply his mechanical skills. (Amelia McKenna.)

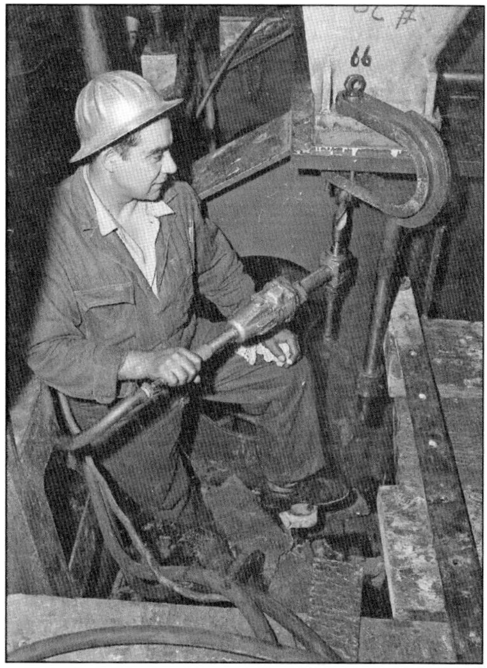

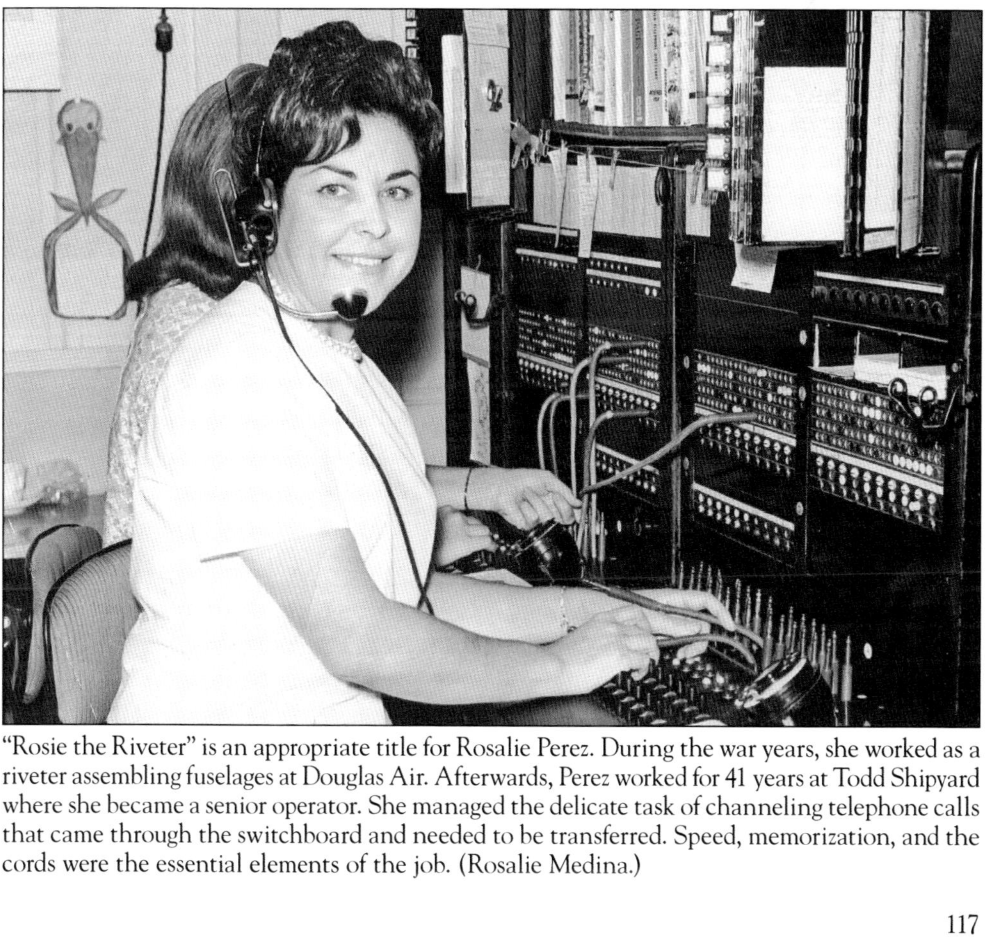

"Rosie the Riveter" is an appropriate title for Rosalie Perez. During the war years, she worked as a riveter assembling fuselages at Douglas Air. Afterwards, Perez worked for 41 years at Todd Shipyard where she became a senior operator. She managed the delicate task of channeling telephone calls that came through the switchboard and needed to be transferred. Speed, memorization, and the cords were the essential elements of the job. (Rosalie Medina.)

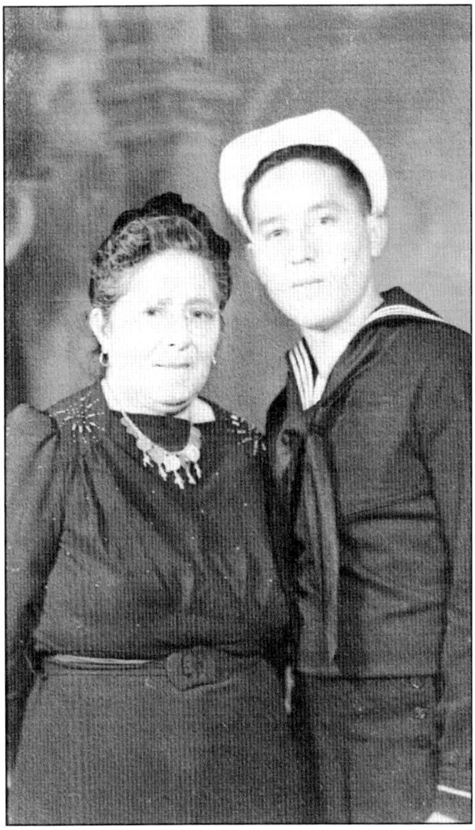

As a wartime memento, Lino Urrea is pictured with his mother, Luisa Urrea, when he joined the navy in October 1942. He participated in the Normandy invasion and South Pacific engagement. After World War II, he worked as a welder for California Shipyard while in the Navy Reserve. Urrea was called back during the Korean conflict. He returned to work and retired from the Long Beach Naval Shipyard. He married Eleanor Madrigal and raised his children in Wilmington. Now in his 90s, he recalls his childhood and military experiences, and he recognizes that over 180,000 Latinos served in the Korean War. Eight of these servicemen were awarded the Medal of Honor, five were awarded the Navy Cross, 37 were awarded the Distinguished Service Cross, and 498 were given the Silver Star. (Lino Urrea.)

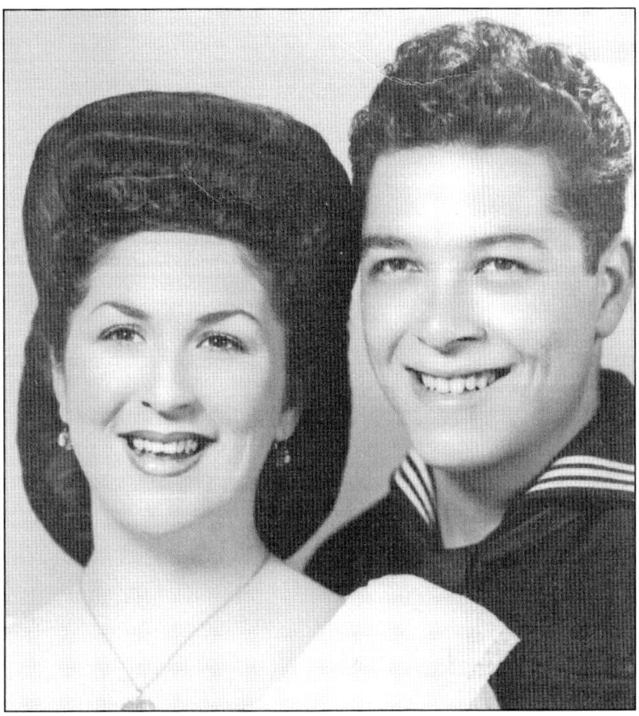

Carlos Rico and Bernice (Lambrini) Stathes graduated from Banning High School in the 1940s and were married before he left for navy duty. Rico was one of 200,000 Mexicans Americans who served in the armed forces during World War II. Most fought as combat troops, receiving more Purple Hearts than any other ethnic group. Rico returned safe, went to college, and became a college art instructor. The teaching profession attracted others from the neighborhood and among them were Frank and Luke Manzo, Henry Granados, Hector Rubio, and Vincent Perez. The teaching profession has continued to draw a large number of individuals from the community. (Carlos Rico.)

The U.S. Maritime Service training station was on Santa Catalina Island. This site trained mariners for deck, engine room, and steward duties on "Liberty ships." Living in a harbor, with military units everywhere, and a strong desire to serve the country, it is only natural that many Wilmington men became merchant marines. Like other armed forces servicemen, they served proudly and encountered many dangerous situations. (Mary Caldera.)

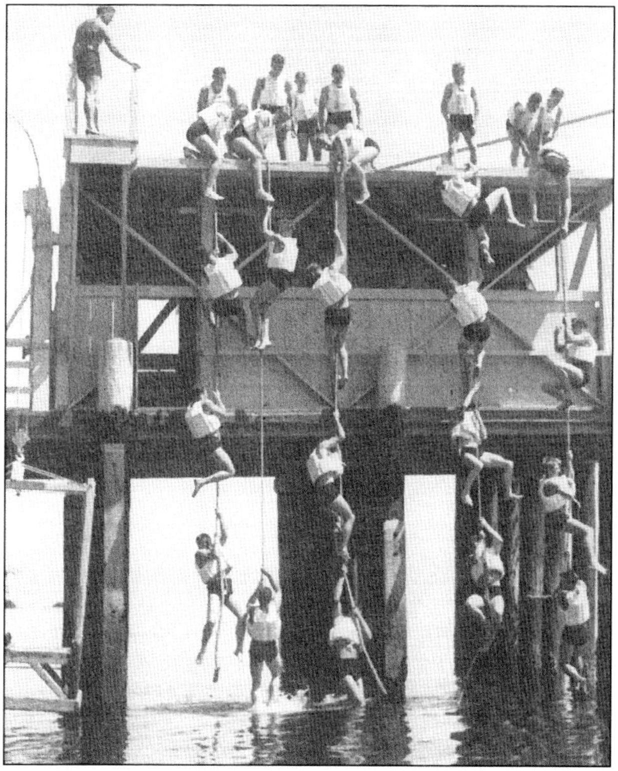

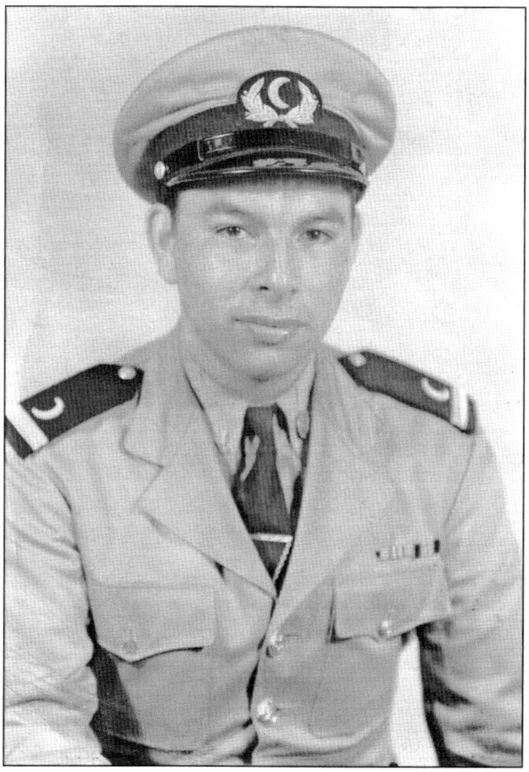

John Caldera saw an informational newsreel at a movie theater about the merchant marines. It inspired him and he joined. Caldera trained at Catalina Island and was on the S.S. *Lane Victory*. During the war, his ship took the first load of coal to Finland and received a Key to the City in appreciation. He worked on Matson Line ships after the war and worked on the S.S. *Catalina* before becoming a longshoreman. His father, Juan Caldera, was one of the first Spanish-speaking disc jockeys and built the Colton Plunge in Colton, California, so that Mexican Americans had a place to swim. (Mary Caldera.)

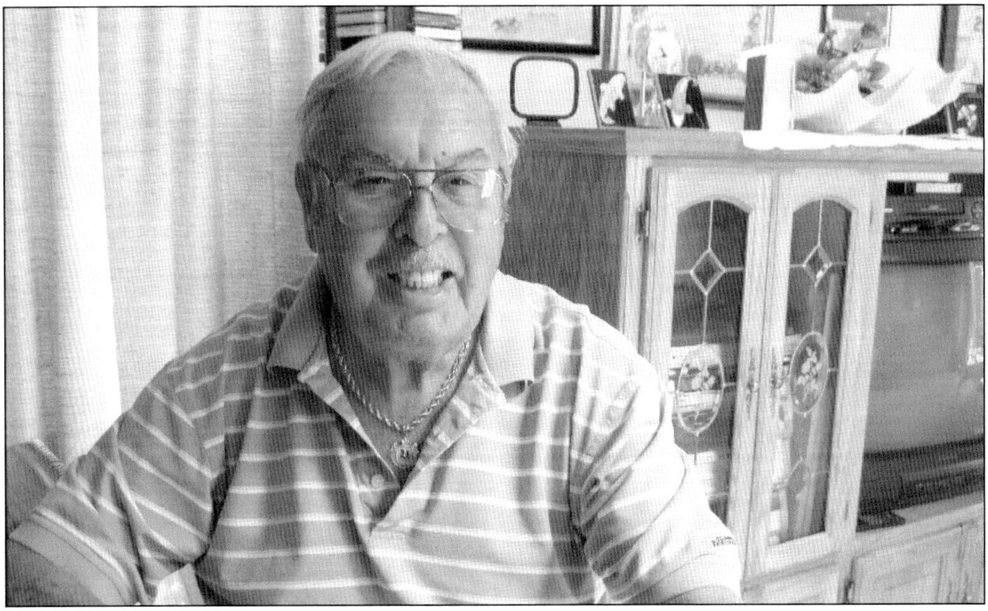

A merchant marine who demonstrates his love of sea and land is Phillip Vaca. He was a seaman for 12 years and was aboard the S.S. *Sackett's Harbor* when it broke in half. The bow of the ship sunk but the stern managed to get to Alaska under its own power. On land, Vaca headed the Cement Masons Union, Local 627, of Los Angeles for nine years and received the "Golden Labor Award" from the Mexican American Opportunity Foundation in recognition of outstanding contributions to the expansion of opportunities for Mexican Americans. He worked tirelessly as a Little League coach, for the Road Kings, City of Hope, and served as building and safety commissioner for Los Angeles. (Author's collection.)

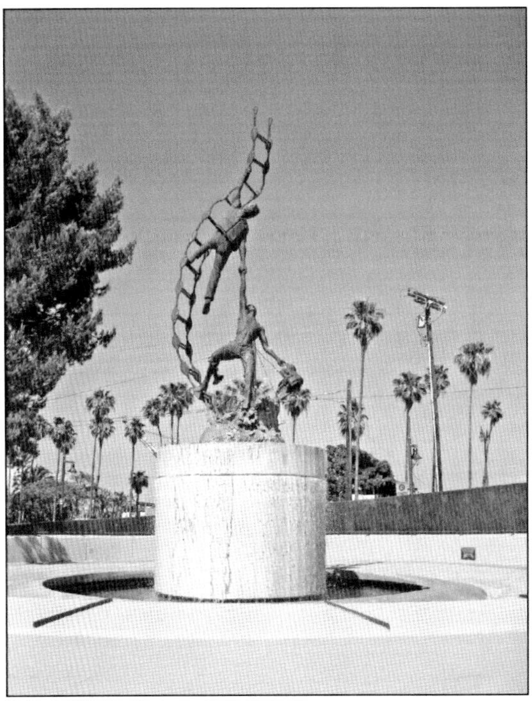

In 1989, the American Merchant Marine Veteran's Monument was dedicated at John S. Gibson Jr. Park in San Pedro. It was trucked to the site from a Wilmington warehouse near the waterfront. The statue depicts two merchant seamen climbing a Jacob's ladder after making a rescue at sea. About 5,600 merchant seamen died during World War II. Many Wilmington men joined and served as seamen both in war and peacetime. Jasper D'Ambrosi, who was born and raised in Wilmington, created the bronze statue with his friends in mind. He died before it was completed, and his sons Marc and Michael, who cast it at the family foundry in Tempe, Arizona, finished the monument as a tribute to their father. (Author's collection.)

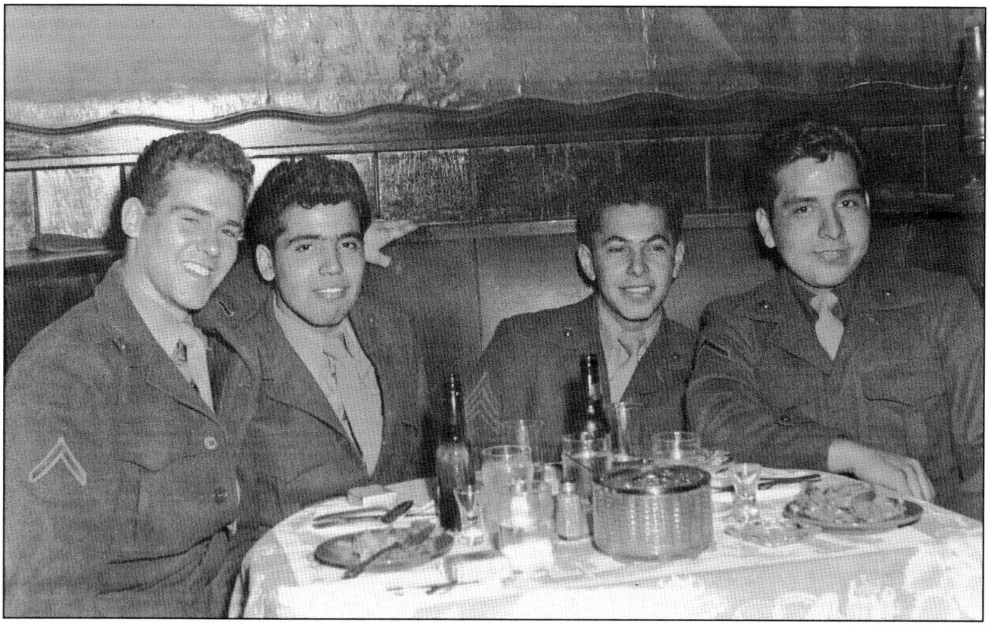

In 1951, four local friends met in San Francisco on their way home from Korea. They are, from left to right, John Reardon, Art Duzal, Henry Gonzales, and Eddie Gutierrez. Gonzales grew up on Robidoux Street with eight siblings and his parents, David and Guadalupe. His father, who had come from Guanajuato in 1915, worked for Santa Fe Railway and retired from the 76 Union Oil refinery. His mother worked in the canneries. (Henry Gonzales.)

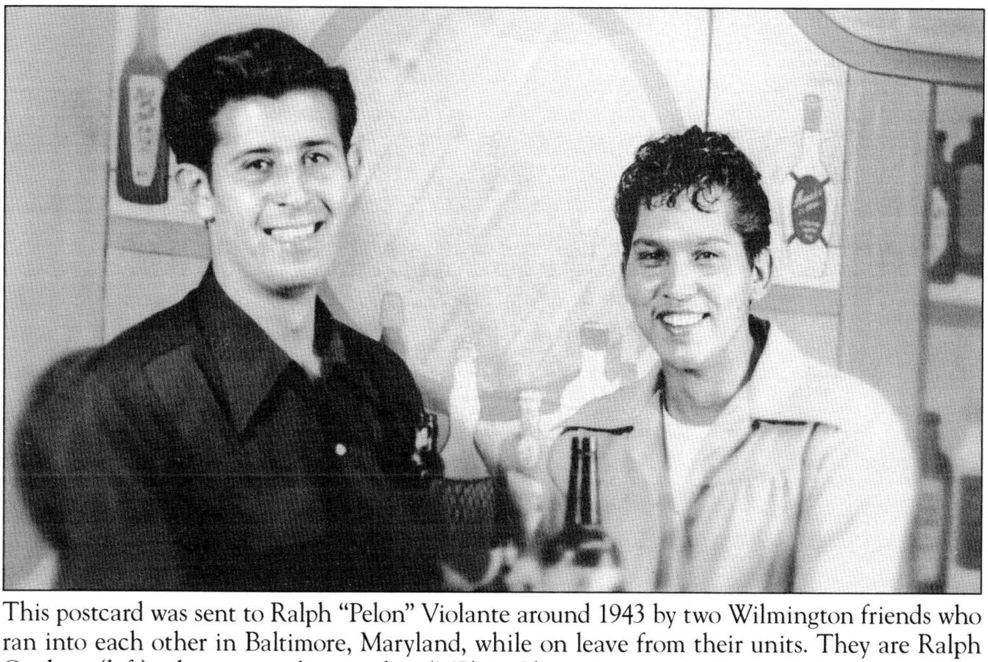

This postcard was sent to Ralph "Pelon" Violante around 1943 by two Wilmington friends who ran into each other in Baltimore, Maryland, while on leave from their units. They are Ralph Cardona (left), who was a military police (MP) in Chicago overseeing German prisoners of war, and Joseph McKenna, who was stationed nearby. Although only one person is identified with a nickname in this caption, it was very common for people to have nicknames, and often this informal name was better known than the given name. (Ralph Violante.)

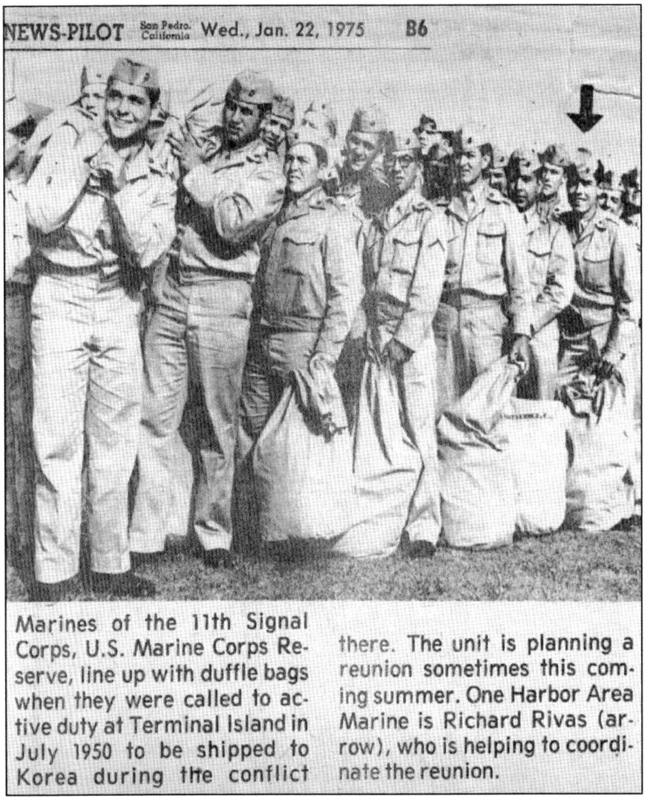

NEWS-PILOT San Pedro, California Wed., Jan. 22, 1975 B6

Marines of the 11th Signal Corps, U.S. Marine Corps Reserve, line up with duffle bags when they were called to active duty at Terminal Island in July 1950 to be shipped to Korea during the conflict there. The unit is planning a reunion sometimes this coming summer. One Harbor Area Marine is Richard Rivas (arrow), who is helping to coordinate the reunion.

The *San Pedro News-Pilot* printed this story of eight Wilmington men in the same marine reserve unit who had a reunion. Their names were Tom Flores, Richard Rivas, Henry Gonzales, Bill Soto, Sam Torres, Bob Menes, Joe P ?, and Frank J. ?. (Henry Gonzales.)

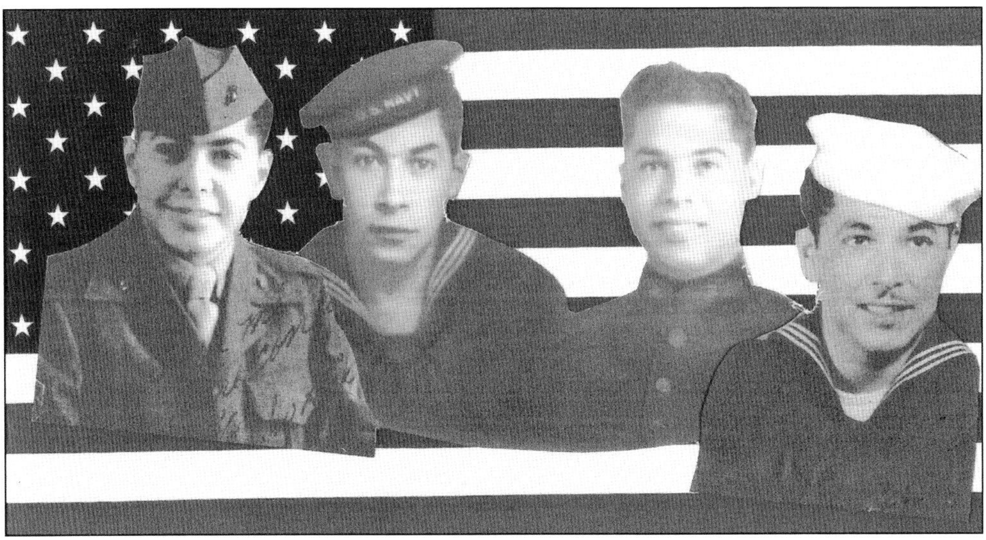

Henry Gonzales (left) was in the Korean War and his three brothers Mike, Peter, and David all served in World War II. Gonzales was a survivor of the troops nicknamed "The Chosin Few." The Battle of Chosin Reservoir was fought in some of the roughest terrain and during brutal winter weather. The troops were surrounded and outnumbered by seven Chinese divisions. In addition, cold weather, as low as -35 degrees Fahrenheit, caused frostbite casualties, icy roads, and weapon malfunctions, and the Chinese, dressed in white, were undetectable against snow. Suffering massive losses, the American convoy pulled out. (Henry Gonzales.)

Jesus Perez was a recipient of the Purple Heart. He was 17 years old when a kamikaze plane hit the USS *California* in January 1945. He became the only survivor of a gun crew, but flames caused burns over his entire body. His sister Margaret hugs him with delight at having him home. However, Wilmington Historical Society records list many Wilmington men who were not fortunate to return home from World War II. Mong them were Pete Lara, Frank Ortiz, Norberto Pasamonte, Bud Soza, Leo Tavera, and Henry Teran. (Margaret Mota.)

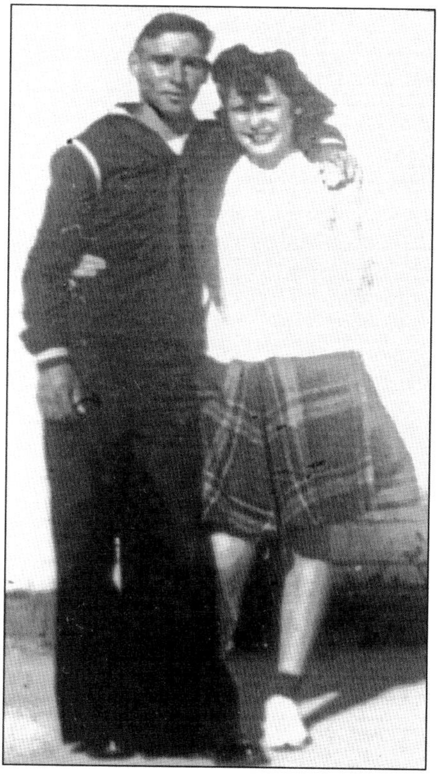

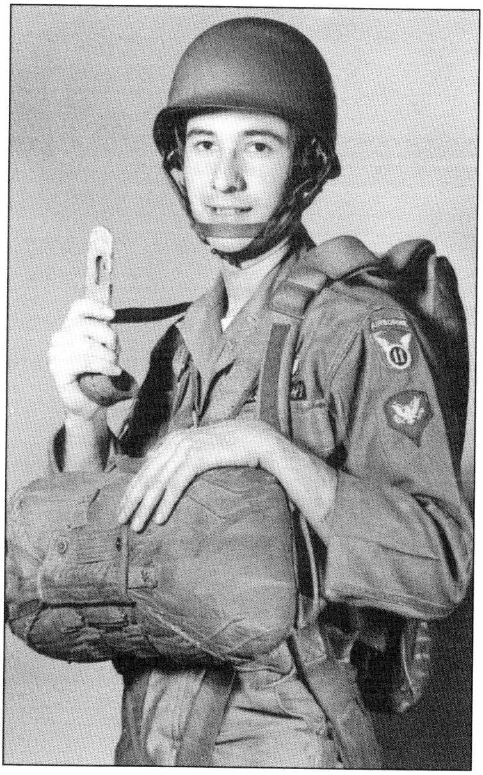

Upon graduation from high school or at age 18, many young men enlisted into the services. Ramon Cruz became a paratrooper in the U.S. Army, 11th Airborne Division. In France, after making a jump and suiting up for another, he was spotted by fellow Wilmington friend Anthony Vargas, who was working on a plane at the air force base. As a Korean veteran, Cruz used the G.I. Bill to attend Long Beach City College. He retired from the Long Beach Naval Shipyard after 31 years. (Ramon Cruz.)

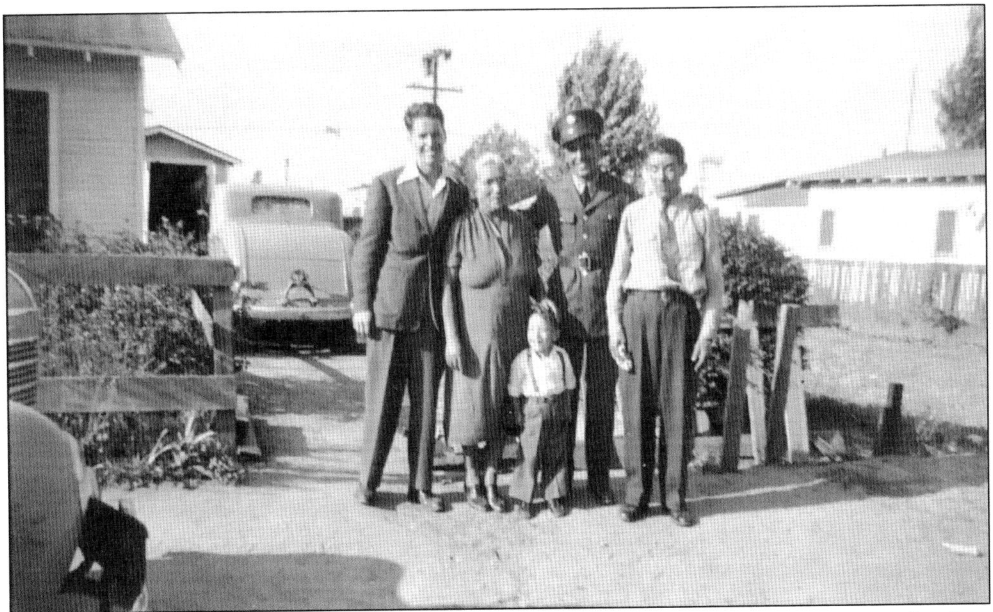

On leave from the U.S. Army, soldier Peter Mota was photographed with his parents, a brother, and son. They are, from left to right, Marcial, Severa, Peter (son), Peter, and his father, Marcelino. Peter's 1934 Plymouth is parked in the driveway of 1123 East Young Street. (Ralph Mota.)

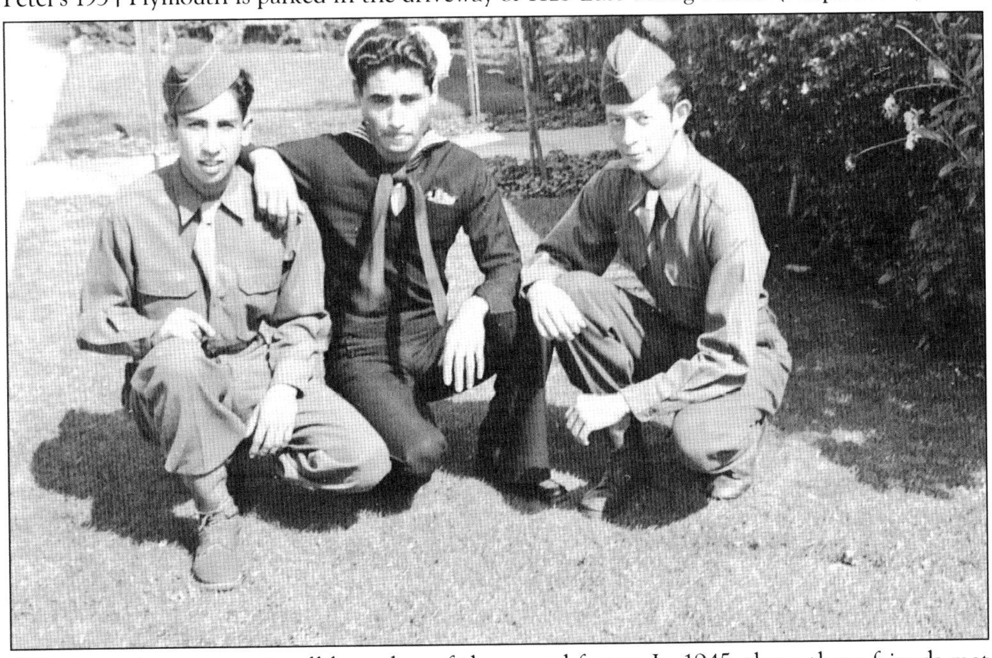

Wilmington's sons were in all branches of the armed forces. In 1945, these three friends met for an afternoon at the park. They had graduated from Banning High School and now faced a new experience. The friends are, from left to right, Ralph Violante, Arthur Ponce, and Silvestre Cardona. Meanwhile, the war effort was evident at the high school. Girls gym classes collected crossword puzzles and pasted them on cardboard with the answers on back. These were sent to soldiers and sailors in hospitals. Also, the Girls' Athletic Association (GAA) encouraged students to buy war stamps. (Maria Enriquez.)

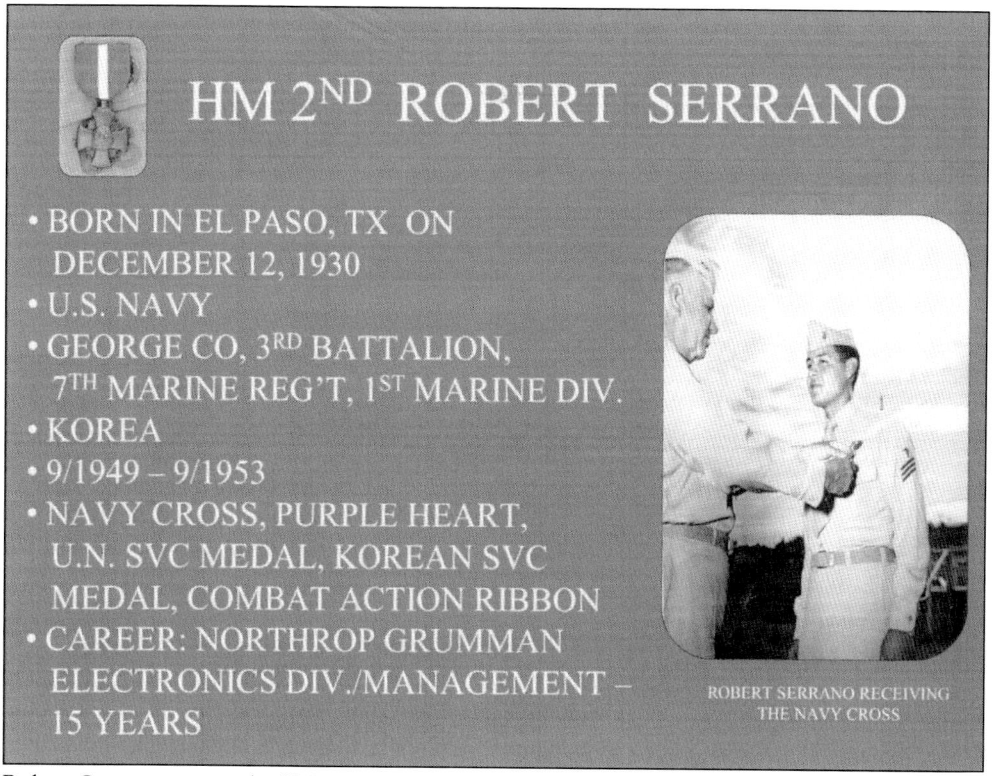

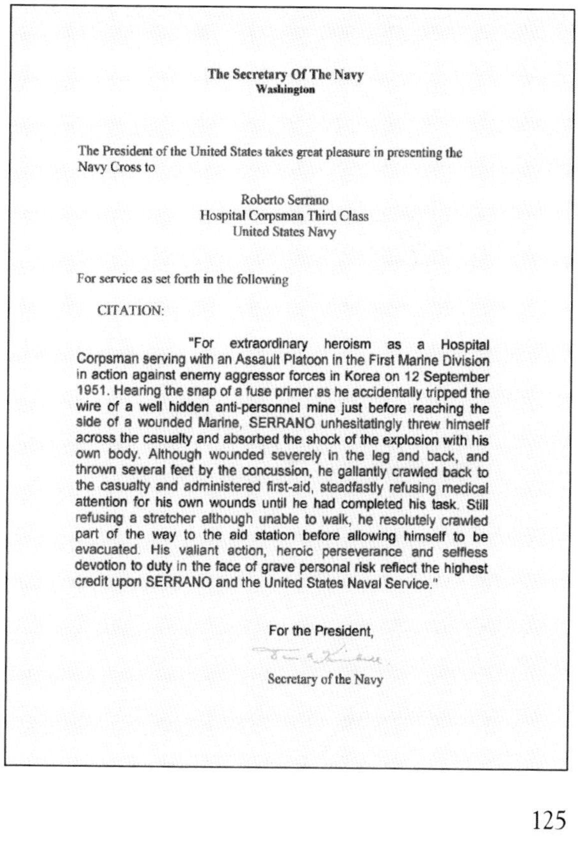

The Secretary Of The Navy
Washington

The President of the United States takes great pleasure in presenting the Navy Cross to

Roberto Serrano
Hospital Corpsman Third Class
United States Navy

For service as set forth in the following

CITATION:

"For extraordinary heroism as a Hospital Corpsman serving with an Assault Platoon in the First Marine Division in action against enemy aggressor forces in Korea on 12 September 1951. Hearing the snap of a fuse primer as he accidentally tripped the wire of a well hidden anti-personnel mine just before reaching the side of a wounded Marine, SERRANO unhesitatingly threw himself across the casualty and absorbed the shock of the explosion with his own body. Although wounded severely in the leg and back, and thrown several feet by the concussion, he gallantly crawled back to the casualty and administered first-aid, steadfastly refusing medical attention for his own wounds until he had completed his task. Still refusing a stretcher although unable to walk, he resolutely crawled part of the way to the aid station before allowing himself to be evacuated. His valiant action, heroic perseverance and selfless devotion to duty in the face of grave personal risk reflect the highest credit upon SERRANO and the United States Naval Service."

For the President,

Secretary of the Navy

Robert Serrano was in the U.S. Navy and served in Korea. Serrano received the Navy Cross as described in the letter from the Secretary of the Navy. He married and had three sons. A UCLA fan and active in the local VFW Post Honor Guard, he was buried in his honor guard uniform and with the UCLA theme song. (Both, Laura Serrano.)

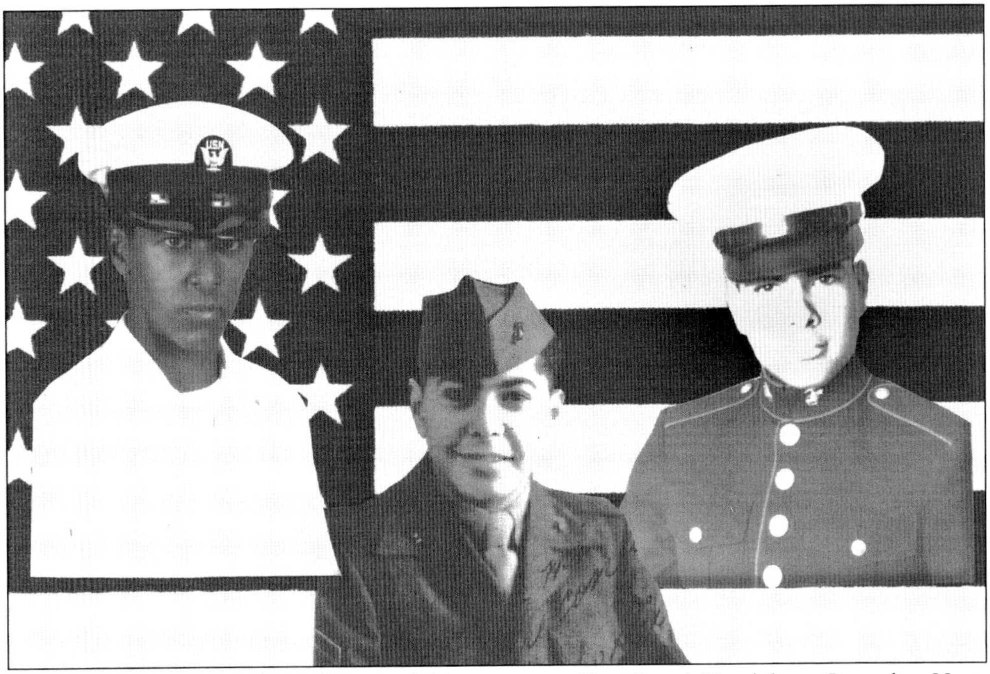

Henry Gonzales (center) was born in Wilmington to David and Guadalupe Gonzales. He is proud of his sons, James (left) and Henry (right). He married Lucille De La O, who grew up near Alameda Street, and they still live in the community. (Henry Gonzales.)

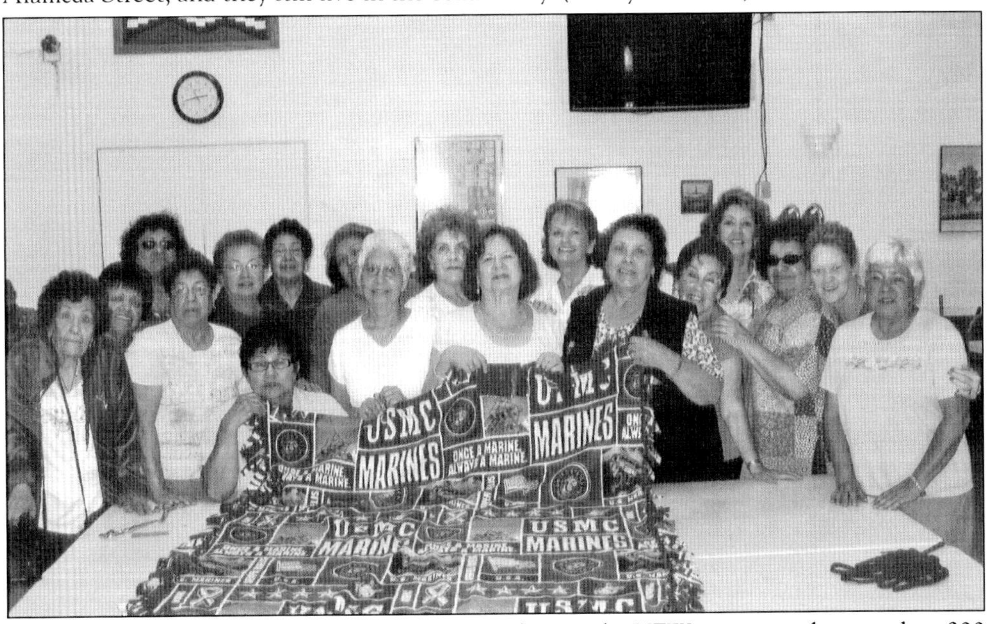

In one year, the Sunshine Seniors, who met as quilters at the VFW center, made more than 300 quilts for hospitalized service personnel in Germany who were injured in Iraq and Afghanistan. They also made lap blankets for patients at the Long Beach Veterans Hospital and baby blankets and hats for infants with cancer at UCLA Medical Center. They were recently honored with the Wilmington Community Service Award and certificates of commendation from various elected officials. (Lourdes Gutierrez.)

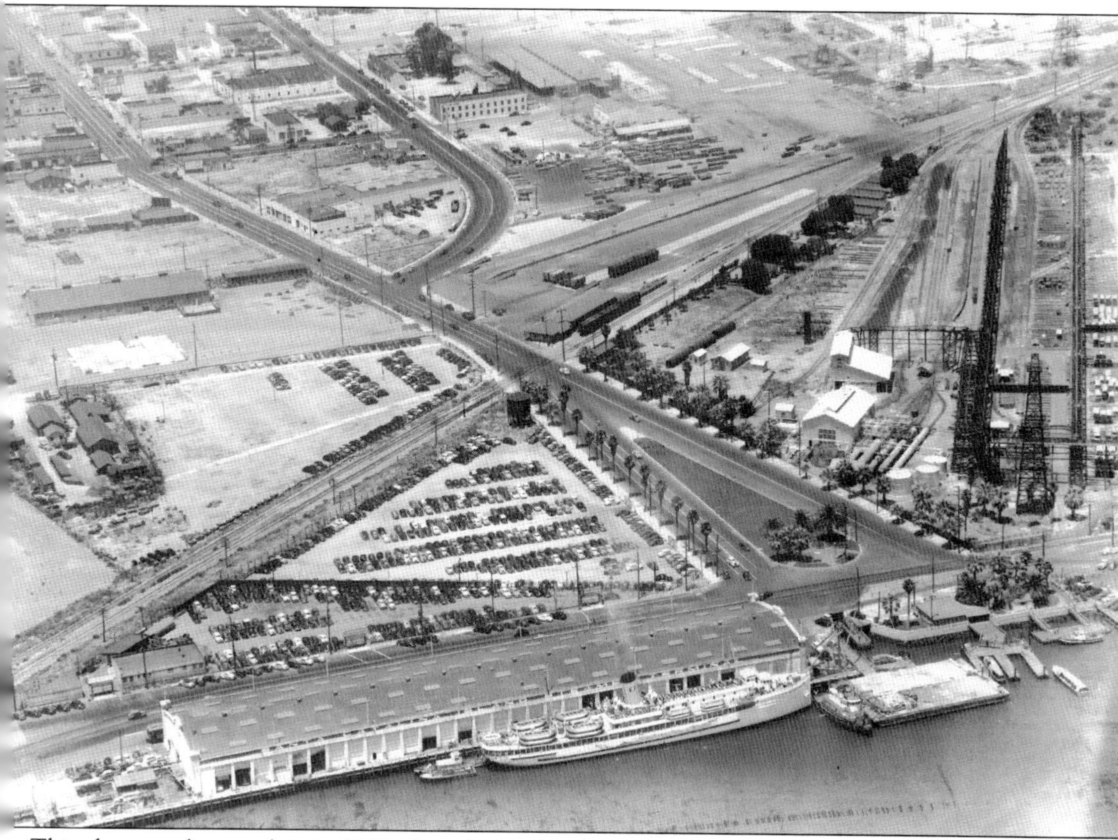

This photograph was taken in 1947, when the SS *Catalina* was moored at the Catalina Terminal. The area that is now known as Banning's Landing is to the right of the terminal. Employment related to the harbor was, and still is, vital to the Wilmington community. Changes have taken place, but the community's strength is in the solid foundation laid down by earlier generations. Wilmington is forging into the next millennium with new developments on the waterfront. (Wilmington Historical Society.)

Discover Thousands of Local History Books Featuring Millions of Vintage Images

Arcadia Publishing, the leading local history publisher in the United States, is committed to making history accessible and meaningful through publishing books that celebrate and preserve the heritage of America's people and places.

Find more books like this at
www.arcadiapublishing.com

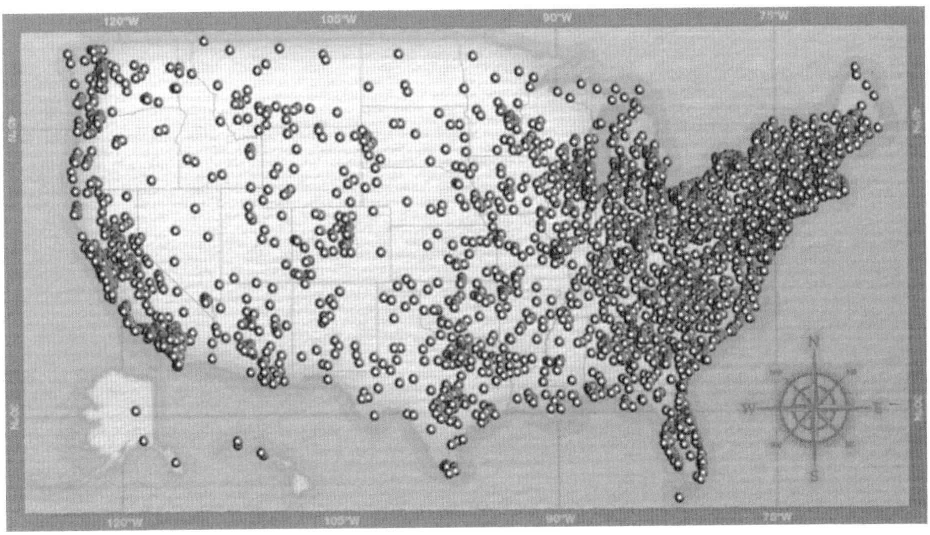

Search for your hometown history, your old stomping grounds, and even your favorite sports team.

Consistent with our mission to preserve history on a local level, this book was printed in South Carolina on American-made paper and manufactured entirely in the United States. Products carrying the accredited Forest Stewardship Council (FSC) label are printed on 100 percent FSC-certified paper.

MADE IN THE USA